DOES GOD EXIST?

This book presents the most recent debates by leading contemporary philosophers of enduring themes and issues concerning the question of God's existence. William Lane Craig and Antony Flew met on the 50th anniversary of the famous Copleston/Russell debate to discuss the question of God's existence in a public debate. The core of this book contains the edited transcript of that debate. Also included are eight chapters in which other significant philosophers – Paul Draper, R. Douglas Geivett, Michael Martin, Keith M. Parsons, William Rowe, William J. Wainwright, Keith Yandell and David Yandell – critique the debate and address the issues raised. Their substantial and compelling insights complement and further the debate, helping the reader delve more deeply into the issues that surfaced. In the two final chapters, Craig and Flew respond and clarify their positions, taking the debate yet one step further. The result of these many contributions is a book which provides the reader with a summary of the current discussion and allows one to enter into the dialogue on this central question in the philosophy of religion.

Dedicated to my tender wife Lori,
and my four wonderful children –
Beth, Brooke, Ryan and Luke

Does God Exist?

The Craig–Flew Debate

Edited by
STAN W. WALLACE
Independent Scholar, USA

ASHGATE

Published by
Ashgate Publishing Limited
Gower House
Croft Road
Aldershot
Hants GU11 3HR
England

Ashgate Publishing Company
Suite 420
101 Cherry Street
Burlington, VT 05401-4405
USA

Ashgate website: http://www.ashgate.com

British Library Cataloguing in Publication Data
Does God exist? : the Craig–Flew debate
 1. Craig, William Lane – Views on existence of God 2. Flew,
 Antony, 1923- – Views on existence of God
 I. Wallace, Stan W.
 212.1

Library of Congress Cataloging-in-Publication Data
Does God exist?: the Craig–Flew debate / edited by Stan W. Wallace.
  p. cm.
 Includes bibliographical references.
 ISBN 0-7546-3189-3 (alk. paper) – ISBN 0-7546-3190-7 (pbk.: alk. paper)
  1. Theism. 2. Atheism. I. Craig, William Lane. II. Flew, Antony, 1923-
III. Wallace, Stan W., 1962-

 BD555 .D64 2002
 212' .1–dc21
                                                                2002074437
ISBN 0 7546 3189 3 (HBK)
ISBN 0 7546 3190 7 (PBK)

Typeset by Tradespools, Frome, Somerset
Printed and bound in Great Britain by Antony Rowe Ltd, Chippenham, Wiltshire

Contents

List of Contributors   vii
Preface   ix

Chapter 1   Some Issues in Theism and Atheism: Setting the Context   1
              Keith Yandell

Chapter 2   The Craig–Flew Debate   17
              William Lane Craig and Antony Flew

Chapter 3   Reflections on the Explanatory Power of Theism   49
              R. Douglas Geivett

Chapter 4   Reflections on the Craig–Flew Debate   65
              William Rowe

Chapter 5   The Burden of Proof and the Presumption of Theism   75
              William J. Wainwright

Chapter 6   Comments on the Craig–Flew Debate   85
              Michael Martin

Chapter 7   Theism, Atheism and Cosmology   95
              Keith Yandell

Chapter 8   The Universe is Probable; The Resurrection is Not   115
              Keith M. Parsons

Chapter 9   Infinity and Explanation, Damnation and Empiricism   131
              David Yandell

Chapter 10   Craig's Case for God's Existence   141
              Paul Draper

Chapter 11   A Reply to Objections   155
              William Lane Craig

Chapter 12   A Reply to my Critics   189
              Antony Flew

Bibliography   221
Subject Index   231

List of Contributors

William Lane Craig is Research Professor of Philosophy, Talbot School of Theology, specializing in philosophy of religion and philosophy of space and time. His publications include *The Kalam Cosmological Argument* (Macmillan, 1979), *Divine Foreknowledge and Human Freedom* (E.J. Brill, 1991) and *God, Time, and Eternity* (Kluwer Academic Publishers, 2001).

Paul Draper is Professor of Philosophy, Florida International University, specializing in philosophy of religion and philosophy of science. His publications include 'The Skeptical Theist', in *The Evidential Argument From Evil*, ed. Daniel Howard-Snyder (Indiana University Press, 1996) and 'Pain and Pleasure: An Evidential Problem for Theists', in *Nous* 23 (June 1989).

Antony Flew is Emeritus Professor of Philosophy, University of Reading, England. His publications include *God and Philosophy* (Harcourt, Brace & World, 1966), *An Introduction to Western Philosophy: Ideas and Argument from Plato to Sartre* (Thames and Hudson, 1971, rev. 1989) and *The Logic of Mortality* (Blackwell, 1987).

R. Douglas Geivett is Associate Professor of Philosophy, Talbot School of Theology, specializing in philosophy of religion, epistemology, ethics, history of modern philosophy and Christian apologetics. His publications include *Contemporary Perspectives on Religious Epistemology*, co-edited with B. Sweetman (Oxford University Press, 1992) and *Evil and the Evidence for God* (Temple University Press, 1993).

Michael Martin is Emeritus Professor of Philosophy, Boston University, specializing in the philosophy of religion, the philosophy of law, and the philosophy of the social sciences. His publications include *Atheism: A Philosophical Justification* (Temple University Press, 1990), *The Case Against Christianity* (Temple University Press, 1991) and *Atheism, Morality and Meaning* (Prometheus Books, 2002).

Keith M. Parsons is Associate Professor of Philosophy at the University of Houston, Clear Lake, specializing in the history and philosophy of science and the philosophy of religion. His publications include *God and the Burden of Proof* (Prometheus Books, 1989) and *Drawing Out Leviathan: Dinosaurs and the Science Wars* (Indiana University Press, 2001).

William Rowe is Professor of Philosophy, Purdue University, specializing in philosophy of religion. Dr. Rowe's publications include *Religious Symbols and God: A Philosophical Study of Tillich's Theology* (University of Chicago Press, 1968), *The Cosmological Argument* (Princeton University Press, 1975) and *Philosophy of Religion: An Introduction* (Dickenson Publishing Co., 1978).

William J. Wainwright is Distinguished Professor of Philosophy, University of Wisconsin-Milwaukee, specializing in philosophy of religion. His publications include *Philosophy of Religion* (2nd edition, Wadsworth, 1998), *Reason and the Heart: A Prolegomenon to a Critique of Passional Reason* (Cornell University Press, 1995) and the *Oxford Handbook of Philosophy of Religion* (Oxford University Press, forthcoming).

David Yandell is Associate Professor of Philosophy at Loyola University of Chicago, specializing in history of modern philosophy and metaphysics. He has published articles in several anthologies and journals, including *History of Philosophy Quarterly* and *British Journal for the History of Philosophy*.

Keith Yandell is the Julius R. Weinberg Professor of Philosophy, University of Wisconsin-Madison, specializing in philosophy of religion, history of modern philosophy and metaphysics. His publications include *Philosophy of Religion: A Contemporary Introduction* (Routledge, 1999), editor of *Faith and Narrative* (Oxford University Press, 2001) and *Comparative Philosophy of Religion* (Kluwer Academic Publishers, forthcoming).

Preface

Antony Flew and William Lane Craig agreed to meet on the evening of 18 February 1998 and debate the question 'Does God Exist?'. Approximately 4000 University of Wisconsin students and faculty attended the debate, which commemorated the fiftieth anniversary of the famous debate between Fredrick Copleston and Bertrand Russell, held in 1948 on BBC radio. In many ways, Craig and Flew stand in the philosophical lineages of Copleston and Russell respectively, and it was for this reason that they were chosen as the best representatives to engage in a similar live debate on this question for a new generation. The University of Wisconsin provided an excellent venue, being an institution with a rich tradition of intellectual discussion and debate concerning important issues central to human flourishing. Finally, the fact that the debate was co-sponsored by the Philosophy Department and a coalition of organizations representing both theistic and atheistic persuasions, furthered the spirit of mutual respect and inquiry into what may well be the most important question ever asked. The edited transcript of this debate is contained here in Chapter 2.

Furthermore, the value of this debate has been greatly enhanced by having other leading thinkers in the philosophy of religion comment on the debate, analysing the approaches and arguments from their philosophical vantage points (Chapters 3 through 10). These eight philosophers were chosen not only because of their expertise in this field of study, but also because of their nuanced positions. Each has substantial and compelling insights, which in many ways complement and further the debate, helping the reader delve more deeply into the issues which emerged. In order to preface this entire discussion among the ten interlocutors, Keith Yandell has provided an overview (Chapter 1) in which he briefly frames the issues of the debate philosophically and offers a point-by-point sketch of the central arguments and responses contained in the pages that follow. Finally, in the last two chapters William Craig and Antony Flew have the opportunity to clarify their positions and offer a final rebuttal to their critics, taking the debate of February 1998 yet one step further. The outcome of these many contributions is a book which allows you, the reader, to enter into the dialogue and hear from some of the most eloquent and well-studied individuals on this most important question – a question so many ask and seek to answer: does God exist?

I wish briefly to acknowledge several individuals who have made this work possible. First, I thank both William Lane Craig and Antony Flew for their willingness to participate in this debate and work so tirelessly with me as we discussed editorial revisions for the publication of the debate transcript. They were both true gentlemen and scholars with whom I am honoured to have worked in this capacity. I also wish to thank Keith Yandell. From the moment that he agreed to moderate the debate he has been a constant source of encouragement and guide throughout this entire project. My sincere appreciation is also due to the eight respondents who have been more than gracious throughout the four years we have been preparing this work for publication. I also wish to thank Mary Wisniewski, JoAnn Angle and Judy Farrar, my administrative assistants, who worked assiduously in the preparation of this manuscript for publication, as well as Tom Aul, who provided important legal counsel at various critical junctures. Finally, to my wife and children – Lori, Bethany and Brooke, Ryan and Luke – thank you for being my strength and joy and thereby enabling me to complete this project.

Stan W. Wallace
Tampa, Florida
March 2002

Chapter 1

Some Issues in Theism and Atheism: Setting the Context

Keith Yandell

Preface

The purpose here is to set the debate, and the discussion to which it gave rise, in philosophical context. Antony Flew and William Lane Craig start from very different philosophical perspectives, and it is helpful to understand something of their overall viewpoints before considering the specifics of their debate.

Furthermore, as the commentators range over a wide variety of issues as the debate unfolds, it seems appropriate to provide a roadmap to most of these issues, and occasionally to comment on the views they hold. This chapter is therefore divided into two principal sections:, 'Perspectives of the Debaters' and 'Roadmap to Issues in the Commentaries'.

Perspectives of the Debaters

I begin by noting some differences in Antony Flew's and William Craig's philosophical perspectives, mentioning some varieties of atheism and theism, and emphasizing the debaters' agreement on whose existence they are debating.

The Humean Theory of Meaning

Antony Flew is a well-known scholar on the philosophy of David Hume (1711–76) and is significantly influenced by his views.

His position is atheistic in what is apparently a 'broad sense' of atheism. An atheist in the broad sense may hold that the proposition 'God exists' is meaningless, that it is false, or that it is neither known nor reasonably believed.

Much of Flew's argument apparently rests on certain views of meaning and verification – an empiricism regarding meaning and verification similar to that of the philosopher David Hume. Hume ties the meaning of words closely to sensory and introspective experience. Broadly, on his view, an indefinable descriptive word gains its sense by corresponding to a perceptual quality (a colour, shape, sound, taste, odour or the like) or else by corresponding to some psychological state. Definable descriptive terms gain their meaning from the meaning of the indefinable descriptive terms that define them. Any mark or sound that supposedly is a descriptive word – that is said to express a descriptive meaning – is then checked to see if its supposed meaning can be defined by reference only to terms that correspond to some perceptual or introspective feature. If it cannot, it is declared to be meaningless.

We have noted that a Hume-like empiricist theory of meaning tells us that the meaning of a descriptive term is given by its association with things that we perceive or introspect. We are offered an account of perception on which what we perceive is sensory qualities. To this an account of introspection is added according to which what we introspect is mental states and never anything that has these states. Colour, shape, taste, odour and tactile words gain meaning, we are told, by being associated with (used as names of?) colour, shape, taste, odour and tactile qualities. That pain, pleasure and emotion words have meaning is explained by their being associated with (used as names of?) pains, pleasures and emotions. If one holds (as Hume did not) that we perceive enduring objects, then the possession of meaning by such physical object words as 'rock' or 'tree' will be explained, on this sort of theory, by (say) 'rock' being associated with observed rocks and 'tree' with observed trees. If one holds (as Hume did not) that we introspect an enduring self, then the possession of meaning by such terms as 'person', 'self', and 'I' will be explained, on this sort of theory, by 'person' being associated with the conscious mind that one is aware of over time. What sort of meaningful terms this sort of theory can explain depends on what sorts of thing it holds that we can be aware of.[1] A narrow, sparse theory of the objects[2] of sense perception and introspection gives a sparse range of meaningful terms. Advocates of the theory will take the theory as a criterion of meaning and dismiss purported counterexamples as instances of terms that some mistakenly take to have meaning. One problem with this sort of theory is that such terms as 'theory', 'meaning' and 'explain' cannot be defined in the terms it accepts. (Looking ahead, the same holds for 'verifies' and 'confirms'.) So one cannot say what the theory means in terms that are allowed by the theory.

The Humean Theory of Verification

A Hume-like theory of verification will contend that a descriptive sentence is verified only if it says that something that can be experienced exists or has some observable property. To verify such a statement is simply to experience the thing in question or to experience it as having the quality in question. A doctrine of experience is required to give the theory of verification specific content, and, for Hume, experience is limited to introspection and sense perception. Hume thus limits the range of what we can verify to matters capable of confirmation by sensory or introspective experience.[3] A problem for this theory of verification is that *the proposition can only verify what can be confirmed by reference to sensory or introspective experience* cannot itself be verified by reference to sensory or introspective experience. So that proposition, which expresses what meaning the theory has is meaningless on the theory that it expresses.

Flew is a Hume scholar who is also significantly influenced by Hume's views. In line with the general tradition of Humean, empiricist theories of meaning and verification, Flew holds that we experience neither disembodied created persons nor God, and so there is no evidence that either exist. Further, he contends, it is doubtful whether the concepts of such things are clear enough even to give sense to the claim that they do exist. Here, Flew walks along a thin line; if we know that we don't experience disembodied minds or God, we must have enough grasp of the relevant concepts for this knowledge to be available. To the degree that we *do not* have such a grasp, it is not clear that we know we don't experience disembodied created persons or God. To the degree that we *do* grasp the concepts of God and disembodied minds, it is at least possible that we can tell whether we experience God or disembodied minds, but then the concepts in question must be clearer than Flew wants to grant. This illustrates some of the tension between a Hume-like empiricist theory of meaning and a Hume-like empiricist theory of verification when both are applied to philosophical and religious matters. Flew's appeal to the existence of evil as evidence against the existence of God also requires that one be able to attach meaning to the word 'God'.

Experience of God is ruled out by a Hume-like theory of verification. To be consistent with the theory, anything that seems to be an experience of God can only be a God-hallucination because God cannot be an object of sense perception or of introspection. Experience of God, if such occurs, is not sensory or introspective because God is not a physical object, a sensory content, a mental state or the content of a mental state. Genuine experiences of God are simply excluded by definition in a Hume-like theory of verification. This is, of course, no argument that they do not occur.[4]

William Craig rejects Hume-like theories of meaning and verification. Given Hume-like theories of meaning and verification, the sort of enterprise in which Craig is engaged cannot get off the ground. There will be no cards dealt to a player like Craig in a Hume-like game; he can only challenge the game's rules.

In a sense, then, Craig and Flew (I take Flew to play by Hume-like rules) do not directly meet each other's perspectives. (A respect in which they do directly meet each other's perspectives is noted shortly.) That would require at least a pair of debates: first, one concerning basic philosophical perspectives; and second, one concerning the existence of God. It is hence particularly useful that there be, as there are here, comments on the debate in which some of the 'first debate' issues also arise.

One of the ways in which Craig's rejection of a Hume-like perspective manifests itself is in his use of the claim that *whatever has a beginning must have a cause*. Craig takes this to be a necessary truth – a proposition that cannot be false under any conditions. He would grant that it is not true by definition and that it cannot be established by appeal to sensory experience or introspection. He notes that we nonetheless take it to be true in our everyday reasoning and sees no reason why it is not perfectly justified to use it regarding such matters as whether the universe, if it had a beginning, must have a cause. Flew's sympathy with a Humean perspective expresses itself in his scepticism about using such a claim so far outside the context of reasoning about the specific items of everyday experience as is required by Craig's argument.

Varieties of Atheism and Theism

Atheism, like theism, has many varieties. One can be an idealist and an atheist, holding (like the philosopher McTaggert) that there exist only uncreated minds and their experiences. One can hold that among the fundamental, not-dependent-on-anything-else items there are inherently conscious things and inherently non-conscious things – souls and physical atoms – that beginning-lessly exist, but no God, as do the Jains.[5] Neither perspective is theistic. One can hold that there are only physical things, perhaps in a sense of 'physical' on which to be physical is (i) to be a spatially extended thing or to be capable of being part of a spatially extended thing, or else (ii) to be a property of, or a relation among, things that are physical by (i). Such physicalism or materialism is the most common sort of contemporary academic atheism, and apparently is the form favoured by Flew.

Theism, too, comes in more than one form. Typically, theists have not been materialists; Craig is not a materialist.[6] Some theists have held that God is creator in the sense that non-divine minds and physical items beginninglessly depend for their existence on God. Other theists hold that God created non-divine things and thereby also created time. Still others hold that time exists independent of created things and, after much time had passed, God created non-divine things. Craig's view is that, in creating a world, the eternal God became temporal.

A different way in which atheism and theism have varieties concerns *modality*. The modalities are:

1   necessary truth: a proposition P is a necessary truth if, and only if, it is impossible that P be false
2   necessary falsehood: a proposition P is a necessary falsehood if, and only if, P's contradictory not-P is a necessary truth
3   contingency: proposition P is contingent if and only if P is neither a necessary truth nor a necessary falsehood
4   possibility: proposition P is possible if and only if P is not a necessary falsehood (that is, P is either a necessary truth or is contingent).

Regarding modality there are two varieties of atheism: one that holds that *Necessarily, God does not exist* and one that holds *That God does not exist is contingent and true*. Flew, insofar as he grants that the word 'God' has meaning, apparently holds that the proposition *God exists* is contingent and false. It is not logically impossible that there be a God, just as it is not logically impossible that there have been unicorns. There just isn't any God, so far as we know.

Regarding modality, theism's versions are *Necessarily, God exists* and *That God exists is contingent and true*. Craig's position is that it is a necessary truth that God exists, but for the purposes of the debate it would not, so far as I can see, matter if Craig held the view *That God exists is contingent and true*. There is one proviso here. On Craig's view it must be logically impossible that God be caused to exist. Otherwise, one could argue as follows:

1 Necessarily, what can have a cause of existence does have a cause of existence.
2 God can have a cause of existence.

So:

3 God does have a cause of existence.[7]

Craig would reject propositions 2 and 3. If Craig's cosmological argument can be offered by theists who hold 2 *That God exists is contingent and true*, then it must be impossible that an omnipotent, omniscient, morally perfect being be caused to exist – it must be impossible that such a being exist dependently, even if it does not exist necessarily.

While both atheism and theism come in various sizes and shapes, there is a broad range of agreement between the debaters concerning the being whose existence they are debating.

'God'

Craig's type of theism concerns an eternal God who becomes temporal by the act of creating, and Flew's atheism concerns a material universe which is all there is. Both mean by 'God' a being who is personal, omnipotent, omniscient and morally perfect, who created the world and governs it providentially. Thus both use the term 'God' in a sense recognizable to monotheistic traditions, and in a manner that is not deistic. It would be otiose to protest that they do not include in the meaning of the term various idiosyncrasies current in the academy. Their use of the term is both that established in popular culture and that embraced by typical recognized representatives of the world's monotheistic religions. Agreement on the use of the term is, of course, a precondition of a debate in which the parties are not arguing past one another. Happily, that condition is met here.

Roadmap to Issues in the Commentaries

It is time to turn from the perspectives of the debaters to a consideration of some of the basic issues that are raised by those who comment on the debate. What follows tracks the course of the comments topic-by-topic and can be read as a prologue to, or as a review of, the arguments of the commentators.

The Cosmological Argument

Craig offers, and Flew critiques, a version of the cosmological argument that runs as follows: the universe has a beginning, whatever has a beginning must have a cause, so the universe has a cause. Craig proposes that this cause is God.

Douglas Geivett takes explanations to be answers to 'why?' questions. A question of the form 'Why X?' assumes that X exists, just as a question of the form 'Why is P true?' assumes that P is true. That X exists, or P is true, is the *topic* of the question or the explanation request. One can reply by claiming that the topic needs no explanation, does not exist, is not true, or is unknown, thereby declining to accede to the request. Or one can offer an explanation.

Geivett claims that:

(G1)   *It is impossible to effectively map the mathematical infinite on to physical reality (the attempt to do so generates paradoxes)*

and

(G2)   *The truth of (G1) provides good evidence for the claim that the physical universe has not always existed*

Thus

(G3)   *There is good evidence that the physical universe has not always existed.*

Flew declines the topic, claiming that the causal principle applies only within the universe. This is arbitrary, and thus Flew fails to deal with a legitimate topic whereas Craig offers a genuine explanation. This is one point in the debate that hinges on whether Flew's Hume-like perspective is defensible.

Michael Martin first claims that, on our ordinary concept of causality, causes are in time. He then argues that if we appeal to that concept, or convictions in which it is embedded, to justify the claim that nothing can begin without a cause, we cannot justify the conclusion that some cause is atemporal. Choices are causes that precede their effect, but choices of an eternal God would have no temporal location. (This objection would not apply to the notion of an everlasting God choosing to create.)

Second, Martin argues that since spaceless atemporal beings can be brute facts, God can be a brute fact. But then so can it be a brute fact that there is a universe.

Third, Martin contends that it is arbitrary to accept

(M1)   *Some spaceless atemporal things have no cause,*
and reject
(M2)   *Some things that begin have no cause.*

To this objection and the preceding, the theist will reply as follows. A brute fact, in the sense relevant here, is a state of affairs that might not have obtained, does obtain, could have been caused to obtain, but was not caused to obtain. If a pink rabbit, composed of material that did not previously exist, simply appeared without a cause, its appearance would be a brute fact.

The existence of God, the theist holds, cannot be a brute fact. Briefly, the relevant reasoning goes as follows.[8] A brute fact is a state of affairs that does obtain and *might* have had a cause, but did not. If it had been caused, it would have depended for its existence on that cause. But *There is a being X that is omnipotent, omniscient, and perfect* and *X depends on something else for its existence* are logically incompatible. A being that cannot depend on anything for its existence cannot be caused to exist. So God's existence cannot be a brute fact.

Fourth, Martin suggests, it is compatible with there being a caused universe that its cause is personal, but is also polytheistic or omnipotent but evil or morally neutral. Keith Parsons and William Rowe make similar remarks.

Fifth, Martin claims, if an atemporal personal cause is possible, so is an atemporal, non-personal cause. These comments seem intended to apply, even assuming that whatever has a beginning must have a cause.

A further question is whether they apply if one assumes a version of the principle of sufficient reason to the effect that *Necessarily, whatever can depend for its existence on something else actually does depend for its existence on something else* or, expressed differently, *Necessarily, whatever is possibly dependent is actually dependent.* If this principle is true, then there cannot be any brute facts. The force of objections four and five depend on whether or not the existence of polytheistic and morally neutral, or non-personal, causes would be brute facts. If, as seems to be the case, their existence would be brute facts, then their existence would also need to be explained.

Parsons adds that:

(P1)   *We have no model for creation-from-nothing*

the idea being that:

(P2)   *A purported explanation of the coming to be of X that includes no model for X's being made to come to be is really no explanation of the coming to be of X.*

The theist's reply will be that omnipotence requires no *modus operandi*, and without a *modus operandi* there is no model.

David Yandell critiques both Craig's position and Flew's. Regarding Craig and the cosmological argument, he focuses on Craig's critique of the notion of an actual infinite, which Craig uses as a basis for his claim that the world cannot fail to have had a beginning. First, if an actual infinite is indeed logically impossible, then the claim *There is an infinite series* entails, for some proposition P, *P is true and P is false.* Thus the idea of such a series is inconsistent and there is, then, no potential for an infinite series. Hence Craig's actual-infinite/ potential-infinite contrast is vacuous. Second, if the notion of an actual infinite is contradictory, God's omnipotence cannot be understood as infinite power and God's knowledge cannot be understood as infinite knowledge. But there are an infinite number of whole positive integers (which ones doesn't God know about?) and one would have thought that an omnipotent God could make a world W such that, in W, there was a one-to-one correspondence between, say, the whole positive integers and persons. How, on Craig's view, are we instead to understand omnipotence and omniscience? Third, there isn't any one answer to the question 'What is infinity minus infinity?'. It depends on which infinites you have in mind, and once one specifies the infinities in question there seem to be perfectly consistent answers to the resulting questions. Fourth, it is highly controversial that there cannot be an actual infinite, so much so that an argument for God's existence that rests on this claim supports a controversial conclusion on a premise arguably at least as controversial as itself. Fifth, there is available a version of the cosmological argument that does not require either that the universe have a beginning in time or that an actual infinite not be possible – so wouldn't it be better to use it? Sixth, it is not obvious that there can be such a thing as a person S such that it is logically impossible that S change in any way, and no such person could become incarnate as Christianity holds God did. Seventh, even if there could be an atemporal, changeless person, Craig claims that this person made an atemporal choice to create the world, not eternally, but at a certain time T. Even if time begins at the creation, how is 'at a certain time T' to be understood here? There is *ex hypothesi* no temporal frame to provide 'at a certain time' with content. Eighth, Craig's position requires that God's existence not be a brute fact – a fact that is possibly explicable but in fact lacks an explanation. One can defend this claim by maintaining that God has logically necessary existence, but Craig offers no ontological argument. One can hold that God is everlasting, and that therefore the question 'Why did God come into existence at all?' reduces without remainder to questions of the form 'Why does God exist at T1?,' 'Why does God exist at T2,' and so on, and that these questions are satisfactorily answered by 'God is beginningless'. As David Yandell notes, Craig does not defend any such reduction. It can be added that Craig is in no position to hold that God is beginningless, having claimed that it is logically impossible that the universe be beginningless because *being beginningless* entails *having existed for an infinitely long time*, which Craig alleges to be logically impossible.

David Yandell also critiques Flew's position. First, his critique of Christianity's view of hell assumes compatibilism – a controversial and powerfully criticized position. Second, he misrepresents the view of hell when he describes it as eternal torture for sheer unbelief. In fact, it is unrepented wrong action that leads to condemnation. But these issues concern particular views of hell rather than, strictly, God's existence. Third, Flew asserts that claims to possess knowledge about the universe as a whole are illegitimate, being beyond the scope of our possible knowledge. This raises two questions. One is: how does Flew know? The other is: how can this claim be reconciled with its own content and with other things Flew says? Taking the second question first, Flew's own claim concerns the universe and would thus appear to eliminate itself. Escape from this problem is not possible by distinguishing between metaclaims (claims about claims) and first-order claims (claims about things). Flew allows the first-order claims that physics makes about the universe as a whole, and physics itself can properly issue Flew's own metaclaim. As to how Flew knows that such things as *The universe has a cause* are unknowable, the answer cannot be that we know it from sensory experience, since no such experience (distributively or collectively) justified this conclusion. He might appeal to conceptual experience, as he does when he claims that there cannot be bodiless persons. But, of course, Craig can also appeal to conceptual experience in favour of his claim that *Necessarily, whatever begins to exist has a cause of existence* and it is common to find philosophers and religious traditions who find no contradiction or unintelligibility in the claim *There are unembodied persons*. Fifth, Flew expresses doubts about the notion of unembodied persons being meaningful. He apparently appeals here to some such view as this: if we commonly appeal to *having some quality Q* as a criterion for *being an X* it follows that *being Q* is an essential property of *being an X*. Or perhaps the idea is that if all experienced Xs have a property Q then *having Q* is an essential part of our concept of an X. But while it is true that all the dogs I've ever seen have been non-purple, it is neither the case that *being non-purple* is as essential property of *being canine* nor of the concept of *being canine*. So the view to which Flew appeals is false. Hence there is no good reason here to reject the notion of an unembodied person.

The Fine-tuning Argument

The fine-tuning argument begins with the claim that the odds of intelligent life arising out of what our best science tells us was the early state of the universe were preposterously low. It continues by claiming that the fact that intelligent life did arise obviously requires explanation, and that reference to God's causing there to be intelligent life is the most plausible explanation.

Geivett notes that Flew here too declines the topic of explaining the appearance of life under conditions that made its occurrence unlikely. Flew claims that such propositions as *The universe exists* and *The universe is orderly* are not candidates for explanation; no proposition of the form *The universe . . .* is explicable. Therefore, the proposition. *The universe produced biological life from sources that made life likely but were themselves unlikely to arise from initial conditions*, on Flew's view, is inexplicable.

Parsons criticizes the fine-tuning argument. First, he rejects the idea of probability having any application to possible universes; any argument that arises from such application he holds to be conceptually perverse. This contrasts sharply with Rowe's claim that, given all the possible universes in which free agents act rightly, it is unreasonable to think that God would not have created one of these.

Second, but closely related to the first point, one can assess the probability of a proposition only given some background of information other than necessary truths, but there is no such background regarding possible worlds.

Third, he contends that the fine-tuning argument requires that the principle of indifference applies to candidate universes – each such universe must be equally probable with every other. He then adds that the principle leads to 'outright inconsistency', referencing Wesley Salmon and John Earman's essay in Salmon's *Introduction to the Philosophy of Science*,[9] and concludes that we are owed a justification of the principle's application to possible universes. If the principle's application leads to inconsistency, presumably the justification is not forthcoming. In *Introduction to the Philosophy of Science*, we are told:

. . . in situations in which we have positive knowledge that we *are* dealing with alternatives that have equal probabilities, the strategy of counting equiprobable favorable cases and forming the ratio of favorable to equiprobable possible cases is often handy for facilitating computations.[10]

Each possible world is equally possible; logical possibility does not come in degrees. Whether each logically possible world is equal concerning the probability of its existence, or that there is any such thing as an intrinsic probability regarding this matter, is something else. Perhaps *if* there is any such thing as the *a priori* probability of the existence of a possible world, then all are tied in this regard. Richard Swinburne would appeal to considerations of simplicity as a reason to doubt this sort of equiprobability. But, as Parson comments, it is hard to see why one should think that there is any intrinsic probability here. Nonetheless, given the initial conditions, one would seem to have background information and not to be relying on considerations of probabilities allegedly attaching to merely possible worlds. Probability calculations, given background information that goes beyond logically necessary truths, seem to be the relevant sort of calculations for a fine-tuning argument.

Fourth, between any two positive numbers there is a non-denumerable infinity of real numbers. Take, then, the tiny range within which a given cosmic constant necessary for life can vary and still make life possible. There is a non-denumerable infinity of values that life-supporting constants can take. As Paul Davies grants in *The Mind of God*, the odds of one of an infinite number of possibilities coming to be realized is zero.[11] Herein lies a *reductio* of the fine-tuning argument.

A problem with this argument, it seems to me, is that, if one identifies *having zero probability* and *being logically impossible*, then it is impossible that any possible world be actual. Yet the actual world is one among the possible worlds. Presumably, then, one will want to characterize *having zero possibility* in terms of *either being logically impossible or being but one of an infinite number of possibilities*.

Assessing the force of this last objection to the fine-tuning argument is tricky. Suppose I get a prize if I throw a baseball through a hoop that is slightly larger than the ball itself. Consider in principle infinitely divisible spaces that have this feature: if I throw the ball through them, I throw the ball through the hoop. For any such space, it is infinitely improbable that I throw the ball through it. In order to throw the ball through the hoop, I must throw it through one or another of those spaces. But it does not follow that it is infinitely improbable that I throw the ball through the hoop.

All of this, however, should not make it impossible for one to tell that the odds against my throwing the ball through the hoop may be wonderfully poor. Suppose the hoop is 100 feet away, there are cross-winds caused by strong fans placed to make throwing the ball through the hoop still harder, I am blindfolded, I am not permitted to throw with the arm I'd normally use for throwing a ball, and the hoop is constantly moving. Anyone who was moved by the argument that, in principle, there are an infinite number of spaces such that, should I throw the ball through one of them, I throw the ball through the hoop, to bet on my doing so would soon be parted from his money. Similarly, the most recent objection to the fine-tuning argument does not seem to remove the improbability of conscious life arising from the initial conditions.

The success, then, of the fine-tuning argument would seem not to be negated by the sorts of *a priori* objection raised, but rather to depend on the reliability of the probability assessments on which it rests and on the view that such large matters as the origin of matter and the arrival of life are not brute facts.

The Moral Argument

R. Douglas Geivett notes that Craig does not argue that there are objective moral values; even his quotations from naturalists are in favour of the view that, if there is no God, then there are no objective values – not that there are, in fact, objective values. Further, *morals are objective* is not identical to *humans are special*.

William Rowe and I both argue that since moral principles are, if true, then necessarily true, there can be no such thing as explaining their truth rather their falsehood. There is no such thing as their possible falsehood which an explanation might eliminate, and hence no such thing as explaining their being true rather than false. One can give an analysis of their truth in terms of something that necessarily exists in virtue of which they are true. The relevant candidates seem to be God and abstract objects. The moral argument contains nothing that would make it clear that, among these candidates, it is God that should be chosen. True, as Geivett notes, abstract objects have no causal powers. But they need not have causal powers in order to ground necessary truths.

Michael Martin argues as follows: moral realism (the view that there exists something in virtue of which one or more moral principles are true) does not entail theism, since there are defences of moral realism that do not appeal to God. If moral realism does not entail theism, the moral argument fails. Hence the moral argument fails. Stated a little differently, the objection is this: there are varieties of moral realism that are theistic and varieties that are not; the moral argument does not succeed unless one can show that moral realism is true, *and among its varieties the true one is theistic*. The argument of the debate does not engage in the latter task.

Concerning the Resurrection

Here one enters a territory that combines historical, hermeneutic (in the old sense of 'concerning textual interpretation'), philosophical and theological considerations. One thing that the discussion of these matters makes clear is that there is a great gulf that divides scholars on these matters as they apply to the Resurrection. Those on the 'there is no reason to think it happened' side quote authors who think there is little basis indeed for giving credence to biblical texts that allegedly provide historical evidence for the Resurrection of Jesus. Those on the 'there is good reason to think it happened' side quote authors who think there is excellent reason for giving credence to the same texts. Rowe suggests that, of course, those who believe will find the relevant texts persuasive, but he knows that there is just as much reason to comment that those who do not believe will not find the relevant texts persuasive. The point here is not, I think, that it is all a matter of taste and sentiment, but that only a very detailed and sustained examination of various issues can present an argument there is much reason to think cogent.

Rowe and Flew emphasize that the texts in question were written down years after the events they purport to describe. In fact, we don't know when they were first written down – for example, was Q, the plausibly posited common source of Luke and Matthew other than Mark, written or oral or some of each? Their emphasis ignores the role of reliable oral tradition in Jewish culture. There thus will have to be a discussion of these matters in an overall assessment of Resurrection-relevant evidence.

Rowe correctly points out that the Christian doctrine of the Resurrection is not that the body of Jesus was resuscitated but that it was brought back to life in such a manner as to be spatially located but not subject to corruption, able to pass through doors but also eat food, and that the bringing back to life was caused by God. Further, the doctrine of the Resurrection is closely associated in Christian thought with the doctrines of the incarnation and the atonement. These doctrines, if I may so put it, provide a good deal of the theological setting and point of the Resurrection.

Rowe offers an interesting argument to this effect. If God does not exist, it is highly unlikely that we survive the death of our bodies. If God does exist, it is highly likely that we do survive the death of our bodies. The claim that Jesus survived the death of his body (which is entailed by Jesus having been resurrected) is highly unlikely to be true unless God exists. Appeal to the Resurrection to provide evidence for God's existence is thus of no avail. Since persons almost certainly do not survive the death of their bodies unless God exists, any claim that any person does survive death will presuppose that God exists, and since it will presuppose that claim it will not present a reason to believe that claim. Craig will grant that it is almost certain that we don't survive the death of our bodies if God does not exist, and will therefore argue that, if we have reason to believe that any person did survive the death of his or her body, that is strong reason to think that God exists. He will then claim that we do have reason to suppose that Jesus did survive the death of his body. Hence we have reason to believe that God exists.

The basic notion of *presupposition* here presumably is expressible in these terms: proposition A presupposes proposition B if, and only if, the falsehood of B entails the falsehood of A. A presupposes B if B's falsehood would prevent A's truth. But then if A presupposes B, A entails B. Adjusted to include probability relations, the idea will be expressible as follows: proposition A presupposes proposition B if, and only if, B's falsehood entails or make probable A's falsehood. A presupposes B if B's falsehood prevents A's truth or makes A's truth improbable. That persons survive death does not entail that God exists – not by itself. So a person's surviving death does not presuppose God's existence via entailment. Thus if it presupposes God's existence then it does so relative to being improbable if God does not exist. So Craig's argument is that, since Jesus survived death and it is improbable that this happens if God does not exist, then probably God exists.

Rowe's objection is that, since it is improbable that Jesus survived death unless God exists, one needs good reason to believe that God exists, independent of claims regarding Jesus' survival of death, in order for it to be reasonable to believe that Jesus did survive death. Suppose Uncle Frank has the habit of eating cucumber and banana sandwiches with mustard on rye, and I find the remains of such a delicacy on my kitchen table. It is improbable that there be these remains unless Uncle Frank has been at work. Can't I then cite the remains as evidence of his activity? Of course. But then I presumably have independent evidence regarding the existence and habits of Uncle Frank. The issue here is this: does one reason properly from *That E occurred is improbable unless G exists, and E occurred* to *Probably, G exists* in cases in which one does not have evidence that G exists independent of the occurrence of E? If not, then the inference from Jesus' survival of death to God's existence will have to be a part of a more general argument – a cumulative case – rather than standing on its own, with other parts of the cumulative case arguing for the existence of God independently of any appeal to anyone's survival of death. On this point, Rowe and Craig may not disagree after all.

Of course, the dispute does not concern the Resurrection of your average Jewish peasant, but one who is alleged to have made astounding claims about himself. Thus the question also arises as to whether Jesus himself made these claims or the Church simply ascribed them to him in the light of the beliefs they came to have about him, and, if the latter, whether those beliefs nonetheless had basis in his actual words and actions. There is also deep disagreement concerning the traditions concerning the appearances of Jesus and the empty tomb. The critical and historical questions quickly multiply and cannot be addressed here.

Geivett notes various positions that Flew might hold concerning the Resurrection: that the historical evidence for the Resurrection would be sufficient for ordinary events but not for an extraordinary event; that no historical evidence could be sufficient for the Resurrection; or that no historical evidence could provide evidence for the existence of God.[12]

The Presumption of Atheism and the Presumption of Theism

William Wainwright raises an issue distinct from those on which the other commentators concentrate. It is often assumed that the burden of proof is on the theist. Wainwright questions this, and indeed argues that if there is a burden of proof in the neighbourhood it rests on the atheist. The basis of this latter contention is that, given the cross-cultural prevalence of religious (and often theistic) belief, it is arguably true that theism is a natural belief – one people naturally tend to have – whereas atheism clearly is not a natural belief.

The arguments that there is no special burden of proof that applies to the theist include these:

1   Both atheism and theism assert positive existential claims – respectively
    That the universe exists is a brute fact and *That the universe exists is a fact
    because God created it.*
2   If the burden of proof is on one who challenges what is taken to be well
    established among those well educated, it is false that atheism is taken to be
    well established among this group.
3   Belief that God exists and life in accord with this belief has high value if
    God exists – a value that surpasses the value of belief that God does not
    exist if God does not exist, let alone if God does exist.

Wainwright ends with the contention that, as James insists, our 'passional
nature' affects our religious beliefs.

Some Concluding Reflections

The theists among the commentators take Craig to have gotten the better of
the argument; the atheists (or agnostics) among the commentators suppose
Flew's arguments to be more powerful. What consensus there is about the
matter suggests that Craig won the debate, but the discussions rightly focus not
on issues of rhetorical skill, but of sound arguments.

Some basic disagreements arise. Do probability considerations apply to
possible worlds? Rowe supposes that they do; he finds it mind-boggling that
among the infinity of possible worlds in which free agents exist, in none of them
do these possible agents act always freely and rightly. This, he thinks, is
logically possible but monstrously unlikely. Parsons thinks that applying
probability considerations to possible worlds is an exercise in futility. How
probable is it, given simply the infinity of possible worlds, that there be an
actual world containing self-conscious life? Well, we take the number of
possible worlds which are such that, if they were to obtain, there would be self-
conscious living creatures – set SC of possible worlds, let's say; and we also
take the number of possible worlds which are such that, if they were to obtain,
there would be no self-conscious living creatures – set SC*, let's say. Then, if
we ask what the proportion of set SC is to the set of all possible worlds – set
PW, let's say – SC is just PW minus SC*. So if there are an infinite number of
possible worlds, what proportion of PW is SC? What is the numerical result of
the formula *PW minus SC*? On Parson's view, these questions are ill-formed;
there isn't any such proportion or equation. Craig himself, as no friend of
infinity, should not have any truck with an infinite number of possible worlds.
If Parsons is right about possible worlds and the probability of self-conscious
life, Rowe is wrong about the possible worlds and free creatures who always
act rightly. In fact, as we noted, Craig's actual argument appeals to
background information about this world – a sort of information not included
in the argument Rowe offers. Thus Craig, apparently, could agree with Parsons
that probability considerations don't apply to possible worlds *per se*.

The issues raised in the comments range widely, covering a host of matters in
epistemology, metaphysics and philosophy of religion. Here, we have tried to
indicate something of their scope, nature, and complexity.

Notes

1   I waive here any problems that arise from the atomistic and naming aspects of this view – from the fact that the view takes it that the locus of indefinable meaning lies in words, one word at a time, and that it takes naming to be a primitive enterprise not itself requiring a context in which meaning is already present.

2   'Constituents' would be a more accurate term for a strictly Humean view.

3   The exception to this is 'relations of ideas' statements, such as 'Every effect has a cause', 'Every cause has an effect' and 'All big dogs are dogs'. Such statements are typically described as 'true in virtue of the meanings of the words they contain' or 'true in virtue of their logical form'.

4   Propositions in traditional metaphysics – claims such as *Necessarily, whatever begins to exist has a cause of existence* and *Necessarily, if something X exists such that it is logically possible that X not have existed, and logically possible that there be a metaphysical explanation of X's existence, then there actually is a metaphysical explanation of X's existence* (*whether or not we know what it is*) are neither true by definition nor verifiable by experience in a manner approved by a Hume-like theory of verification. They, too, are out of the question as premises in any argument if one accepts such a theory. But a Hume-like theory of verification can no more satisfy its own criterion than can such metaphysical propositions as those mentioned.

There is also the matter of Hume-like theories of necessity. The proposition *All bachelors are male* is identical to *All unmarried adult males are male* and is hence of the form *All X,Y,Z are Z*. The fact that the words 'All bachelors are male' has this form – that the sounds or marks in questions are words and that so put together they express something of the indicated structure – is a matter of convention; we made that true. The fact that propositions with that structure are necessarily true is not something we made true. Further, there are necessary truths that lack that structure and any other structure that guarantees truth. *If Richard draws a triangle, then Richard draws a figure* is a necessary truth, but true by content rather than structure. That the words in question express the content they do is a matter of convention; we made that true. That the contents in question are so related as to constitute a necessary truth is not something we made true.

Hume-like theories of necessity are conventionalistic. They hold that necessity arises from conventions. A proposition is necessarily true only if it is impossible that it be false or lack truth-value. For any convention you like, it could have been avoided – its non-adoption is a possibility. If the necessity of necessarily true propositions depends on conventions, then those propositions could have been false (had certain other conventions been adopted instead) or lacked truth value (as they would had no conventions been adopted). Since necessary truths cannot be false or lack truth value, they do not rest on conventions.

It is crucial here as elsewhere in considering conventionalism to distinguish between whether the proposition expressed by a sentence is a necessary truth – which is not conventional – and whether the sentence happens to express a necessary truth – which is conventional. We decide what proposition a sentence expresses; we do not decide whether that proposition is true, unless it concerns what decisions we make (as it typically will not, and as no necessary truth will).

There are further inelegances in a conventionalist theory of necessity. Whatever the correct theory of necessity is, it will be a necessary truth. A conventionalist account of necessity will say that for any necessary truth T, it is true due to the adoption of a convention C. But then the conventionalist account itself is true only due to some convention. The convention might never have obtained. Hence the theory is possibly false. If it is possibly false, it is not a necessary truth. If it is not a necessary truth, it is not true at all – not because all truths are necessary truths (that is plainly false) but because any account of necessity is either necessarily true or necessarily false. So conventionalism, being possibly false, is not a necessary truth. In addition, then, to being possibly false, it is also a necessary falsehood. (One needs here to remember that *P is possibly false* means *Either P is logically contingent (neither a necessary truth nor a necessary falsehood) or a necessary falsehood, being necessarily false* entails *being possibly false*).

5 Jainism is an atheistic South Asian Indian religion.
6 Nonetheless various contemporary theists hold that a theist can be a materialist at least about non-divine persons; if it is logically possible that a person be wholly material (a controversial issue), then a theist can be a materialist concerning non-divine persons.
7 The argument can be more cautiously put as follows:

   1. Necessarily, what can have a cause of existence does have a cause of existence.
   2. If God exists, then God can have a cause of existence.

   Thus

   3. If God thus exists, then God does have a cause of existence. Craig will still need to reject, and will reject, 3.

8 It is more fully presented in the present author's comments in Chapter 7.
9 See *Introduction to the Philosophy of Science* (Indianapolis: Hackett Publishing Co., Inc., 1999), with multiple authors: Salmon, Earman, Glymour, Lennox, Machamer, McGuire, Norton, Salmon, Schaffner. Its predecessor was by Wesley Salmon, and published in 1992 by Prentice-Hall. The passage quoted below is from page 77.
10 Ibid., p. 77.
11 Paul Davies, *The Mind of God: The Scientific Basis for a Rational World* (New York: Simon & Schuster, 1992), pp. 204–5.
12 *The Epistemology of Religious Experience* (Cambridge: Cambridge University Press, 1993) critically assesses, but does not support, the claim that one's prior conceptual apparatus explains why things appear as they do in religious experience.

Chapter 2

The Craig–Flew Debate

William Lane Craig and Antony Flew

(Keith Yandell moderating)

Introduction (Keith Yandell)

I want to join Stan Wallace in welcoming you to this event and begin with a story told to me by one of my graduate students who is now teaching philosophy at a college just outside of Atlanta, Georgia, having received his Ph.D from our department. The story goes like this.

> My advisee and his family were at church one morning and the son, Mark, was attending a Sunday School class. Topic of the morning: the Power of God. Old Testament story: God parts the Red Sea. Question from one of the students, 'Is God so powerful that God does not even have to exist in order to part the Red Sea?' Teacher's response: 'Why don't we discuss this?' So they did. Having discussed it for a while, they took a vote. The vote was overwhelmingly that God was so powerful that God did not have to exist for God to part the Red Sea. Mark was not satisfied with the vote and, after class, ran into the sanctuary where his father was talking to the pastor and said in a voice loud enough for the entire room to hear, 'Dad, you know about this stuff, you do philosophy of religion. Is God so powerful God does not have to exist in order for God to act?' Having been well taught, my advisee answered, 'Not even God can do anything if God doesn't exist.' At which point Mark turned to his teacher across the room and shouted out 'See, I was right.'

My colleagues, William Craig and Antony Flew agree, I assume, that if God does not exist, God does no acting. They disagree about whether or not God exists. They are professional colleagues. It is a distinct pleasure for me to introduce them.

Dr Flew earned his BA and MA degrees at Oxford and received a D. Litt. from the University of Keele. He has published some 23 authored books on topics ranging from *An Introduction To Western Philosophy* through *Darwinian Evolution* to *Agency and Necessity*, a discussion with co-philosopher Godfrey Vesey. He has published some 72 articles and pamphlets. He co-edited a book entitled *New Essays in Philosophical Theology* with Alasdair MacIntyre, which was the major textbook in the only philosophy of religion course I have ever taken, and, in addition, has edited 11 more volumes. Perhaps most relevant to tonight's discussion are his *God and Philosophy*, published in 1966, *The Presumption of Atheism*, published a decade later, and *Atheistic Humanism*, published in 1993. Dr Flew has been a regular member of the faculty at Oxford University, the Universities of Aberdeen, Keele and Reading and the University of Calgary and York University in Canada. He has been visiting professor at New York University, Swarthmore College, the Universities of Minnesota, Pittsburgh, Maryland, New Buffalo, Southern California at Los Angeles and California at San Diego, as well as at the Universities of Adelaide, Melbourne and the Australian National University. This cumulative record of publication and teaching is impressive enough not to need me to comment on it.

Dr Craig has a BA from Wheaton College in Illinois, two Master's degrees from Trinity Evangelical Divinity School and two doctorates, one in philosophy from the University of Birmingham in England and one in theology from the University of Munich. He has taught at Trinity Evangelical Divinity School and Westmont College and done research at the Catholic University of Louvain, and currently he is research professor at Talbot School of Theology. Leaving aside his forthcoming publications, he has authored some 70 articles or book chapters which have appeared in such refereed journals as *Analysis, Faith and Philosophy, International Journal for Philosophy of Religion, British Journal for Philosophy of Science, American Philosophical Quarterly, International Philosophical Quarterly* and, *Australasian Journal of Philosophy* and *Religious Studies*. He has given distinguished lecture series at various colleges and universities and, in addition to having written several more popular books, he has published some seven scholarly books on topics ranging from *The Problem of Divine Foreknowledge and Future Contingents from Aristotle to Suarez* through *The Historical Argument For The Resurrection of Jesus during The Deist Controversy* to *Theism, Atheism and Big Bang Cosmology*, co-authored with Quentin Smith. This last book, along with *Assessing the New Testament Evidence for the Historicity of the Resurrection of Jesus* (1989) and *The Kalam Cosmological Argument*, published in 1979, are perhaps those of his books which relate most closely to tonight's discussion. This cumulative record of publication and lecturing is impressive enough not to need me to comment on it either.

This evening's participants, then, are professionally trained, well-published scholars. They know that either God exists or else God does not exist. They disagree about where the truth of that matter lies. Our debate format is simple. There are four rounds of descending length; two 20-minute opening statements, two 12-minute comments on the opening statements, two eight-minute responses to the previous remarks, and two five-minute closing statements. After a very brief break, we will begin a half-hour session of questions and answers. There is no need for me to make any further introductions and Professors Craig and Flew will proceed through the four phases of their remarks without any interruption. Then I will formally close the debate and shortly thereafter open the question and answer session.

It is, then, my genuine pleasure to introduce Professor William Craig and Professor Antony Flew. As is traditional, the affirmative side starts. Let the debate begin.

Craig's Opening Statement

Good evening! I want to begin by expressing my thanks for the privilege of participating in this event on the fiftieth anniversary of the famous Copleston–Russell debate, and it's a special honour to be sharing the platform tonight with Dr Flew.

Now, in order to determine rationally whether or not God exists, we need to conduct our inquiry according to the basic rules of logic and ask ourselves two fundamental questions: (1) Are there good reasons to think that God exists? And (2) Are there good reasons to think that He does not?

Now with respect to that second question, I'll leave it up to Dr Flew to present the reasons why he thinks that God does not exist. But notice that, although atheist philosophers have tried for centuries to disprove the existence of God, no one's ever been able to come up with a successful argument. So rather than attack straw men at this point, I'll just wait to hear Dr Flew's answer to the following question: what good arguments are there to show that God does not exist?

Let's look, then, at the first question: are there good reasons to think that God exists? Tonight I am going to present five reasons why I think theism is more plausibly true than atheism. Whole books have been written on each of these, so I can only present here a brief sketch of each argument and then go into more detail as Dr Flew responds to them. These reasons are independent of one another, and, taken together, they constitute a powerful cumulative case for the existence of God.

I. The Origin of the Universe

Have you ever asked yourself where the universe came from? Why anything at all exists instead of just nothing? Typically, atheists have said that the universe is just eternal and uncaused. As Russell remarked to Copleston: 'The universe is just there and that's all.'[1] But is that really all? If the universe never began to exist, then that means that the number of events in the past history of the universe is infinite. But mathematicians recognize that the existence of an actually infinite number of things leads to self-contradictions. For example, what is infinity minus infinity? Well, mathematically you get self-contradictory answers. This shows that infinity is just an idea in your mind, not something that exists in reality. David Hilbert, perhaps the greatest mathematician of this century, states, 'The infinite is nowhere to be found in reality. It neither exists in nature nor provides a legitimate basis for rational thought .... The role that remains for the infinite to play is solely that of an idea.'[2] But that entails that since past events are not just ideas but are real, the number of past events must be finite. Therefore, the series of past events can't go back forever. Rather, the universe must have begun to exist.

This conclusion has been confirmed by remarkable discoveries in astronomy and astrophysics. The astrophysical evidence indicates that the universe began to exist in a great explosion called the 'Big Bang' 15 billion years ago. Physical space and time were created in that event, as well as all the matter and energy in the universe. Therefore, as the Cambridge astronomer Fred Hoyle points out, the Big Bang theory requires the creation of the universe from nothing. This is because as you go back in time, you reach a point at which, in Hoyle's words, 'The universe was shrunk down to nothing at all'.[3] Thus the Big Bang model requires that the universe began to exist and was created out of nothing.

Now, this tends to be very awkward for the atheist for, as Anthony Kenny of Oxford University urges, 'A proponent of the [Big Bang] theory, at least if he is an atheist, must believe that ... the universe came from nothing and by nothing'.[4] But surely that doesn't make sense? Out of nothing, nothing comes. So why does the universe exist instead of just nothing? Where did it come from? There must have been a cause which brought the universe into being.

We can summarize our argument thus far as follows:

1   Whatever begins to exist has a cause.
2   The universe began to exist.
3   Therefore, the universe has a cause.

Now from the very nature of the case, as the cause of space and time, this cause must be an uncaused, timeless, changeless and immaterial being of unimaginable power which created the universe. Moreover, I would argue, it must also be personal. For how else could a timeless cause give rise to a temporal effect like the universe? If the cause were an impersonal set of necessary and sufficient conditions, then the cause could never exist without the effect. If the cause were timelessly present, then the effect would be timelessly present as well. The only way for the cause to be timeless and for the effect to begin to exist in time is for the cause to be a personal agent who freely chooses to create an effect in time without any prior determining conditions. Thus, we are brought, not merely to a transcendent cause of the universe, but to its personal creator.

Isn't it incredible that the Big Bang theory thus confirms what the Christian theist has always believed – that 'In the beginning God created the heavens and the earth'?[5] Now I simply put it to you: which do you think makes more sense – that the theist is right, or that the universe just 'popped' into being, uncaused, out of nothing? I, at least, don't have any trouble assessing these alternatives.

II.   The Complex Order in the Universe

During the last 30 years scientists have discovered that the existence of intelligent life depends on a delicate and complex balance of initial conditions simply given in the Big Bang itself. We now know that life-*prohibiting* universes are vastly more probable than any life-*permitting* universe like ours. How much more probable? Well, the answer is that the chances that the universe should be life-permitting are so infinitesimal as to be incomprehensible and incalculable. For example, Stephen Hawking has estimated that if the rate of the universe's expansion one second after the Big Bang had been smaller by even one part in a hundred thousand million million, the universe would have recollapsed into a hot fireball.[6] P.C.W. Davies has calculated that the odds against the initial conditions' being suitable for later star formation (without which planets could not exist) is one followed by a thousand billion billion zeros, at least.[7] Davies also estimates that a change in the strength of gravity or of the weak force by only one part in 10^{100} would have prevented a life-permitting universe.[8] There are around 50 such quantities and constants present in the Big Bang which must be fine-tuned in this way if the universe is to permit life. And it's not just each quantity which must be finely tuned. Their ratios to one another must also be exquisitely fine-tuned. So improbability is multiplied by improbability by improbability, until our minds are reeling with incomprehensible numbers.

There is no physical reason why these constants and quantities possess the values they do. The one-time agnostic physicist Paul Davies comments, 'Through my scientific work, I have come to believe more and more strongly that the physical universe is put together with an ingenuity so astonishing that I cannot accept it merely as a brute fact.'[9] Similarly, Fred Hoyle remarks, 'A common sense interpretation of the facts suggests that a super-intellect has monkeyed with physics.'[10] Robert Jastrow, the head of NASA's Goddard Institute for Space Studies, calls this the most powerful evidence for the existence of God 'ever to come out of science.'[11]

So, once again, the view that Christian theists have always held – that there is a designer of the cosmos – seems to make much more sense then the atheistic view that the universe, when it 'popped' into being uncaused out of nothing, just happened to be, by chance, fine-tuned to an incomprehensible precision for the existence of intelligent life.

We can summarize our reasoning as follows:

1   The fine-tuning of the initial conditions of the universe is due to either law, chance or design.
2   It is not due to either law or chance.
3   Therefore, it is due to design.

III.   Objective Moral Values in the World

If God does not exist, then objective moral values do not exist. Many theists and atheists alike concur on this point. For example, Russell observed:

> Ethics arises from the pressure of the community on the individual. Man ... does not always instinctively feel the desires which are useful to his herd. The herd, being anxious that the individual should act in its interests, has invented various devices for causing the individual's interest to be in harmony with that of the herd. One of these ... is morality.[12]

Michael Ruse, a philosopher of science at the University of Guelph, agrees. He explains:

> Morality is a biological adaptation, no less than are hands and feet and teeth ... considered as a rationally justifiable set of claims about an objective something, [ethics] is illusory. I appreciate that when somebody says 'Love thy neighbour as thyself', they think they are referring above and beyond themselves .... Never-

theless, … such reference is truly without foundation. Morality is just an aid to survival and reproduction, … and any deeper meaning is illusory ….[13]

Friedrich Nietzsche, the great nineteenth-century atheist who proclaimed the death of God, understood that the death of God meant the destruction of all meaning and value in life.[14] I think that Friedrich Nietzsche was right.

But we've got to be very careful here. The question here is *not*: 'Must we believe in God in order to live moral lives?'. I'm not claiming that we must. Nor is it the question 'Can we recognize objective moral values without believing in God?'. I think that we can. Rather, the question is: 'If God does not exist, do objective moral values exist?'

Like Russell and Ruse, I don't see any reason to think that, in the absence of God, the herd morality evolved by *Homo sapiens* is objective. After all, if there is no God, then what's so special about human beings? They're just accidental by-products of nature which have evolved relatively recently on an infinitesimal speck of dust lost somewhere in a hostile and mindless universe and which are doomed to perish individually and collectively in a relatively short time. On the atheistic view, some action – say, rape – may not be socially advantageous and so in the course of human development has become taboo. But that does absolutely nothing to prove that rape is really wrong. On the atheistic view there is nothing really wrong with your raping someone. Thus, without God there is no absolute right and wrong which imposes itself on our conscience.

But the problem is that objective values *do* exist and, deep down, I think we all know it. There's no more reason to deny the objective reality of moral values than the objective reality of the physical world. Actions like rape, cruelty and child abuse aren't just socially unacceptable behaviour. They are moral abominations. Some things are really wrong. Similarly, love, equality and self-sacrifice are really good.

Thus we can summarize this third consideration as follows:

1 If God does not exist, objective moral values do not exist.
2 Objective values do exist.
3 Therefore, God exists.

IV.   The Historical Facts Concerning the Life, Death and Resurrection of Jesus

The historical person Jesus of Nazareth was a remarkable individual. New Testament critics have reached something of a consensus that the historical Jesus came on the scene with an unprecedented sense of divine authority – the authority to stand and speak in God's place. He claimed that in himself the Kingdom of God had come, and as visible demonstrations of this fact he carried out a ministry of miracles and exorcisms. But the supreme confirmation of his claim was his Resurrection from the dead. If Jesus did rise from the dead, then it would seem that we have a divine miracle on our hands and, thus, evidence for the existence of God.

Now, most people would probably think that the Resurrection of Jesus is something you just either believe in by faith or not. But there are actually three established facts, recognized by the majority of New Testament historians today, which I believe are best explained by the Resurrection of Jesus.

- Fact 1. *On the Sunday following his crucifixion Jesus' tomb was found empty by a group of his women followers.* According to Jacob Kremer, an Austrian scholar who has specialized in the study of the Resurrection, 'By far most scholars hold firmly to the reliability of the biblical statements about the empty tomb'.[15]
- Fact 2. *On separate occasions different individuals and groups saw appearances of Jesus alive after his death.* According to the prominent German New Testament critic Gerd Lüdemann, 'It may be taken as historically certain that … the disciples had experiences after Jesus' death in which Jesus appeared to them as the Risen Christ.'[16] These appearances were witnessed not only by believers, but also by unbelievers, sceptics and even enemies.
- Fact 3. *The original disciples suddenly came to believe in the Resurrection of Jesus despite their having every predisposition to the contrary.* Jews had no belief in a dying, much less a rising, Messiah. And Jewish beliefs about the afterlife precluded anyone's rising from the dead before the end of the world. Nevertheless, the original disciples suddenly came to believe in the Resurrection of Jesus so strongly that they were willing to die for the truth of that belief. Luke Johnson, a New Testament scholar from Emory University, muses, 'Some sort of powerful, transformative experience is required to generate the sort of movement earliest Christianity was.'[17] N.T. Wright, an eminent British scholar, concludes, 'That is why, as a historian, I cannot explain the rise of early Christianity unless Jesus rose again, leaving an empty tomb behind him.'[18]

Attempts to explain away these three great facts – like the disciples stole the body or Jesus wasn't really dead – have been universally rejected by contemporary scholarship. The simple fact is that there just is no plausible, naturalistic explanation of these three facts. And therefore, it seems to me, the Christian is amply justified in believing that Jesus rose from the dead and was who he claimed to be. But that entails that God exists.

V. The Immediate Experience of God

This isn't really an *argument* for God's existence. Rather, it's the claim that you can know that God exists wholly apart from arguments, simply by immediately experiencing Him. This was the way in which people in the Bible knew God. As Professor John Hick explains:

> God was known to them as a dynamic will interacting with their own wills, a sheer given reality as inescapably to be reckoned with as destructive storm and life-giving sunshine …. To them, God was not … an idea adopted by the mind but an experiential reality which gave significance to their lives.[19]

Now, if this is the case, then there is a danger that proofs for God could actually distract your attention from God Himself. If you are sincerely seeking God, then God will make His existence evident to you. The Bible promises: 'Draw near to God and He will draw near to you.'[20] We mustn't so concentrate on the external proofs that we fail to hear the voice of God speaking to our own hearts. For those who listen, God becomes an immediate reality in their lives.

In conclusion, then, we have yet to see any arguments to show that God does not exist, and we have seen five reasons to think that God does exist. Together these constitute a powerful, cumulative case for the existence of God, and therefore I think that theism is the more plausible world-view.

Flew's Opening Statement

I thought I was going to have to begin as Socrates ended, with an apology, because I thought I was going to have to explain that I wasn't going to try to show that there is no God. I was going to try to show that there are no sufficient reasons for believing that there is. And Dr Craig apparently was wanting to maintain the exact opposite: that I wouldn't be able to establish that there is no God, but he thinks he's provided sufficient reasons for thinking that there is.

He has offered so many arguments that it will be impossible for me in any reasonable amount of time to answer them all. But what I am going to say, if it's correct, will provide a sufficient reason for thinking that he and others are altogether too bold in thinking that they know what caused the universe or even that they *could* know what caused the universe. My fundamental point is that we are, all of us, creatures whose entire knowledge and experience has been of the universe. It is, after all, the only one there is and certainly the only one we have experience of. So why should anyone think that they are able to provide an answer to the question that Dr Craig posed: '*Where did the universe come from?*'

Take this business about whether God caused the Big Bang or whether the universe just 'popped' into existence. Why are we offered only two possibilities here? Why does anyone think that these are the only two possibilities?

I think there are two things one needs to say about this. One concerns the ultimates of explanation. Every explanation of why anything is the case is given an answer in terms of something else, some general or more general law, which at that stage is taken as a brute fact – the fact that explains other things. This is surely the nature of the case: you cannot have an end to all explanations that is anything other than a brute fact. Of course, some people find some sort of brute fact satisfactory and think: 'That's a good place to stop.' And one can't say its absolutely *wrong* to stop at that point. So it seems to me that you can't rule out the possibility that our knowledge of the universe or all knowledge must stop with the Big Bang; that this itself is the ultimate fact; that, if there's any first cause, it's the beginning or something some microseconds away from the beginning (because after all, everything else in the universe is being explained now).

Of course, the whole of cosmology may be different next year, but we're debating in Wisconsin tonight. So one has at least to entertain the possibility that it's not ridiculous for the universe to pop into existence out of nothing. If someone was there beforehand, watching, they'd say, 'Gosh! It's started out of nothing.' But we're just not in a position to answer the question. And concerning the fact that one is unable to suggest a cause for the Big Bang, why should you think that anyone but a physicist is going to explain that? And if physics stops there, isn't that the end of human knowledge?

Now let's consider the alternative. Let us actually produce a definition of 'God,', the supposed explanation of everything. This is the definition offered by a Richard Swinburne, which is generally accepted as the standard definition within the English-speaking countries:

> ... a person without a body, (i.e., a spirit), present everywhere, the creator and sustainer of the universe, a free agent, able to do everything, (i.e., omnipotent), knowing all things, perfectly good, a source of moral obligation, immutable, eternal, a necessary being, holy, and worthy of worship.[21]

Well, that's a lot of characteristics for this cause, and some of the audience clearly think, 'Got it! That's what must have caused the whole universe.' Well, it would be perfectly possible that there should be a being that was omnipotent and omniscient and created the universe, but wasn't particularly interested in human conduct. Of course, everyone thinking of creation is thinking of the first two chapters of Genesis. This God created the whole universe in order to have some human beings created in His image. But why should we assume, in this definition of God as first cause, that He has this interest in human behaviour – in morality and so on? And if this God was omnipotent and omniscient and wanted people to behave in a certain way, why couldn't he accomplish this? If you were omnipotent wouldn't you expect results and expect people to do exactly what you wanted? And shouldn't our presumption be, looking at human behaviour, that as far as omnipotence is concerned, He is not interested in human behaviour? You might well have an argument that might show there was an existing being possessing some of these characteristics but not others, but not an argument for a being with all these characteristics.

The second thing I want to say is that these characteristics are at least compatible, but the God that I understand Dr Craig to believe in is one who is described as good and benevolent Himself but is also described as a being who expects that He is going to torture forever the majority of the creatures He has created. Well, if you think these characteristics are compatible with benevolence, if your absolute values hold that torturing anyone at all, apart from forever, is OK, then we have different ideas of benevolence. I regard it as morally compulsory not to torture anyone at all.

I'm not saying that this is a reason for not believing there is a torturer who runs the universe. I am saying that these two characteristics are incompatible. I think actually that Dr Craig is sometimes a little anxious about these things. He says:

If we take Scripture seriously, we must admit that the vast majority of persons in the world are condemned and will be forever lost, even if in some relatively rare cases a person might be saved through his response to the light that he has apart from special revelation.[22]

He then goes on to indicate that 'No orthodox Christian *likes* the doctrine of hell or delights in anyone's condemnation. I truly wish that universalism were true, but it is not.'[23] Well, I regard that as a sign of grace, that he says that, but I still have to say that these two things are simply incompatible – it's a nightmare. As for the idea that such a punishment could be just, don't you know what justice is? Of course, the right ones are getting the punishment. But justice isn't a matter of simply getting the right ones punished for the crime. The punishment needs to be to some extent proportionate to the seriousness of the crime. And how can there be any offence committed by a human being in a short life that deserves a literally infinite punishment?

So what I am basically trying to show is that there aren't good reasons for believing in God, and my very fundamental contention is that one shouldn't expect to be able to know things outside the universe. And, if you like, the burden of proof lies on the person who says that one can know such things. So, no number of arguments from Dr Craig which I leave unanswered will be sufficient grounds to ignore my argument by saying, 'Well, that's no use – I've produced all these arguments he hasn't answered'. No one could answer in the available time all the great, long lists of arguments he has produced. But this is the answer that I think couldn't be answered – the argument, if you like, against the presumption of thinking that we're in a position to say what was going on (if anything was going on) outside the universe.

But let's look at what I believe is called the *kalam* argument, which is a great favourite of Dr Craig's: 'The universe must have had a beginning because nothing could exist without beginning and without end.' Fair enough, I think this is a good argument. But this is supposed to be an argument for a creation by a bodiless person (a notion I find very difficult to understand anyway, as all the people I know are creatures of flesh and blood) who apparently was himself uncreated and eternal. Now I don't doubt that the universe had a beginning because this is the present view of physical science. It looks as if at least this part of the Big Bang theory is likely to be with us permanently (although some further things may be added). But surely, if time had to have a beginning, how do we explain that beginning by saying 'Oh well, the beginning was started off, the whole universe was created by a being that existed eternally'? Well, if this argument assumes that time must have had a beginning, then how is it that the same is not true of God? Of course, one may respond that God never had a beginning and will never have an end. But this simply won't do: the argument that gets us to the creation is inconsistent with the desired explanation of it.

So, I think we come back again to a decent ignorance. I'm often thought to be a rather arrogant chap (how wrong people can be!), but I've never believed that I could give you a sort of guidebook outside the universe. I've been a bit hard-pressed to give you a guidebook to a fairly small area inside the universe. But this idea that we could gather a group of rational chaps and expect that they could all recognize an argument showing that this is how the universe began, that we know something about what must exist behind the universe, is absurd. I don't think this argument will work at all.

What about my contention that an omnipotent being, if he wanted people to behave in a certain way (as devoted and obedient children), could perfectly well make them that way? Ordinary human parents would love their children to be obedient and virtuous and so on. Wouldn't we all, being parents? And we have all, I suspect, been rather unsuccessful. But granted the resources of omnipotence, I think I could manage to have such perfectly obedient children.

But apparently the God whom Dr Craig is asking us to believe is the creator very much wants people to believe in a certain way and He wants this so much that He's prepared to torture them forever to punish them for not obeying 'Me'. Well, it seems to me that anyone who knew that this was what this cosmic 'Saddam Hussein' wanted would behave like the sensible subjects of Saddam Hussein. They would say anything about His merits and goodness. Wouldn't you if you were going to fall into the hands of his torturers? But omnipotence could avoid all this by simply making them such that they would choose to obey Him. This is an argument which I think may give Dr Craig a little pause.

About design: everyone has heard of the argument to design – about how if we found a watch in the bush, we'd infer that this was a product of design, and so on. But surely the reason why we infer that something was made by an intelligent being is not its complexity. It's simply that it is obviously an artifact and not a natural phenomenon. The most complicated, sophisticated entities in the whole universe are entities of a sort of which I see about 3000 around here. They were not, at least within the universe itself, designed. They (we) were, at least within the universe itself, products of unconscious physical and mechanical forces.

As this argument from design concerns design within the universe, the argument from design concerning design outside the universe is another one of like kind. And in the remaining 30 seconds, I won't try to deal with that one now. Another time, another argument.

Craig's First Rebuttal

You will remember that, in my first speech, I argued that there are no good reasons to think that atheism is true and that there are good reasons to think that theism is true. Now I asked Dr Flew to give us good arguments to show that God does not exist. As I listened to his first speech, I distilled basically three arguments that he offered. The first argument is that, if God is omnipotent, then why don't things turn out as God wills? It seems to me that the answer to that question is evident: namely, God's omnipotence does not mean that He can do things that are logically impossible. It is logically impossible to *make* someone *freely* do something. Libertarian freedom *entails* freedom from causal restraints. Therefore, if we are truly free and God has willed to create free creatures, then He *cannot* guarantee how free creatures will choose. In other words, Dr Flew's fallacy is thinking that, because there are logically possible worlds in which everyone always does what God wants, those worlds are feasible for God to create. But it may well be the case that any time God would try to create such a logically possible world the creatures would freely go wrong and would not do what God wants. And even an omnipotent being cannot *make* someone freely do something. So I think the first argument is simply fallacious.

Second, Dr Flew argued that the doctrine of God's love and justice is incompatible with the doctrine of hell, particularly because the punishment is not proportionate to the crime. Well, let me say two things about that. First of all, this isn't the topic of the debate this evening. The subject of the debate is the existence of God. What this argument would show is that the doctrine of hell is false, not that God does not exist. Nevertheless, as a Christian theist who believes in the doctrine of hell, let me say something in its defence anyway.

First, this problem is related to the one that we mentioned a moment ago, namely: people freely separate themselves from God forever. It isn't that God sends people to hell. Rather, people freely reject God's grace and forgiveness, and so separate themselves from God forever. If eternal punishment were for finite sins in this life, then I agree it would be disproportionate. But the biblical view is that people of their own free will reject God and His forgiveness, and so they separate themselves from God forever.

The second point I'd like to make is, if a person committed an infinite number of sins, then he would deserve eternal punishment. Now obviously no one commits an infinite number of sins in this life, but what about in the afterlife? Insofar as the damned in hell continue to hate and reject God, they continue to sin, and thus they incur further punishment. And thus, in a real sense, hell is self-perpetuating: because the sinning goes on forever, the punishment goes on forever.

Finally, I want to suggest that there may be in fact a sin of infinite gravity and proportion which does merit eternal punishment, and this would be the sin of irrevocably rejecting God and His forgiveness. It seems to me that for the creature to spit in the face of God, his Creator – to reject God irrevocably – is a sin of infinite proportion and could well merit eternal punishment.

So even though this isn't the topic of the debate tonight, I think that no arguments have been given to show that the doctrine of hell is incompatible with God's love and justice. The biblical view is that God wants every single person to know Him and His love and His salvation forever, and the only reason that will isn't fulfilled is because of human freedom.

The third argument offered by Dr Flew was that the notion of a bodiless person is impossible. I have two responses to this. In the first place, notice that he gave no proof of this. He gave no argument; he just asserted that it's impossible. I want to see a proof of that. Second, I would argue that we are acquainted with our own selves as immaterial persons. Reductive materialism, which says that the mind is the same as the brain, just doesn't work because mental properties are clearly distinct from physical properties. For example, the brain is not sad, but a person is sad. A thought doesn't have a weight or a spatial location. So reductive materialism just won't work. What about another view called 'epiphenomenalism' – the idea that the physical brain has mental properties which supervene on it? Well, this is simply incompatible with such things as self-identity over time or intentional states (where one intends to do something), because, on this view, mental states are just sort of an 'excretion' of the brain, not really a self which intends to do anything. It's incompatible with free will, because there's no way in which these mental epiphenomenal states can freely choose anything or do anything to affect the brain. So that view seems to me to be implausible. I think the best view is some sort of dualism–interactionism: that we act as agents to cause physical events in the world. We ourselves are immaterial selves, embodied, and God would be an immaterial Self or Mind which is not embodied. And so, far from being implausible, I think that this is the most plausible view of human beings, and it applies to God as well.

So I don't think any of these reasons for atheism that we've seen tonight are very compelling – I don't find them persuasive. Now what about my arguments for the existence of God – are they any better?

First I argued (I) that the origin of the universe points to the existence of God and gave a deductive argument: whatever begins to exist has a cause; the universe began to exist; therefore the universe has a cause. Now Dr Flew, in response, said: 'But we must explain things in terms of other things which are simply brute facts.' But my argument is that because the universe began to exist it cannot plausibly be our stopping point as that brute fact. Why is that? Because of that first premise – that whatever begins to exist has a cause. Dr Flew has to refute that first premise if he thinks that the universe is going to be the brute fact and the stopping point. That first premise, I think, has two lines of support behind it. First would be the metaphysical intuition that something cannot come out of nothing. Out of nothing, nothing comes. And that's why if the universe began to exist, it cries out for a cause. Second, that causal premise is constantly confirmed in our experience. Nobody believes that, say, a raging Bengal tiger or an Inuit village could suddenly 'pop' into existence out of nothing right here in the Fieldhouse. So it seems to me that the first premise is very plausible and that therefore, if the universe began to exist, it must have a cause.

Now Dr Flew admits the universe began to exist. In his book *Atheistic Humanism* he says, 'We ... now have excellent, natural scientific reasons for believing that the Universe did in fact have an explosive beginning.'[24] And therefore it follows logically and inescapably that the universe has a cause.

Now he asks: 'Does the cause of the universe have the attributes of God?' And he suggested that it doesn't. Let me make two responses. First, I am using the definition of God that was used in the original Copleston–Russell debate. In that debate, Copleston proposed: 'By God we mean a supreme personal being distinct from the world and the creator of the world.' And Russell responded, 'I accept this definition.'[25] On that definition, I have given evidence for the existence of God. Second, remember that I am offering a cumulative case. The first argument gives us an immaterial, timeless, changeless, spaceless, beginningless, uncaused, personal creator of the universe. The second argument gives us an intelligent designer of the universe. The third argument gives us a source of moral value and all goodness. The fourth argument gives us a God who is active in history in the person of Jesus. And the last one gives us a God who can be immediately known and experienced. And I think the cumulative force of these arguments does indeed give us many of the attributes of God.

My second argument (II) was based on the complex order of the universe, and here I argued that the fine-tuning of the initial conditions is due to either law, chance or design. It's not due to law or chance, because these are *initial* conditions and they cannot be explained by scientific law. Paul Davies, in his book *The Mind of God*, says there is 'absolutely no evidence' in favour of these conditions being necessary.[26] He says:

> Even if the laws of physics were unique, it doesn't follow that the physical universe itself is unique .... The laws ... must be augmented by cosmic initial conditions .... There is nothing in present ideas about 'laws of initial conditions' remotely to suggest that their consistency with the laws of physics would imply uniqueness. Far from it.[27]

It seems, then, that the physical universe does not have to be the way it is – it could have been otherwise. And I showed that, in fact, the universe is balancing on a razor's edge. That cries out for some sort of explanation. It can't be from law. It can't be from chance because the chances of this occurring are simply incomprehensible. And therefore the best explanation is design.

Now Dr Flew says, 'But we don't infer design because of complexity – we infer design because something is an artifact.' But, of course, the question is: how do we recognize something as an artifact? Well, we do so by recognizing a specified improbability concerning the complexity of that thing. For example, two archaeologists, digging in the ground and finding certain rocks shaped like arrowheads or other implements, don't say, 'Ha! Look how the processes of sedimentation and metamorphosis have created these uncanny rocks!' They immediately recognize the presence of design because of the improbability of that specified complexity. Or consider the Search for Extra-Terrestrial Intelligence. If we were to receive from outer space a message listing the first 100 prime numbers in sequence, we would instantly recognize that as the product of intelligent design (just like in the movie *Contact*). These specified probabilities are the way in which we detect design all the time in ordinary life and experience. And those specified probabilities are present in the Big Bang itself. And thus, in the absence of an explanation by law or chance, it seems to me that the best explanation is design.

My third argument (III) was based on objective moral values. I showed that, in the absence of God, everything becomes socioculturally relative. There is no absolute right and wrong unless you have a transcendent vantage point to transcend sociocultural relativism. Dr Flew made no response to this argument at all.

I also argued (IV) that the facts of the empty tomb, the appearances of Jesus and the origin of the disciples' faith are best explained by the hypothesis of the Resurrection of Jesus. I await any alternative naturalistic hypothesis which is more plausible than that.

Finally (V), my immediate experience of God allows me to know that He exists. In the absence of good arguments for atheism I see no reasons to deny my immediate experience of God and my belief that He exists.

Flew's First Rebuttal

Regarding immediate experience of God, we need a distinction between two senses of the word 'experience'. There is the philosophers' sense in which things like dreams, visions, hallucinations and sense data are experiences, and there is the experience of things where a person who has had experience of things has actually had dealings with them. Now it seems to me that for people to say that they've had experience of either the Christian God or of Shiva the Destroyer or any other god, it is, as Thomas Hobbes said, 'To say He hath spoken to him in a dream, is no more than to say he dreamed that God spake to him ...'.[28]

I have no doubt at all that Dr Craig's experience appears to *him* to be of God, but this is a matter in which the subject's honest testimony is not authoritative. Of course, it's authoritative if we're asking whether they had the experience in the philosopher's sense – the owner's testimony is the last word in that case. But when someone says they've had an experience of dealing with cows and so on, that means they've actually had dealings with real cows. Well, so much for the appeal to religious experience. (I was deeply unimpressed by Hywel Lewis's book about experience of God[29] in which he never confronted this obvious difficulty.)

Then about the argument that whatever begins to exist has a cause. Yes, absolutely. This is not a truth of logic, however. This, like the principle that every event has a cause, is an experienced truth *within* the universe and it is *wholly* arbitrary and prejudicial to think, 'Oh well, therefore clearly the universe – the whole universe – must have had a cause' so we now look for it.

Why do I have difficulty with the idea of an incorporeal person? Well, if I was asked to explain the meaning of the word 'person' to someone who didn't know the meaning, I'd point around the place here. And if someone said a person has called at their house, I would think that someone with a body had called.

The second thing I would say about this is that no one has (well maybe some of my Australian friends have) said that the *brain* has experiences. I think that conscious experiences are experiences of a material thing, namely a personal material object, because they are experiences of a human being (or, in some cases, of animals).

Then about the tortures of the damned being self-incurred, so that's all right. It seems to me that anyone who, with his eyes wide open, refused to do what an omnipotent being said, knowing that he was going to be tortured just not for a few days, like the earthly Saddam Hussein's victims were and are, but forever, would be someone who had lost the balance of his mind.

Dr Craig's response misunderstood my point. On another occasion he wrote:

But so long as people are free, there's simply no guarantee that everyone in that world would be freely saved. To be sure, God could force everyone to repent and be saved by overpowering their wills, but that would be a sort of divine rape; not a free acceptance of salvation. It is logically impossible to *make* someone do something *freely*.[30]

Yes, of course it is, but I didn't say that God should *coerce* people – force them to do it. I said that the omnipotent God would be able to make people such that they would freely choose to do what He desired. Now you may say that this is the doctrine of predestination, and, of course, only Calvinists believe that. Not true. This view that God guided the wills both of the saved and the damned is found in, for instance, Aquinas. He writes:

God alone can move the will as an agent without doing violence to it .... Some people, not understanding how God can cause a movement of our willingness without prejudicing the freedom of the will, have tried to explain ... authoritative texts wrongly, that is, they would say that God 'works in us and to wish and to accomplish' means that He causes in us the power of willing, but not in such a way that He makes us will this or that .... These people are, of course, opposed quite plainly by authoritative texts of Holy Writ. For it says in Isaiah: 'Lord you have worked all your work in us'. Hence we received from God not only the power of willing but its employment also.[31]

Calvin, of course, and Luther, too, maintained substantially the same position. But, to his great credit, we need to take special note of Luther's insistence that this total divine control abolishes none of the familiar humanly crucial differences. Thus, in his *De servo arbitrio*, concerning this enslaved will he wrote:

Now by 'necessarily' I do not mean 'compulsory' .... A man without the Spirit of God does not do evil against his will under pressure as though he were taken by the scruff of his neck and dragged into it, like a thief or a foot pad being dragged off against his will to punishment; but he does it spontaneously and voluntarily.[32]

But, again to his credit and unlike Aquinas, the reformer was appalled by the so pellucidly perceived implications. And his response was:

The highest degree of faith is to believe He is just, though His own will makes us ... proper subjects for damnation and seems (in the words of Erasmus) 'to delight in the torments of poor wretches and to be a fitter object for hate than for love'. If I could by any means understand how this same God could yet be merciful and just, there would be no need for faith.[33]

So, Luther addressed himself to the question: 'Why, then does He not alter these evil wills in which he moves?' He addressed himself to precisely the question that I was raising. Understandably, if unsatisfactorily, the person Erasmus, who'd raised the question, simply gets the answer:

It is not for us to inquire into these mysteries, but to adore them. If flesh and blood take offense here and grumble, well, let them grumble. They will achieve nothing; grumbling will not change God! And, however many of the ungodly stumble and depart, the elect will remain.[34]

Had we pressed Luther further, he would undoubtedly have referred to a key passage from his favourite epistle, the epistle to the Romans:

Therefore hath He mercy upon whom He will have mercy, and whom He will He hardeneth. Thou wilt say unto me 'Why doth He yet find fault, for who hath resisted His will?' Nay but, O man, who art thou that repliest against God? Shall the thing formed say to Him that formed it, 'Why has thou made me thus?' What if God, willing to show His wrath ... and to make His power known, endured with much long-suffering the vessels of wrath fitted for destruction: and that He might make known the riches of His glory on the vessels of mercy which He hath before prepared ....[35]

Well, I think that would be a useful thing to have on the record in this discussion, lest we have any more of this suggestion that an omnipotent being could not cause people to freely choose Him. It's an absurd idea that He could not produce people to do freely exactly what He wanted them to do, because here you have biblical authority and the authority of three of the great doctors of the Church – Luther, Aquinas and Calvin.

Craig's Second Rebuttal

Let's review those three reasons that Dr Flew offers for thinking that God does not exist. The first argument is that, if God is omnipotent, then He should be able to make creatures such that they would always freely choose the way that He would like them to choose. And as Dr Flew's last speech made very clear, he's presupposing here a Thomistic/Calvinistic doctrine of divine conservation and concurrence. Now bear with me because this is a very subtle theological point. I do not agree with Thomas Aquinas on this issue. I agree with a Molinist doctrine of divine concurrence and conservation. This is a doctrine laid out by Luis Molina, who was a sixteenth-century Jesuit Counter-Reformer. Molina's view of concurrence differed from Aquinas's in the following way: Aquinas thought that God moved the will of persons to do certain effects, so that God would move my will to will to, say, lift my arm. And, I agree, if that's the way you think of God's working, then Dr Flew is right – omnipotence could bring it about that everyone would freely do what God wants him to do. But, on Molina's view, God's concurrence acts to produce the secondary effect *with* my will, but He does not move *on* my will to produce the effect because, Molina argued, that would be incompatible with human freedom. In these circumstances, I would have no ability to do otherwise – if it is God who is moving me to that effect. Let me quote from the introduction to Molina's treatise *On Divine Foreknowledge* by Alfred

Freddoso. He explains that debates in sixteenth-century theology over the nature of freedom came to a focus on God's general concurrence:

> Molina's conception of freedom is strongly indeterministic; in modern terms, He is an unremitting libertarian ... Molina insists that God's general concurrence is an action of God's *directly on the effect* and not on the secondary agents themselves, whereas his ... opponents [that is, the followers of Thomas Aquinas] take [it] to be a divine action *directly on the secondary agents* ('premoving' them) and *through* them on the effect. Molina thus denies ... that secondary causes must be *moved* by God ... to exercise their causal power. In this way he stresses their autonomy .... This ... has an immediate and profound impact on the analysis of free choice and of causal indeterminism in general.[36]

In other words, if you have a Molinist doctrine such as I have, then it may in fact be impossible for God to create a world of genuinely libertarian free creatures who always do the right thing. Dr Flew is in the paradoxical position of having to prove to us that Thomas Aquinas's doctrine of divine concurrence is true if God exists! And I can't imagine how he is going to do that (or even that he would want to do that)! But it seems to me that Molinism provides the right analysis of freedom and concurrence and shows that even an omnipotent being cannot guarantee that free creatures will always do what He wants.

That answers immediately the second objection about hell, because God *cannot* freely make people believe in Him and go to heaven. The Bible says that 'God is not willing that *any* should perish but that *all* should reach repentance'.[37] It says His desire is that '*all* persons should be saved and come to a knowledge of the truth.'[38] Those are direct quotations. The only reason why universal salvation is not true is because of human free will.

What about the third argument concerning the possibility of a bodiless person? Well, here I didn't really understand Dr Flew's argument. He simply said that he takes our mental experiences to be the experiences of a material object. But he didn't answer my objections to epiphenomenalism. On that view you cannot explain self-identity over time, you cannot explain intentionality, you cannot explain free will – none of that makes sense. So I think epiphenomenalism is an inadequate view. In any case, he's never shown that there cannot be an unembodied Personal Mind, and therefore I don't think he's shown that God cannot exist. So none of these arguments are very powerful against God's existence.

Do we have reasons to think that God exists?

With regard to the argument based on the origin of the universe (I), Dr Flew grants the second premise – that the universe began to exist. Therefore, the whole question hinges on that first premise: whatever begins to exist has a cause. And here Dr Flew says, 'Yes, absolutely.' But, he says, this principle only operates *within* the universe. Well, I'd like to know *why*, without begging the question, he refuses to apply this principle to the universe as a whole. As I said, this principle is based on the metaphysical intuition that something can't come out of nothing. Does Dr Flew *really* believe tonight that the universe just 'popped' into existence, uncaused, out of nothing? Is *this* his alternative to theism? I find that incredible! Moreover, we see, all the time that, in our experience, this doesn't happen. Why, when you get to the universe, should you suddenly dismiss that experience like a cab and refuse to ask for the cause of the universe? So, given the plausibility of that premise (and, I think that it's clear that it's more plausible than its negation), the conclusion follows that, therefore, a personal Creator of the universe exists.

Nor have the rest of the arguments been refuted.

The argument from complex order in the universe was not addressed (II).

The argument from objective moral values (III) is one of the most important, and that hasn't been addressed. J.P. Moreland, who is a Christian philosopher, underlines this point. He states:

> On an evolutionary secular scenario, ... human beings are nothing special. The universe came from a Big Bang. It evolved to us through a blind process of chance and necessity. There is nothing intrinsically valuable about human beings in terms of having moral non-natural properties .... The view that being human is special is guilty of specie-ism – an unjustifiable bias toward one's own species.[39]

On the atheistic view, human beings are just animals, and animals don't have morality. When a lion kills a zebra it doesn't murder it – it doesn't do anything evil. And we are just animals.

But I think it's evident that this gives us a patently inadequate view of ethics. Some things are really wrong. Other things are really good. And if you agree with me about that, then you should agree that God exists as a transcendent anchor for those values.

Finally, let me just say one thing about the life, death, and Resurrection of Jesus (IV). Dr Flew had a debate a couple of years ago with someone on this subject, and it was published as the book, *Did Jesus Rise from the Dead?*[40] In that book my doctoral father, Wolfhart Pannenberg, wrote a response to the debate, and this is what he said:

> [Professor] Flew argues that there is simply not enough evidence ... to tell what really happened, but one expects that he should at least take notice of the evidence at hand and that he should do so in detail as well as by informing himself on the scholarly discussion of it. Otherwise the skeptical claim that the evidence is insufficient smacks of the kind of *a priori* rejection that [Professor] Flew disclaims .... The weakness of [Dr] Flew's argument in terms of historical detail damages his position because he admits that no *a priori* decision of the issue is acceptable ....[41]

And, again, in tonight's debate Dr Flew has refused to engage the details of the historical evidence.

As for the immediate experience of God (V) I admit that the question is: is my experience of God veridical? But what I want to know is, in the absence of good arguments for atheism, why deny my experience? God is real to me, just as the external world is real. In the absence of good reasons to deny that experience, why am I not rational to go on believing in God?

Flew's Second Rebuttal

Well, about human beings being merely animals. It is a fallacious form of argument to say that anything is *merely* this and nothing else. Of course, human beings are members of the animal kingdom, but that *doesn't* mean they don't have special characteristics, and characteristics of enormous importance. So it's ridiculous to say that anyone who doesn't believe in God believes, or should believe, that human beings are merely bags of bone or something like that. For a start there is an enormous difference between what's in a body bag and a living human being. It's the difference between life and death. A dead body is not merely a body, it's a dead human body that was something else before. It simply does not follow that because human beings are animals they're merely animals and so they've no importance and you shouldn't think of them as important. This just won't do at all.

About the Resurrection. Yes, I did say there was insufficient evidence to come to the desired positive conclusion. The most recent documentation after the alleged events was 30 or so years afterwards. When I was an active member of the Society for Psychical Research we would have had grave doubts about taking as an absolutely faithful record documents that were written, say, a year or so later than the actual event. And what have we got here by way of evidence? Again, if an omnipotent being wanted to establish that it had become incarnate in a way in which He would be sure that the maximum number of people would come to believe in this and accept what He wanted them to believe, wouldn't He have done this in a place where there were public records? All of whatever records the Romans had left in Jerusalem were destroyed after the suppression of the Jewish uprising in 70 AD. So, my reason for saying that there was insufficient evidence was simply that there *was* insufficient evidence. And my failure to accept the conclusion that the Resurrection happened on the basis of historical evidence is simply that the evidence is insufficient. After all, my whole argument is that the evidence for a desired conclusion is insufficient in this other case. Do you expect me now to say, 'Oh but I'm perfectly prepared to say, indeed I *ought* to say, that if there's any evidence *at all* (it doesn't have to be sufficient) I ought to reach your conclusion'? I didn't want to refer to the Resurrection because it seemed to me that this claim lacks anything remotely like sufficient evidence. It's of enormous importance to discover what did happen at that time, but when you consider the basis of what you've got there is little evidence. The first New Testament documents were Pauline epistles rather than the Gospels. What is so remarkable about the Pauline epistles is what they *don't* say about the detail, and how the appearances recorded were apparently visions, which is a very different thing from a body into the wounds of which you can poke your fingers and that sort of thing.

About morality. Of course, I don't accept the sort of subjectivism which most people call relativism – the idea that there's really no right and wrong, and it's a matter of what's right for him is wrong for you. For years I've been used to having students thinking I was a progressive sort of chap and being astounded to hear that I thought this was simply false. Well, I think it's false because the moral words simply do not have relativistic meanings. As Hume put it in one of his less quoted passages:

> When a man denominates another his *enemy*, his *rival*, his *antagonist*, his *adversary*, he is understood to speak the language of self-love and to express sentiments peculiar to himself and arising from his particular circumstances and situation. But when he bestows on any man the epithets of *vicious* or *odious* or *depraved*, he then speaks another language and expresses sentiments in which he expects all his audience are to concur with him. He must here, therefore, depart from his private and particular situation and must choose a point of view common to him with others; he must move some universal principle of the human frame and touch a string to which all mankind have an accord and symphony.[42]

I am perfectly prepared, happy to believe and constantly maintaining that things are really wrong. But I don't think they're wrong and only wrong and only really wrong because God said so. And I certainly don't think that you can argue that this belief (which I hope many of you share with me) that there's a real difference between right and wrong, and between justice and injustice, could only be so if God prescribes it, and therefore this is evidence for the existence of God. I think it is not that at all. You can only take it that these things are approved by God if you know that they were approved by God. Again, if you are working from within the universe, you've got to find some other account for the evolution of norms. And, of course, in the times of Hume, Adam Smith, Adam Ferguson and the other founding fathers of social science, the first work was being done on trying to provide an account of the evolution of norms.

Craig's Closing Statement

In my closing statement, I'd like to draw together the threads in this debate and try to come to some conclusions. You'll remember I said that the decision as to whether or not God exists will be a matter of weighing the reasons to think that God exists against the reasons to think that God does not exist. Now have we seen compelling reasons in tonight's debate to think that God does not exist? Well, it seems to me not. Most of the arguments that Dr Flew gave were based on the incompatibility of omnipotence with God's not getting His way in the world, but he never refuted my explication of the Molinist doctrine of conservation and concurrence, which explained why there may be worlds that are not feasible for God because He cannot guarantee how free creatures will choose.

With respect to God's being incorporeal, I explained that we have an acquaintance of ourselves as immaterial agents, and this gives us a good explanation of things such as intentionality, freedom of the will and so forth, and that there's no reason to think God can't be an unembodied mind. Little response has been made to those arguments. So I think there is negligible, if any, weight to the arguments for atheism tonight.

Now, what about the five reasons I gave to think that God does exist? I. First, I argued that there is a deductive argument for God as the explanation of the origin of the universe. First of all, we saw that the universe began to exist and that whatever begins to exist has a cause. And the whole debate has really hinged upon whether that causal premise is more plausibly true than not. It seems to me clearly that it is. Kai Nielsen, who is an atheist philosopher at the University of Calgary, would agree with me on that score. Nielsen says: 'Suppose you suddenly hear a loud bang ... and you ask me, "What made that bang?" And I reply, "Nothing, it just happened". You would not accept that. In fact, you would find my reply quite unintelligible.'[43] Well, what is true of the little bang is also true of the Big Bang: it must have had a cause. Something cannot come out of nothing, and therefore there must exist a timeless, spaceless, immaterial and personal Creator of the universe.

My second argument (II), based on the fine-tuning of the universe, has gone completely unrefuted in tonight's debate.

My third argument (III) from objective moral values finally elicited a response in the last speech. Dr Flew said that it's fallacious to think that, if God does not exist, objective moral values do not exist because human beings are not merely animals: there is a difference between life and death. But I fail to see why that's important. There is a difference between live zebras and dead zebras, but a lion doesn't do anything wrong when it kills a zebra. Richard Taylor, an eminent ethicist, asks us to imagine a race of people living without customs or laws, and he asks us to suppose that one person kills another one and takes his goods. He says:

> ... such actions, though injurious to their victims, are no more unjust or immoral than they would be if one animal did it to another. A hawk that seizes a fish from the sea *kills* it, but does not *murder* it; and another hawk that seizes the fish from the talons of the first *takes* it, but does not *steal* it – for none of these things is forbidden. And exactly the same considerations apply to the people we are imagining.[44]

Dr Flew admits there are objective moral values, and I say 'that's great'; but his world-view lacks any *foundation* for why human beings have objective worth and inherent dignity. I offer you a foundation in a trans-subjective, objective foundation – in God.

What about the life, death, and Resurrection of Jesus (IV)? Again, Dr Flew did exactly what Professor Pannenberg accused him of doing. He simply says the evidence is insufficient, but he doesn't engage himself with the evidence. Remember I pointed out that critical New Testament historians agree that the empty tomb, the post-mortem appearances and the origin of the disciples' faith are all established historical facts. So I ask Dr Flew: what is a better explanation of those facts than the fact that these men were telling the truth – that Jesus did rise from the dead? Is he going to defend that it was a conspiracy? Is he going to say that Jesus wasn't really dead? What is his alternative? It seems to me that there is no plausible naturalistic alternative.

Finally, let me just say a word about the immediate experience of God (V). I myself wasn't raised in a Christian home or churchgoing family. But when I became a teenager, I began to ask the 'big questions' in life: 'Why am I here?' 'Where am I going?' And as I read the New Testament for the first time, I was arrested by the person of Jesus. His words had the ring of truth about them, and there was an authenticity about his character that I couldn't deny. After a six-month period of intense soul-searching, I finally came to the end of my rope and cried out to God. And I experienced a spiritual rebirth. It was as though someone turned on the light inside, and God became an immediate reality to me – a reality that I've walked with day-by-day for the last 30 years. If you're searching for God in this way, I want to encourage you to do the same thing I did – pick up the New Testament and read it and ask yourself, 'Could this really be true?'. It could change your life in the same way that it changed mine.

Flew's Closing Statement

Oh, that someone could believe the evidence for an empty tomb was sufficient evidence recorded years after the event by we know not whom, and so on. This is hopeless. Then Kai Nielsen wants to make out that there's no difference between the 'little bang' and the Big Bang. The whole difference is that the 'little bang' occurs within the universe; the Big Bang is of the universe *itself*. And Taylor says that there is no difference between what a lion or a fish does and what a human being does. The difference is the difference between human beings and other animals! The fact that we are animals does *not* justify a direct inference that we're nothing but animals, that we're no special sort of animals. It doesn't justify any inferences to these manifestly false conclusions.

The one thing that I feel guilty about not doing anything about is the probabilistic arguments. Well, applying probabilities, again, outside the universe makes it impossible, I think, to apply either sort of probability theory. We can't apply the propensity theory, because we don't know anything about the propensities of the objects considered. And we certainly can't apply a frequency theory, because we haven't got any other universes to count.

This may not be satisfactory but it's impossible, I think, to give complete satisfaction on every issue within these limits. So I think the least useless thing I can hope finally to do is to stress once again that I have not, from the beginning, tried to persuade you of the non-existence of God. Suppose you'd recently visited, as I have done, the Metropolitan Museum in New York and you'd seen a statue of the Egyptian god, Horus. One of the interesting things about this god was that the Egyptians in those days believed that every successive Pharaoh was an incarnation of that god. Now, would you like to provide proof of the non-existence of that god? The reason why you don't believe in that god is that no one's ever mentioned this being before, and no one could produce any compelling reasons for believing that there was this god. So I haven't been trying to prove God does not exist. What I have been trying to persuade you of is that we are finite, limited human beings. All our knowledge, all our theories, are contained within the only universe that, as far as we know, there is and certainly the only one we know. Any move we try to make to find out what is and is not going on outside the universe is, in the last degree, speculative. It may be right, it may be wrong, but we haven't got any evidencing, as opposed to motivating, reason for believing that there is such a being as God.

Questions and Answers

Question: Dr Craig, you stated in your first premise that infinity can only be an idea in our heads and therefore the past can't go back forever. And because of that you believe that God created the Big Bang. But you never explained what came before God. What created God? If God exists, something must have existed before Him that created Him.

Craig: Remember that the initial premise in my argument is that whatever *begins* to exist has a cause. Since God did not begin to exist, God would not need to have a cause. And that isn't special pleading, because that's what the atheist has always said about the universe. Remember Russell's comment in the original debate with Copleston – 'the universe is just there and that's all'.[45] The atheist has always thought that the universe is eternal and uncaused, but now that's become untenable. So my argument is that anything that begins to exist has to have a cause. In the absence of a beginning, God doesn't need a cause, and in fact I argued that, as the creator of space and time, He would himself have to be timeless. So the question of what is before God is meaningless because there is no 'before'. God exists timelessly without creation, and time comes into existence at the moment of creation. So God would be timeless, uncaused and necessary in His existence and therefore would not Himself need to have a cause.

Flew: When atheists like Russell said that the universe had no beginning, they were arguing already against the inference to a cause of the universe that had no beginning. And the objection is, I think, that explanation has to end at some point. And to infer a cause for the universe and then to announce, 'Oh, well I've done it now. That cause had no beginning and therefore, it doesn't need a cause' seems to me wrong. Why shouldn't you simply stop at 'the universe had a beginning and didn't have a cause'? If you like, it's first cause was the universe itself.

Question: Dr Flew, do you believe that there is a historical person that once lived on this earth named Jesus of Nazareth?

Flew: I should have thought the evidence for this is pretty good but by no means decisive. It's not as clear a case as Caesar or Napoleon. It is a matter of controversy among some clearly reasonably well informed and not obviously perverse people.

Craig: There isn't any historical scholar who denies that Jesus of Nazareth actually existed. Indeed, as I've argued, such things as the crucifixion of Jesus are indisputable facts of history, just as much as the existence of Julius Caesar. And when you compare the New Testament writings to other ancient sources for Greco-Roman history, the New Testament comes out looking very, very good in comparison to the normal sources for Greco-Roman history that we have to work with. They are earlier in terms of their date of origin compared to the events that they record. They are attested in more abundant manuscripts, and they are written by people who were within the first generation and had a familiarity with the eyewitnesses. Many historians of Greco-Roman history would be green with envy to have sources for their history that New Testament historians have for the life and the teachings of Jesus.

Question: Dr Craig, I question how you can reconcile the Big Bang with free will. You said that every event has a cause and that nothing comes out of nothing. Well, any action has to have a cause and that cause has a cause. Thus, you can't have free will if everything has a cause.

Craig: Let's be careful now about what my premise was. My premise is that everything that begins to exist has a cause. Now, I think that, in the case of actions, they do have causes in agents, and it's the same kind of causality that I appeal to as the cause of the Big Bang. You must get back to a personal agent endowed with free will who is able to bring about new effects without prior determining conditions. That's the whole notion of agent causation. And if that applies in our case as human beings – if we act as agent causes – then I see no reason at all why we cannot appeal to agent causation as well to explain the origin of the universe.

Question: Dr Flew, I was wondering why is it that the universe models that you are using are closed universes – have a definite beginning point and presumably a definite ending point – whereas the idea of cyclical universes might fit better into an argument against God or an argument of agnosticism. How does a cyclical universe model, one which opens and closes and opens and closes, change a view concerning God?

Flew: Well, I was thinking that the discussion here tonight had to start from what is clearly the main accepted view among cosmologists at this time. If it was a matter of my preference, I would certainly prefer a cyclical universe exploding and contracting, and so on. This idea has apparently been empirically ruled out. But I think all the arguments about the Big Bang are, of course, arguments about something which is – like almost all major cosmological theories – provisional. But it's certainly the dominant theory today and the one, therefore, that we have to work with.

Craig: I really appreciated Dr Flew's forthrightness in that response because he is absolutely correct. In my opening speech I said that I can only share the tip of the iceberg and go into more detail as people ask questions. And in fact, the empirical evidence that Dr Flew alludes to, ruling out the oscillating model, is threefold.

First, the density of the universe is not great enough to halt the expansion and cause the universe to recontract again. In fact, the evidence indicates the universe would have to be ten times denser than it is in order for the universe to recontract. And I have here an AP news release dated 9 January 1998, in which it reports that five teams of astronomers from Princeton, Yale, the Lawrence Berkeley National Laboratory and the Harvard Smithsonian Astrophysics Institute reported that, using five different methods, they all arrived at a common conclusion: the Big Bang will not be followed by a Big Crunch. It is quite clear now that the universe will expand forever – that it doesn't have sufficient density to close itself.[46] So that's the first empirical problem.

Second, there's no known physics that could reverse a catastrophic Big Crunch and make it bounce back to a new expansion anyway.

Third, the thermodynamic properties of an oscillating universe show that, even though it has an infinite future, as you trace the cycles back in time they become smaller and smaller until you reach a first cycle and an absolute origin of the universe. So, observationally, physically and thermodynamically the model is ruled out.

Question: Dr Craig, I was wondering how you reconciled your argument against Russell's assertion that the universe just is and has always existed eternally (and eternal existence implies an infinite amount of events) with your argument for the eternal existence of God in time? Even if His existence in time only began with the creation of the universe, He'll exist forevermore. Hence an infinite amount of events. And as you said, the idea of an infinite amount of events is ridiculous according to mathematicians.

Craig: Right. Remember that my argument is that we must get back to a cause of the universe which is timeless. So we shouldn't think of God as enduring through infinite time up until the moment of creation. As Augustine says, that would raise the problem of what was God doing all that time prior to creation, waiting around until He created it.[47] Rather, time itself begins with the universe, and God without the universe is simply timeless. So it makes no sense to talk about 'before' the beginning of time.

Now, with respect to God's enduring forever into the infinite future, the crucial distinction here is that the future is merely potential in a way that the past is not. The past is actual. It has existed. It's instantiated. But the future does not yet exist. So God's existing forever into the future is merely a potential infinite. It means that He will endure indefinitely into the future. But one will never actually arrive at infinity. Infinity is just a conceptual limit that one approaches, but at which one never arrives. At any point in time, the number of days, the number of years, that have existed, that one has lived through, will always be finite but always be increasing. So the key distinction to keep in mind here is the difference between the actuality of the past and the mere potentiality of the future.

Question: Dr Flew, I would like to ask a question based on your rebuttal of the evidence presented by Dr Craig about the evidence of Christ: his Resurrection and the overnight change in the apostles' behaviours. There is a lot of documented evidence about these things, and yet your argument seems to be lacking in that you say that there's not a lot of evidence. Why is that?

Flew: Well, for a start, this is not like the evidence of an occurrence of a battle. This is all evidence of what happened in a small area, like your next-door neighbour's house. And the sort of evidence that you require for this, for heaven's sake, needs to be contemporary, rather than from people who, some years afterwards, say they remembered it happening. These alleged events (which are, of course, miraculous if they occurred), therefore require very much more evidence than pedestrian, ordinary events like someone finding the door of a tomb open without a previously known opening. And we don't have that here; there is simply not adequate evidence *for this sort of event.*

Craig: Let me try to explain this argument a little bit further. We have indisputable evidence, as the questioner indicates, that these early disciples underwent a sudden and drastic change – a transformation in their lives. Remember that statement I quoted from Luke Timothy Johnson that some sort of powerful, transformative experience must have occurred to generate this religious movement.[48] Now any responsible historian investigating the history of the first century in Palestine has to ask: where did this religious movement come from? What caused it to come into being? And what you discover is that, at the root of this movement, was this strange conviction that this man had risen from the dead. And you have to ask yourself: what brought about this belief in this group of people, such that they were willing to go out and die for this belief? Now the fact is that you can't explain this belief in terms of either Jewish influences on them or pagan influences on them. There were absolutely no pagan parallels in first-century Palestine that would have caused them to believe such a thing. And, as I alluded to in my first speech, Jewish beliefs ran decidedly against the idea of someone's being raised from the dead as an isolated individual before the end of the world. So here is a belief which cannot be accounted for in terms of any antecedent historical influences in either Judaism or pagan religions. And this raises the question: why not believe these men?

Question: Dr Craig, I have a major concern with the fact that you consider God timeless and apparently spaceless – above and beyond the constraints of the universe – but yet He is somehow limited by free will, some sort of mortal free will. Dr Craig, is free will more powerful than God?

Craig: In the sense that God didn't have to create free will, no. He could have created puppets or robots. But in the sense that He decreed to create a creature in His image, having moral autonomy and the freedom to do as it wills, then, yes, God limits His control over that creature. Now, He could have controlled him in the sense of coercing him, but God chose to create moral agents who are reflections of Himself in having this kind of libertarian freedom. And then He cannot guarantee what they will do. And that's just a point of logic – you can't make someone freely do something.

Flew: Notice that the arguments I've produced were not confined to those of Aquinas and Luther and Calvin (which I thought were pretty good to go on), but Aquinas quoted one biblical passage and I quoted another with great enthusiasm – one which Luther often repeated. It apparently didn't occur to anyone until this chap Molina, centuries later, that this was a crucial notion which showed that God didn't really cause people freely to choose this or that. It's rather a long time afterwards. And it doesn't seem to me that there's evidence that there is such a thing as – what do you call it? – libertarian free will, because actually freedom indicates that someone was not compelled, that they did these things of their own free will. It doesn't have anything to do with unpredictability.

Question: Dr Flew, you stated that the mere fact that humans are animals gives no basis for an assertion that an atheist must assume that humans and animals are not different. You later made it clear that your position is that humans indeed *are* special. From an atheist perspective, what makes humans special in comparison to animals?

Flew: Well, the list is enormous. One of the things is that we are members of a kind of creature that can, and therefore cannot, make choices. This is the fact about human beings that was ignored by Thomas Malthus in his first *Essay on Population*. There are many other features that are peculiar. If you like, take the one that Aristotle used: that men were rational animals. He didn't mean that everyone was a reasonable person. He meant that we were capable of rationality, and only capable of actual irrationality because we are capable of rationality, in the way that only people who are capable of being immoral are capable of being moral and only people who are capable of being moral are capable of being immoral.

Craig: Well, I find it ironic that Dr Flew wants to appeal to our ability to make choices – that we can make choices is what makes us special – because in his previous answer to the questioner he denied that we have this sort of libertarian free will, arguing that we just have freedom from coercion. And as for rationality, that, of course, is a relative thing. Suppose there were extraterrestrials who came to earth who were as superior to us in intelligence as we are to animals such as cows and pigs, and they began to farm the earth and use us for labouring animals and began to eat human beings for food. What would we say to them to convince them that human beings are special, that we are of intrinsic value? Why should they treat us any differently than we treat horses and cows and pigs? On the atheistic view, I can't think of any reason. It seems to me that to think humans are special is just specie-ism.

Question: Dr Craig, you mentioned that God is our transcendental anchor of morality and that He is the means by which we develop our moral standards. Well, we have moral standards as Christians, and other religions have moral standards, and they differ from our moral standards. How do we know which moral standard is the right moral standard?

Craig: This is a question not of the *existence* of objective moral values, but a question of the *knowledge* of them. And I don't have any special insight on that – about how one knows them. I think that, in many cases, we would simply say that we intuit morally the intrinsic worth and dignity of human beings, and that therefore anything that would tend to depreciate the value of human beings or contravene their rights would be immoral. In other cases, we may need to find revelation from God of what His moral will is for us in certain circumstances. So I would say that you would do the project based both on these sorts of moral intuition and then on divine revelation. That's how you would try to discern what God's will is with respect to what is right and wrong. But that's a wholly separate question from the ontological foundation of moral values, which is what my argument tonight was about.

Question: Multiple cultures believe that there's a god. Some have pantheistic beliefs, some believe that its a creator and that its not a ruler, that it's not a personified god. Why were such beliefs ignored on both parts when they could have been used to refute the opposing side?

Flew: I am not sure that this is right in the first place. An historical incident which is worth mentioning is that when the first Jesuit mission arrived in China, they could not find any Chinese character to stand for God in the translations they wanted to make of the scriptures. So they used the character 'T'ien' (which is the 'T'ien' of 'T'ien-an men Square') and is normally translated 'heaven'. And when news of what they had done got back to Rome they were reprimanded for doing this because this was going too far in making concessions to the heathen. The point is that the intended referent of this character was not, and is not, a personal, omnipotent, creator God.

Craig: I think that I implicitly mentioned these views in the sense that, if my arguments are correct, it refutes pantheistic views. Pantheism regards the universe itself as divine and necessary and absolute. But the fact that the universe began to exist and was designed points to the contingency of the universe – that it's not divine, it's a creature, and therefore depends on a transcendent creator. So if those arguments that I gave are correct, they do limit the field to the great monotheistic traditions of Judaism, Christianity, Islam and perhaps deism.

Yandell: Please allow me, then, to bring the formal event to a conclusion and ask you to join with me in thanking the participants of this evening.

Notes

1   Bertrand Russell and F.C. Copleston, 'A Debate On The Existence of God', reprinted in John Hick (ed.), *The Existence of God*, Problems of Philosophy Series (New York: Macmillan Publishing Co., 1964), p. 175.

2   David Hilbert, 'On the Infinite,' in Paul Benacerraf and Hilory Putnam (eds), *Philosophy of Mathematics* (Englewood Cliffs, NJ: Prentice-Hall, 1964), pp. 139, 141.

3   Fred Hoyle, *Astronomy and Cosmology* (San Francisco: W.H. Freeman, 1975), p. 658.

4   Anthony Kenny, *The Five Ways: St. Thomas Aquinas Proofs of God's Existence* (New York: Schocken Books, 1969), p. 66.

5   Genesis 1:1.

6   Stephen W. Hawking, *A Brief History of Time* (New York: Bantam Books, 1988), p. 123.

7   P.C.W. Davies, *Other Worlds* (London: Dent, 1980), pp. 160–61, 168–69.

8   P.C.W. Davies, 'The Anthropic Principle', *Particle and Nuclear Physics* 10 (1983), p. 28.

9   Paul Davies, *The Mind of God: The Scientific Basis for a Rational World* (New York: Simon & Schuster: 1992), p. 16.

10 Fred Hoyle, 'The Universe: Past and Present Reflections', *Engineering and Science* (November 1981), p. 12.

11 Robert Jastrow, 'The Astronomer and God', in Roy Abraham Varghese (ed.), *The Intellectuals Speak Out About God* (Chicago: Regenery Gateway, 1984), p. 22.

12 Bertrand Russell, *Human Society in Ethics and Politics* (New York: Simon and Schuster, 1955), p. 124.

13 Michael Ruse, 'Evolutionary Theory and Christian Ethics', in *idem, The Darwinian Paradigm* (London: Routledge, 1989), pp. 262–9.

14 Friedrich Nietzsche, *The Gay Science*, in *The Portable Nietzsche*, trans. and ed. W. Kaufmann (New York: Viking, 1954), p. 95.

15 Jacob Kremer, *Die Osterevangelien Geschichten um Geschichte* (Stuttgart: Katholisches Bibelwerk, 1977), pp. 49–50.

16 Gerd Lüdemann, *What Really Happened to Jesus?*, trans. John Bowden (Louisville: Westminster/John Knox Press, 1995), p. 80.

17 Luke Timothy Johnson, *The Real Jesus* (San Francisco: Harper, 1996), p. 136.

18 N.T. Wright, 'The New, Unimproved Jesus', *Christianity Today* (13 September 1993), p. 26.

19 John Hick, 'Introduction', in Hick, *The Existence of God*, p. 13.

20 James 4:8.

21 Richard Swinburne, *The Coherence of Theism* (Oxford: Clarendon Press, 1977), p. 2.

22 William Lane Craig, 'No Other Name: A Middle Knowledge Perspective on the Exclusivity of Salvation Through Christ', *Faith and Philosophy*, 6 (1989), p. 176.

23 Ibid., p. 186.

24 Antony Flew, *Atheistic Humanism* (Buffalo, NY: Prometheus Books, 1993), p. 47.

25 Russell and Copleston, 'A Debate On The Existence of God', p. 167.

26 Davies, *The Mind of God*, p. 168.

27 Ibid.

28 Thomas Hobbes, *Leviathan*, ed. C.B. Macpherson (Harmondsworth and Baltimore: Penguin, 1968), p. 411.

29 Hywel D. Lewis, *Our Experience of God* (London: Allen and Unwin, 1959).

30 William Lane Craig, 'Politically Incorrect Salvation', in T.P. Phillips and D. Ockholm (eds), *Christian Apologetics in a Post-Christian World* (Downers Grove, IL: InterVarsity Press, 1995), pp. 91–92.

31 Thomas Aquinas, *Summa contra Gentiles*, Book III, Part II, chs 88–89, trans. Vernon J. Bourke (Doubleday Image, vol. 4, 1956).

32 Martin Luther, *De servo arbitrio, Luther and Erasmus: Free Will and Salvation* (ed). E.G. Rupp, A.N. Marlow, P.S. Watson and B. Drewery (Philadelphia: Westminster, 1969), p. 139.

33 Ibid., p. 138.

34 Ibid., p. 137.

35 Romans 9:18–23, King James version.

36 Alfred J. Freddoso, 'Introduction', in Luis de Molina, *On Divine Foreknowledge* (Ithaca, NY: Cornell University Press, 1988), pp. 24, 18–19.

37 2 Peter 3:9, author's translation.

38 1 Timothy 2:4, author's translation.

39 J.P. Moreland and Kai Nielsen, *Does God Exist?* (Nashville: Thomas Nelson, 1990), p. 112.

40 Gary Habermas and Antony Flew, Terry L. Miethe (ed.), *Did Jesus Rise From The Dead?* (San Francisco: Harper and Row, 1987).

41 Pannenberg's response in Miethe, *Did Jesus Rise From The Dead?*, p. 128.

42 David Hume, 'An Inquiry Concerning the Principles or Morals', in *Hume's Inquiries*, ed. L.A. Selby-Bigge, with revisions by P.H. Nidditch (Oxford: Clarendon, 1975), IX (i), p. 272.

43 Kai Nielsen, *Reason and Practice: A Modern Introduction to Philosophy* (New York: Harper & Row, 1971), p. 48.

44 Richard Taylor, *Ethics, Faith, and Reason* (Englewood Cliffs, NJ: Prentice Hall, 1985), p. 14.

45 Russell and Copleston, 'A Debate On The Existence of God', p. 175.

46 'Studies Find Universe Will Expand Forever and Not Collapse,' AP News Release, 9 January 1998.

47 Augustine, *Confessions*, XI.

48 Johnson, *The Real Jesus*, p. 136.

Chapter 3

Reflections on the Explanatory Power of Theism

R. Douglas Geivett

Robert of Sorbonne observed that 'nothing is known perfectly which has not been masticated by the teeth of disputation.'[1] In the spirit of this observation, I offer the present critical commentary on the existence-of-God debate between William Lane Craig and Antony Flew.

On Methodology

General Observations

This debate begins with William Lane Craig's opening statement. His contribution here and throughout the debate is carefully researched and supremely well-organized. He begins by clarifying the division of labour. His basic aim is to present 'good reasons to think that God exists'. To Flew he assigns the task of developing whatever good arguments there are that God does not exist. Craig then devotes the balance of his own time to an exposition of five theistic evidences. He claims that these reasons, though independently effective, 'constitute a powerful cumulative case for the existence of God'.

Antony Flew's opening statement begins with a bit of redistricting. He shuns Craig's invitation to present arguments for the non-existence of God and proposes instead to show that the reasons Craig offers are not sufficient for believing that God exists. This is reminiscent of Flew's work on the 'presumption of atheism'. Although he says nothing about it here, Flew holds that, in the absence of good reasons to believe in God, one should accept a certain kind of atheism – what he calls 'negative atheism'.[2] Flew's remarks throughout the debate are more meandering and disjointed than Craig's, and this creates the risk of leaving his audience a bit bewildered about how to connect the dots.

Since Craig's case is so well-organized, and since Flew conceives of his basic aim as one of crafting defeaters for Craig's evidences, we can be reasonably secure in the verdict that Craig's agenda and method largely determine the trajectory of the debate. Even when it comes to the occasional argument for the non-existence of God, it is Craig, rather than Flew, who is most effective in clarifying what is at stake. Given the basic thrust of the debate, the few direct arguments that Flew sketches on behalf of atheism play a subordinate role. At any rate, I restrict my commentary to the shape of debate about Craig's five evidences for theism. Four of these evidences are developed into arguments, in the proper sense of the term. The remaining category of evidence – namely, religious experience – I discuss in the final section of this commentary.[3]

Inference to the Best Explanation

Craig's case for the existence of God is predominantly explanatory in nature. His four arguments for theism scrupulously follow the pattern of inference to the best explanation.

The history of the theory of explanation is almost hopelessly convoluted. Even today there are rivalries that show no promise of abatement.[4] In my commentary on the debate I simply bypass these controversies and adopt a manner of talking about inferences to the best explanation that has been developed by Bas van Fraassen.[5]

Van Fraassen maintains that 'an explanation is an answer to a why-question'. Sometimes the request for an explanation of some phenomenon is expressed explicitly in the form of an explanation-seeking question. But even if it is not, how to paraphrase the request for an explanation as an explanation-seeking question is often a fairly straightforward matter.

This is certainly the case with Craig's explanatory arguments for theism. For example, the why-question embedded in Craig's request for an explanation of the beginning of the universe is 'Why did the universe begin to exist?'. Notice that the question implies or presupposes that the universe began to exist. The proposition that the universe began to exist is what is sometimes called 'the presupposition of the question'. Van Fraassen elects to call it 'the topic of the question'. I adopt this terminology here.

In the following analysis of the debate I identify in various places the several explanation-seeking questions that William Craig formulates for Flew, note the topic corresponding to each question, and attempt to pinpoint the nature of Flew's response by examining whether he accepts or refuses the explanation-seeking question, and what form his refusal takes when he does not accept the question. Examples of his strategies of refusal include the following:

1 accept the topic but refuse the need for (or aptness of) an explanation;
2 refuse to accept the topic by denying that it is true;
3 refuse to accept the topic by withholding judgement on the truth-value of the topic.

As I hope to show, various complications and permutations of these options emerge along the way.

Turning now to the details of give and take between Craig and Flew, let us be mindful of the basic aim that each has charted for his contribution to the debate.

On the Explanatory Evidence for Theism

The Origin of the Universe

In William Craig's first argument for theism the topic of his explanation-seeking question is 'The universe began to exist'. In this debate, Craig, who has done more than any other figure to rehabilitate the *kalam* cosmological argument for the existence of God, develops two independent arguments for the topic of the question.

The first argument is *a priori*. It is borrowed from the mathematician, David Hilbert. Hilbert was an instrumentalist about the infinite. He denied that the infinite really exists and conceived of it as a heuristic device that made it possible to perform certain mathematical operations. A major motivation behind his instrumentalism was his interest in preventing mathematics from being engulfed in the flames of paradox. He reasoned that mathematics is the one domain in which there remains the prospect for knowledge of the most exalted variety – namely, certainty – and he took the prospect of irreducible paradox to be an unacceptable threat to the premier standing of mathematics within the architectonic of knowledge. Hilbert devised a scheme for shielding mathematics from paradox and inconsistency by treating one of mathematics' most fruitful entities – namely, the infinite – as a useful fiction. As a consequence of his analysis of the infinite, the whole realm of numbers was judged to be unreal. Yet, for all of his mathematical brilliance, Hilbert never succeeded in settling the controversy swirling about the status of the infinite.[6] Many have been convinced by Georg Cantor's famous diagonal argument that an infinity of infinities involves no contradiction after all, and hence that the existence of such is at least possible.[7]

It is not entirely unreasonable to affirm the actual existence of the mathematical infinite. This does not mean, however, that the peculiarities of infinity have no bearing on the topic of Craig's explanation-seeking question, for the impression of ineluctable paradox is enhanced by the effort to map the infinite on to the world of physical objects. Perhaps the paradox that rises as an unsavoury spectre to overshadow the whole field of mathematics comes to little more than this. Realists about mathematical entities do not expect these entities to behave like physical objects. My inclination is to think of the impossibility of effectively mapping the infinite on to physical reality as good evidence that the physical universe, with its temporal series of physical events, had a beginning. At any rate, we need not think of the behaviour of the infinite as such a paradoxic. Rather, it is the attempted mapping of the infinite on to physical objects that generates paradox. And this is reason enough to deny that the universe has always existed.[8]

Craig's second argument for the topic of the question is empirical; it exploits the evidence supporting the Big Bang cosmology for the physical universe. My only comment about this is that, for Hilbert himself, the more compelling evidence that the universe had a beginning was that it had been demonstrated empirically. He seems to have thought that the empirical argument was fully sufficient for this purpose.[9]

Flew's response to Craig's argument is (a) to accept the topic of the question, but (b) refuse the request for explanation, by (c) stipulating that the principle of causality applies only to entities within the universe and not to the universe as a whole, thus (d) concluding that the universe itself is a brute fact.

Flew is quite willing to accept that the universe had a beginning. But he favours the notion of 'the universe popping into existence out of nothing'. Pretty obviously, this notion has not one iota of explanatory power. What, then, does it have going for it, according to Flew? The main thing is that the possibility that the universe exploded willy-nilly into existence is not ridiculous, he says.[10] And we certainly don't know that it isn't the case. If I detect revelry here, I'm at a complete loss to recognize its justification.

My own view is that we are in a very good position to make a responsible judgement about what counts as the most reasonable terminus of explanation. Craig's theistic hypothesis certainly does the trick; Flew's does not. One unsettling thing about Flew's 'brute facts' is that they are entities for which we are able to find deeper explanations but whose explanations he arbitrarily excludes from consideration. This is an odd way to make pariahs out of true believers.

Craig rightly rejects Flew's unsupported axiom that a cause isn't needed for the whole universe. But all is not lost even if we accept the axiom. What *is needed*, Flew claims, is a cause for all the *parts* of the universe. But I maintain that there is a perfectly apt description of the physical universe according to which the beginning of the universe, as the first event in a long series making up the entire history of the universe, is itself a *part* and not the whole.[11]

Thus, when Flew reasons that the causal principle applies only to objects within the universe and not to the universe as a whole, he misses the real force of the argument for a cause. Since the principle of causality maintains that every event has a cause, it follows that every event in the history of the universe has a cause. The great chain of events constituting the total history of the physical universe is finite. This much Flew concedes when he acknowledges that the universe had a beginning. Since the beginning of the universe was the first event in the history of the universe, there is nothing untoward about invoking the causal principle in order to explain this event. As an *event*, it is metaphysically the same sort of entity as is any other event within the history of the universe. As a *big bang*, it is empirically of like kind to all other members of the class of 'bangs' (at an appropriate level of generality, of course). Otherwise, the label 'Big Bang' would be utterly metaphorical, which it is not.

Carl Sagan has been credited with the aphorism 'If you want to make an apple pie, you must first create the universe'.[12] If, *per ardua ad astra*,[13] cosmologists were to take the individual constituents of the physical universe at the Big Bang singularity and combine them in accordance with all the other initial conditions of the actual universe, they would be able to replicate the Big Bang. Any agent having this recipe for creating universes and the resources to produce the ingredients themselves would be a prime candidate for being the best causal explanation for the existence of a universe like our own.

The Complex Order of the Universe

Next, Craig introduces a version of the design argument for the existence of God. Pre-Darwinian expositions of the design argument now seem quaint and anachronistic. But, owing to various developments in the sciences, there has been a resurgence of interest in this type of argument. William Craig quite understandably focuses on the evidence of design at the level of astrophysics and cosmology, where a mind-boggling array of 'cosmic constants' is so finely calibrated as to make human biological life possible in a physical universe that would otherwise preclude the existence of organisms such as ourselves.

What is Flew's response? It is both remarkable and disappointing that he simply ignores the one category of evidence that seems to have attracted the most sympathetic notice from other naturalists.[14] What accounts for this? Here I'll venture a guess. First, Flew says early in his opening statement that his fundamental point is 'that we are, all of us, creatures whose entire knowledge and experience has been of the universe'.[15] This thesis leads him to conclude that humans are simply unable to address in a meaningful way questions that cannot be answered on the basis of our empirical experience of the world. (Call this his 'verificationist thesis'.) This means that we cannot hope to explain the origin of the universe. Presumably, we are in precisely the same position relative to explaining apparent design in the universe. (The only difference may be that whereas Flew is perfectly willing to concede that the universe probably did begin to exist a finite time ago, he probably would not be prepared to say that features of apparent design are features of bona fide design.) Second, in the same way in which Flew's verificationism prevents him from making the inference to God's existence, it apparently also forbids his endorsement of the most typical naturalist objection to this version of design argument: the many-universes objection. In sum, although Flew is not explicit about this, I suppose that, when pressed, he would simply acknowledge the existence of complex features of the universe, unified in a way that is conducive to the flourishing of living organisms, and beg off answering the explanation-seeking question by noting that it cannot be meaningfully answered. Thus, he would settle for calling these phenomena 'brute facts'.

The many-universes objection, which Flew does not mention, suggests that if we suppose our universe to be only one physical system within a grand ensemble of universes, then it is unremarkable that this particular one should evince design. If our universe is but one of a huge number of universes, the odds are greatly increased that at least one of them will exhibit the complexity we find in our universe. (Further, since intelligent organisms such as ourselves happen to inhabit this particular universe within the ensemble, we are naturally – albeit inordinately – impressed by those features that are life-enhancing.)[16] Of course, since there is no empirical evidence to support the many-universes hypothesis, serious sponsorship of it against the design argument can seem to be an act of desperation.[17] But what is of interest here is that Flew does not rehearse this type of response. Again, this may be a consequence of his positivist tendencies to restrict explicanda to the empirically verifiable.

Before moving on, there is one more point about contemporary design arguments that deserves notice. Certainly, developments in astrophysics have given theists a crowbar to pry open fresh consideration of the design hypothesis. But also in the realm of biology there have been novel developments that cannot simply be ignored by naturalists accustomed to reposing in the explanatory power of Darwinian or neo-Darwinian natural selection.[18] For example, a fair amount of dust has recently been kicked up in connection with the emerging research programme of *intelligent design*. This programme purports to exhibit biochemical and information-theoretic evidence in favour of the design hypothesis relative to living organisms. Of course, it takes time for the scholarly community to digest unprecedented empirical and theoretical developments having large-scale ramifications and achieve something resembling consensus. So my recommendation is to watch closely as the debate about intelligent design unfolds and withhold a verdict until specialists on all sides have had ample opportunity to subject their research to peer review and scout the strength of the opposition.[19]

The Existence of Objective Moral Values/Properties

Craig's third explanatory argument for theism is an argument from 'objective moral values in the world'.[20] I find that the exposition of this argument suffers from a certain lack of clarity, which in turn leads to a misunderstanding of Flew's response.

Here is Craig's summary of the argument:

1   If God does not exist, objective moral values do not exist.
2   Objective values do exist.
3   Therefore, God exists.

As an inference to the best explanation argument, the logically first step is to establish the existence of objective moral values (to establish premise 2). Craig attempts to do this by identifying a set of actions that are 'really wrong' (rape, cruelty, child abuse) and a set of actions that are 'really good' (love, equality, self-sacrifice). He is counting on his audience to agree with him about the objective rightness and wrongness of these sets of actions respectively, although he does add that there is no reason to *deny* the objective reality of moral values. Perhaps the idea here is that we know intuitively what is right and what is wrong in these cases, and that anyone who disagrees bears the burden of proof.

That moral values exist is, then, the topic of the question. In the second step, Craig simply quotes atheist philosophers who agree with premise 1.

Now it happens that the passages that Craig quotes indicate not only agreement with premise 1 but the denial of premise 2. Bertrand Russell calls ethics an invention, and Michael Ruse says 'morality is a biological adaptation'.[21] This presents a slight problem. First, Craig's expressed conviction that we all know that objective values exist follows immediately upon the heels of these quotes from Russell and Ruse whose comments imply that they think they do not know this and who probably think that anyone who thinks he knows this is simply mistaken. Second, the naturalists quoted by Craig would probably argue that the evidence for naturalism – which does not rely on a dubious faculty of intuition – is what leads them to deny premise 2 in the same breath that they acknowledge premise 1. In their case, then, we can expect a refusal of the request for explanation since they deny the topic of the question.

Turning to Flew's response we find remarks that lead Craig, in his closing statement, to suppose that Flew, in contrast to Ruse and Russell, accepts premise 2, the topic of the question. Flew does say at one stage late in the debate that he rejects relativism and that 'I am perfectly prepared [*sic*], happy to believe and constantly maintaining that things are really wrong'.[22] This does initially look like an acceptance of premise 2 – that objective values do exist. On the assumption that it is, the only thing left for Craig to do is to repeat the request for an explanation, but by this late stage in the debate it is too late for Flew to oblige. When an explanation is not forthcoming, the natural feeling may well be one of exasperation.

But there are reasons to wonder whether Flew really accepts premise 2. There are two problems with knowing what to say about this. First, although he does seem to indicate approval of premise 2 in the way described above, he creates considerable room for doubt when he speaks, Ruse-like, of the need to explain 'the evolution of norms'.[23] I wouldn't have thought that this was quite what Craig had in mind in asserting premise 2. Notice also that Flew is explicit about rejecting only a particular variety of subjectivism, namely, relativism,[24] which leaves open the possibility that he is a subjectivist of a different sort. Given his evident commitment to the evolution of norms, I can only surmise that Flew's moral theory somehow contrives to combine the evolution of norms, perhaps socially, with the denial of relativism. His position is unclear and of doubtful plausibility.

The second problem, however, is that William Craig is not very clear about what affirming the existence of objective moral values actually amounts to. Initially, those who traffic in moral arguments for the existence of God may assume that Craig is committed to a realm of abstract moral truths or moral facts that exist independently of contingent human circumstances and actions. But at one point he paraphrases the relevant explanation-seeking question as follows: 'What's so special about human beings?'[25] The problem is that 'Human beings are special' and 'Objective moral values exist' are not equivalent formulations of the topic of the question. In addition to the moral worth of persons and the objective existence of moral values, Craig speaks of *actions* being (objectively) right or wrong.[26]

On the whole, Craig's emphasis seems to be on the need to explain how it is that humans 'have morality' whereas animals do not. In context, this looks like a need to explain human moral accountability. I can appreciate that humans, unlike animals, have moral responsibilities, and that humans' treatment of one another must be governed by a respect for their moral worth. But this does not necessitate our tying objective moral values generally to what it is that makes humans special. For one thing, we seem to have moral responsibilities towards animals. I don't see that that has anything to do with what makes *humans* special.

At any rate, a case can certainly be made for the *analyticity* of moral principles. This is what has prevented Richard Swinburne, an enthusiastic proponent of natural theology, from sponsoring any argument for God's existence from 'the existence of morality'.[27] Still, to my mind, the analyticity of moral principles does not forbid an inference to the existence of God as the best explanation for various features of human moral experience. It may even be that moral principles, analytic and necessary though they may be, depend ontologically (though not causally) on the existence of God. At any rate, we should take an interest in explaining how creatures such as ourselves happen to be the fitting subjects of moral appraisal (in terms of objectively existing, analytic moral principles, if you like) that we are. (This, of course, involves a shift in the topic of the question from the one in William Craig's argument.) One consequence of conceiving of moral truths as existing in a peculiar realm of abstract objects is that they are probably causally inert, incapable of explaining the existence of contingent states of affairs where morality has scope and application. This would be a problem for naturalism-cum-Platonism.

The Resurrection of Jesus

Finally, Craig argues for the existence of God from the miracle of the Resurrection of Jesus. He says, 'If Jesus did rise from the dead, then it would seem that we have a divine miracle on our hands and, thus, evidence for the existence of God.'[28] Again, the argument fits the pattern of inference to the best explanation. Certain facts are presented and an explanation-seeking question is asked and answered in favour of theism as the best explanation. This suggests that there are two basic steps in the argument.

In the first step, Craig presents evidence that Jesus did in fact rise from the dead. To this end he identifies 'three established facts':[29]

1 'On the Sunday following his crucifixion Jesus' tomb was found empty by a group of his women followers.'
2 'On separate occasions different individuals and groups saw appearances of Jesus alive after his death.'
3 'The original disciples suddenly came to believe in the Resurrection of Jesus despite their having every predisposition to the contrary.'

While it may be thought that each of these facts by itself invites an explanation-seeking question (where each is the topic of an independent explanation-seeking question), Craig's emphasis in the debate is on the need to explain all three together. The topic of the question, then, is the conjunction of facts 1–3.

At step two the inference is made to the existence of God as the best explanation for these facts. But notice, the inference is not direct. For Craig, what warrants the conclusion that God exists is this set of facts 1–3 *together with* the claim that Jesus made during his life to have unique authority to speak for God. The three facts enumerated are set forth as evidences that Jesus did rise from the dead. That Jesus rose from the dead is, in turn, evidence corroborating Jesus' claim to be God's special emissary. This, in turn, entails that God exists (for Jesus cannot have been God's emissary if God does not exist). The thesis that Jesus claimed special divine authority during his life plays a crucial role in Craig's argument, and it must be supported by independent evidence. Thus, the argument really involves three steps.

My first substantive comment about Craig's argument from the Resurrection is to suggest that the step involving Jesus' claim to have special authority from God may actually be gratuitous relative to Craig's purposes and given what else he says in exposition of the argument.

I am not suggesting that there is good reason to doubt that Jesus actually made the sort of claim indicated. Of course, by making Jesus' claim crucial to the success of the argument, raising questions about the evidence for – *and about the significance of* – this claim is one way for a naturalist to pursue a rejoinder to this particular argument.[30] But my main point is different: why make Jesus' alleged claim a premise in the argument when the very evidence that corroborates Jesus' alleged claim also indicates that a miracle has occurred, thus paving the way for a more direct inference to the existence of God? After all, Craig himself says, 'The simple fact is that there just is no plausible, naturalistic explanation of these three facts.'[31] If this is true, doesn't the inclusion of the premise about Jesus' claim take the argument on a needless detour?

My second comment about this argument is closely related to the first. For someone who already believes in God, the evidence that Craig presents for the Resurrection of Jesus may well have the effect of vindicating Jesus' claims about himself. There are at least three reasons for this. First, a theist who happens to be agnostic about the identity of Jesus may, when confronted with the evidence for his Resurrection, think that God must have had something to do with his rising from the dead. A theist has at his disposal a perfectly plausible explanation for an event that would otherwise be an anomaly of the highest order. Second, a theist might doubt the wisdom of God's permitting the Resurrection of Jesus if God did not intend the corroboration of Jesus' claims. And it does not seem likely that God would intend the corroboration of Jesus' claims if those claims were false. Third, a theist might reasonably suppose that God can be expected to act in an identifiable way to rectify the human predicament in all of its complex dimensions, and to suppose that the surest way to recognize God's remedy would be for it to be accompanied by an inimitable miracle enjoying strong historical attestation.[32] The point is, the evidence Craig presents may be more aptly deployed for different purposes than as evidence for the existence of God.[33]

My third and final comment about this argument relates to Antony Flew's response. His most general reply is that the evidence Craig presents is insufficient 'to come to the desired positive conclusion'.[34] There can be little doubt that by 'the desired positive conclusion' he means the conclusion that God exists. But what does Flew mean when he says the evidence is insufficient? Here are a few of the more interesting possibilities.[35]

First, he may mean that the evidence for each of Craig's three factual claims may be as strong as Craig pleases as evidences that Jesus rose from the dead, but not strong enough to warrant the conclusion that God exists, *because there exists an equally plausible (or even more plausible) naturalistic explanation for the event of the Resurrection*. If this is Flew's position, it is incumbent on him to describe the alternative explanation that he finds so much more attractive.

Second, he may allow that the evidence for each of Craig's three factual claims is as strong as Craig pleases as evidences that Jesus rose from the dead, but deny that it is strong enough to warrant the conclusion that God exists, *even if Jesus' Resurrection from the dead is best explained by the existence of God*. This stance might be deemed reasonable if there is such strong evidence against the existence of God that it is more likely that Jesus did not in fact rise from the dead, despite the historical evidence to the contrary. On this scenario, the historical evidence that Jesus rose from the dead is not strong enough to outweigh the evidence for the non-existence of God. The decree that the evidence is insufficient for the conclusion here would depend on an assessment of the total evidence for and against theism. Thus, if this is Flew's intent, it is incumbent upon him to exhibit the relevant evidence against theism. He cannot settle for rebutting theistic arguments, but must launch his own atheistic argument.

Third, Flew may hold that there is indeed good evidence for each of Craig's three factual claims, and allow that, if Jesus did rise from the dead, the existence of God would be part of the best explanation, *and yet refuse to believe that Jesus rose from the dead*. Without the conviction that Jesus rose from the dead there is no basis for inferring the existence of God. This type of manoeuvre may initially seem wildly implausible. One would think that if Flew judged the evidence for each of Craig's three factual claims to be good, then he would be prepared to accept the bridge proposition that Jesus rose from the dead. And if Flew believed that the Resurrection of Jesus would justify the inference to God's existence, then surely he would also affirm the existence of God. The catch, one might suppose, is that relative to forming beliefs about historical events, the evidence for each of Craig's factual claims appears strong, but that relative to forming beliefs about the existence of God, historical evidence cannot carry the day. Historical evidence is just not the right type of evidence to support belief in God. Perhaps belief in God is just too momentous for it to be grounded in our fallible acquaintance with the vicissitudes of history, and especially ancient history. Of course, a theist confident of the existence of other good reasons to believe in God will not be disturbed by this sort of claim. For it may be that against the background of independent evidence for the existence of God, historical evidence for an event like the Resurrection begins to look like additional evidence for the existence of God. In that case, however, the evidence of the Resurrection does not stand alone as evidence for theism.

William Craig seems to think that Flew is stuck with option one from the list above. He repeatedly implores Flew to offer a naturalistic explanation for the Resurrection of Jesus, supported by his three historical facts, as if Flew does accept the topic of Craig's explanation-seeking question. This is understandable given Craig's conviction about the current consensus among historians of the New Testament. How could one not accept the topic of Craig's explanation-seeking question given this consensus?

As I explained in the section on general methodology, one way to respond to a request for explanation is to refuse to accept the topic of the question. And refusal to accept the topic of the question leaves two possibilities: deny the topic of the question, or withhold judgement. To sustain a denial of the topic, Flew's evidence would have to be strong enough to overturn the evidence Craig presents in support of his factual claims. It is hard to imagine what this evidence could be.

On the other hand, if Flew merely intends to withhold judgement and remain agnostic about the topic of Craig's explanation-seeking question, then the historical counterevidence need not be so strong. At most, all he would need is evidence strong enough to neutralize Craig's claim to be justified in believing his three propositions to be true. Apparently, Flew thinks that the problems he raises for Craig's factual claims do effectively neutralize Craig's case.[36]

Flew does not leave matters there, for he also maintains (in response to a question from the audience[37]) that the degree of strength of evidence required for affirming the occurrence of an event *varies with the nature of the event.* The range and type of evidence Craig presents in support of his three factual claims may be sufficient to warrant belief in the occurrence of 'pedestrian' events, but they do not warrant belief in the occurrence of an event like a Resurrection from the dead. As a thesis about epistemic justification, Flew's claim is *epistemological*, not historical. Hence, my sympathy for Pannenberg's complaint against Flew is moderate.[38] If something like Flew's epistemological thesis is correct, then perhaps he need not have the detailed grasp of historical data that Pannenberg and Craig demand if he is to be justified in refusing the request for an explanation. Much depends on whether Flew's thesis involves a *de jure* claim or a *de facto* claim. If Flew means that, as a matter of fact, the historical evidence available in this case just isn't sufficient to warrant belief in the Resurrection, then he cannot escape the responsibility to demonstrate a more expansive grasp of the details of historical evidence in this matter. (And it is not at all certain that Flew, if he takes the time to investigate the historical details, will find what he needs to make his argument work.) But if Flew means that, as a matter of principle, no historical evidence could be sufficient to warrant belief in the Resurrection, then he might well refuse the need to stock up on specialized historical knowledge. In that event, however, he would need to say far more than he has in defence of his epistemological thesis.

On the Immediate Experience of God

In addition to his four explanatory arguments, Craig appeals to his own immediate awareness of God in support of his own belief in the existence of God. I conclude with a few comments about this aspect of the debate.

First, while it certainly is legitimate to set an explanation-seeking question for religious experiences, Craig does not do so here. Perhaps one reason for this is that various naturalistic explanations have been devised to account for the phenomenology of religious experiences and the inclination to treat religious experiences as veridical by the subjects who have had them. In his exposition of the four explanatory arguments for theism, Craig expresses a high degree of confidence that naturalistic explanations for each of the phenomena do not so much as exist. The availability of a theistic explanation in each case makes it pretty obvious that it is the best explanation. Exhibiting the superlative explanatory power of theism in relation to religious experience, however, would require a comparison with naturalistic accounts that have enjoyed a measure of support among opponents of theism. The mere existence of several varieties of naturalistic accounts may suggest a greater challenge for the theist in this particular arena.

But I think the main reason for Craig's way of handling the evidence of religious experience has to do with his conception of the way in which experience typically grounds belief in God. He emphasizes that the sort of experience he has in mind is direct or immediate awareness of God. And certainly it is quite common – and, I would add, also natural and appropriate – for believers in God to characterize their experiences in this way.

Second, the emphasis on direct experience of God leads Craig to claim only that his own belief in God is justified by his experience of God. He very carefully avoids suggesting that his experience of God is evidence for others. Instead, he encourages others to attend to the possibility of their having experiences of the same kind in the future so that they, too, might have this sort of justification for belief in God.

Nevertheless, it makes sense to ask why Craig's own immediate experience of God shouldn't provide some justification for others to believe in God. Some philosophers have argued that direct awareness of God is analogous to perceptual awareness of physical objects.[39] If a subject's beliefs about some physical object are grounded in the subject's perceptual experience of the object so that the subject is justified in believing as she does, and if the subject herself is trustworthy with regard to reports of her experience to others, then her testimony about her experience is normally thought to provide some justification for others to hold the same beliefs about that object. Perhaps the same holds for religious experience. Furthermore, if William Craig's experience of God conforms to a pattern of experience widely exhibited within the community of believers in God, then perhaps the aggregate of such relatively uniform experiences is evidence for outside observers.[40]

Craig does refer to the fruit of his experience of God under the description of a changed life. For those who know him best, such transformation may be something that invites an explanation-seeking question in its own right. A genuine experience of God may prove to be the best explanation for the personal transformation that he has experienced and that others have witnessed. There are, then, several ways in which the direct awareness of God on the part of a person or group of persons may contribute to the justification that others have for believing that God exists.

Third, Craig seems quite willing to allow that the evidence of immediate experience is defeasible. What he says is that 'In the absence of good arguments for atheism I see no reasons to deny my immediate experience of God and my belief that He exists'.[41] This suggests that perhaps the only kind of defeat to which his experiential evidence is subject is defeat by 'good arguments for atheism'. But other philosophers, some of them proponents of the epistemic value of religious experience, have taken other sorts of threat seriously. The availability of naturalistic explanations for religious experience has already been mentioned.[42] Some have emphasized the role of conceptualization in interpreting religious experience, suggesting that one's prior conceptual apparatus explains why things appear the way they do in religious experience.[43] Others have worried that the practice of relying on religious experience within diverse and incompatible religious traditions precludes the conferring of justification on religious beliefs by religious experience.[44] It would be interesting to have Craig's response to these challenges.

My own view is that appeals to religious experience are more credible against the background of other evidences for the existence of God. A successful programme of natural theology may support appeals to religious experience in a couple of ways. First, the evidence of natural theology may support a policy of seeking God in a manner that could – on the hypothesis that theism is true – be expected to result in religious experiences. The experiences themselves could function as the occasions for actually forming the belief in God. Second, the conceptual framework underwritten by natural theology would tend to legitimate an interpretation of religious experience by means of theistic concepts that are independently plausible. These benefits may accrue even for one who does not quite believe in the existence of God on the basis of the evidences of natural theology. For the evidences may be compelling enough to commend the *experimental* adoption of the theistic world-view. This may involve a belief-like condition that H.H. Price called 'assiduous supposing', where one embarks upon a devotional experiment, suitably grounded in evidence favouring theism.[45] Such an experiment would include, among other things, the sorts of practice that William Craig commends in the context of his own appeal to direct experience of God.

On this matter, I close with a passage from Anthony Kenny, a noted agnostic philosopher of religion:

> There is no reason why someone who is in doubt about the existence of God should not pray for help and guidance on this topic as in other matters. Some find something comic in the idea of an agnostic praying to a God whose existence he doubts. It is surely no more unreasonable than the act of a man adrift in the ocean, trapped in a cave, or stranded on a mountainside, who cries for help though he may never be heard or fires a signal which may never be seen … if there is a God, then surely prayer for enlightenment about his existence and nature cannot be less pleasing to him than the attitude of a man who takes no interest in a question so important.[46]

Notes

1 Quoted in Christopher Dawson, *Religion and the Rise of Western Culture* (New York: Image Books, 1958), p. 191.

2 See Flew's article, 'The Presumption of Atheism', *Canadian Journal of Philosophy*, 2 (1972), reprinted in R. Douglas Geivett and Brendon Sweetman (eds), *Contemporary Perspectives on Religious Epistemology* (New York: Oxford University Press, 1992), pp. 19–32. I develop a response to Flew's thesis in R. Douglas Geivett, 'A Pascalian Rejoinder to the Presumption of Atheism', *The Journal for the Critical Study of Religion*, 2 (Fall/Winter 1997), pp. 19–35; reprinted with revisions in *God Matters: Readings in the Philosophy of Religion*, ed. Raymond Martin and Christopher Bernard (New York, NY: Longman 2003), pp. 162–175.

3 While Craig's strategy for assessing the evidence for theism parallels my own, there are differences between our approaches. This commentary naturally draws attention to the differences.

4 For helpful historical perspective and exposition of the major theories, see Wesley C. Salmon, *Decades of Scientific Explanation* (Minneapolis, MN: University of Minnesota Press, 1989). For analysis of inference to the best explanation, see especially Peter Lipton, *Inference to the Best Explanation* (London: Routledge, 1991).

5 See Bas van Fraassen, *The Scientific Image* (Oxford: Clarendon Press, 1980), ch. 5.

6 See A.W. Moore, *The Infinite* (London: Routledge, 1990), pp. 133–37 and 178–79.

7 See D.M. Armstrong, 'A Naturalist Program: Epistemology and Ontology', *Proceedings and Addresses of American Philosophical Association*, 73 (November 1999), pp. 77–87.

8 For interesting discussion of the relation between the empirical world and mathematics, and on the practical value of mathematics, see Eugene Paul Wigner, *Symmetries and Reflections: Scientific Essays of Eugene P. Wigner* (Bloomington, IN: Indiana University Press, 1967) and Michael Guillen, *Bridges to Infinity: The Human Side of Mathematics* (Los Angeles, CA: J.P. Tarcher, 1983).

9 See David Hilbert, 'On the Infinite', *Mathematische Annalen*, 95 (1926), p. 186, reprinted in Paul Benacerraf and Hilary Putnam (eds), *Philosophy of Mathematics*, 2nd edn (Cambridge: Cambridge University Press, 1983), pp. 183–201. Citations are from this reprint.

10 See p. 25.

11 See R. Douglas Geivett , *Evil and the Evidence for God* (Philadelphia, PA: Temple University Press, 1993), pp. 103–12.

12 Gabriel Robins, 'Good Quotations by Famous People', http://www.cs.virginia.edu/ ~robins/quotes.html 9 September 1999.

13 'Through difficulties to the stars', the motto of the Royal Air Force.

14 See, for example the favourable notice this evidence receives from philosopher Armstrong, 'A Naturalist Program: Epistemology and Ontology', p. 88.

15 See p. 24.

16 See the seminal article by Brandon Carter, 'Large Number Coincidence and The Anthropic Principle in Cosmology', in M.S. Longair (ed.), *Confrontation of Cosmological Theories with Observational Data* (Dordrecht: D. Reidel, 1974), pp. 291–98.

17 See Stephen T. Davis, *God, Reason and Theistic Proofs* (Edinburgh: Edinburgh University Press, 1997), p. 114.

18 It is not as if the Grand Evolutionary Story has ever enjoyed a period of total respite from cogent criticism. Given its relatively short life-span so far, and the many permutations it has gone through in order to withstand criticism along the way, it would be remarkable that it has achieved the hegemony it presently enjoys were it not for the fact that from a naturalistic point of view it is, in the words of Alvin Plantinga, 'the only game in town'.

19 For a detailed presentation of the case for intelligent design on the biological level, see especially Michael J. Behe, *Darwin's Black Box: The Biochemical Challenge to Evolution* (New York: The Free Press, 1996); William A. Dembski, *The Design Inference: Eliminating Chance Through Small Probabilities* (Cambridge: Cambridge University Press, 1998); and William A. Dembski, *Intelligent Design: The Bridge Between Science and Theology* (Downers Grove, IL: InterVarsity Press, 1999); and Michael J. Denton, *Nature's Destiny: How the Laws of Biology Reveal Purpose in the Universe* (New York: The Free Press, 1998) is also of interest. For a negative assessment of the intelligent design movement, see Robert T. Pennock, *Tower of Babel: The Evidence Against the New Creationism* (Cambridge, MA: The MIT Press, 1999).

20 See p. 21.

21 Russell and Ruse are quoted by Craig (ibid. above). Craig also notes that Friedrich Nietzsche lamented the destruction of meaning and value in life that resulted with the death of God.

22 See p. 37.

23 Ibid.

24 See p. 3b

25 See p. 22.

26 Ibid.

27 See Richard Swinburne, *The Existence of God* (Oxford: Clarendon Press, 1979), pp. 176–79; and idem, *The Coherence of Theism* (Oxford: Clarendon Press, 1977), pp. 179–209. Swinburne's view does not entail that God cannot issue commands that result in moral obligations; nor does it entail that God is not the source of our moral knowledge.

28 See p. 22.

29 See p. 23.

30 It would be interesting to explore the details of scholarly consensus on the question of Jesus' claims and self-understanding, and the precise significance critical scholars attach to this aspect of Jesus' life and persona. Since every factual premise in the argument does find support among critical scholars who would refrain from making Craig's inference to God's existence, one might suspect that critical scholars mean something different when they affirm that Jesus made such-and-such a claim for himself. Only careful research will reveal the answer to that question.

31 See p. 23.

32 For more on these types of considerations, see R. Douglas Geivett, 'The Evidential Value of Miracles', in R. Douglas Geivett and Gary R. Habermas (eds), *In Defense of Miracles* (Downers Grove, IL: InterVarsity Press, 1997).

33 Of course, if theism supports the strong expectation that God would produce a miracle such as the Resurrection of Jesus, then historical evidence for the Resurrection would tend to confirm theism, all other things being equal. See ibid.

34 See p. 36.

35 The list is not intended to be exhaustive.

36 See p. 36.

37 See p. 43.

38 See p. 35 where William Craig quotes Wolfhart Pannenberg.

39 See, for example, William P. Alston, 'Religious Experience and Religious Belief', *Nous*, 16, reprinted in Geivett and Sweetman, *Contemporary Perspectives on Religious Epistemology*, and William P. Alston, *Perceiving God* (Ithaca, NY: Cornell University Press, 1991).

40   R. Douglas Geivett, 'The Evidential Value of Religious Experience', in P. Copan and P.K. Moser (eds), *The Rationality of Theism* (New York and London: Routledge, forthcoming).
41   See p. 31.
42   See Caroline Franks Davis, *The Evidential Force of Religious Experience* (Oxford: Clarendon Press, 1989), pp. 193–238.
43   For example, see Wayne Proudfoot, *Religious Experience* (Berkeley, CA: University of California Press, 1985), pp. 216–27; Caroline F. Davis, *The Evidential Force of Religious Experience*, pp. 143–65; Keith E. Yandell, *The Epistemology of Religious Experience* (Cambridge: Cambridge University Press, 1993), pp. 185–87 and pp. 322–61. The material by Proudfoot is reprinted in Geivett and Sweetman, *Contemporary Perspectives on Religious Epistemology*, pp. 336–52.
44   For example, see Alston, *Perceiving God*, pp. 255–85 and Davis, *The Evidential Force of Religious Experience*, pp. 166–92.
45   See H.H. Price, *Belief* (London: George Allen & Unwin, 1969), pp. 481–87. For further development of the idea of a devotional experiment, see Caroline Franks Davis, 'The Devotional Experiment', *Religious Studies*, 22 (March 1986).
46   Anthony Kenny, *The God of the Philosophers* (Oxford: Clarendon Press, 1979), p. 129.

Chapter 4

Reflections on the Craig–Flew Debate

William Rowe

Craig

Craig begins his first speech by indicating, rightly enough, that the issue is whether there are good reasons to think that God exists, and whether there are good reasons to think that God doesn't exist. And he is fairly careful in presenting arguments on the side of the affirmative, indicating that he will leave it to Flew to present the reasons for thinking that God does not exist. But immediately after saying he will leave the case for atheism to Flew, he then asserts, 'But notice that although atheist philosophers have tried for centuries to disprove the existence of God, no one's ever been able to come up with a successful argument'.[1] Surely, that all the arguments against the existence of God are unsuccessful is not something that we can 'notice', like we might notice that the weather has been unusually warm? That the arguments for the non-existence of the theistic God are unsuccessful is something one needs to *establish*; it is not something that Craig and all the members of the audience (including, presumably, Flew) can simply *notice*. Imagine Craig's reaction if, after he presented his five reasons in favour of the existence of God, Flew were then to stand up and simply declare: 'Notice that although theist philosophers have tried for centuries to prove the existence of God, no one's ever been able to come up with a successful argument.' Of course, we must remember that this is a live debate where a rhetorical flourish, now and then, may play a useful role. But one cannot help but be surprised when Craig begins his second speech by remarking, 'You will remember that, in my first speech, I *argued* that there are no *good* reasons to think that atheism is true and that there are good reasons to think that theism is true'.[2] It is, I submit, one thing to simply *assert* your view (no one's ever been able to come up with a successful argument for the non-existence of God), but quite another thing to refer your audience back to your assertion and then tell them that you have *argued* that there are no good reasons to think that atheism is true. Even in a live debate one should take some care not to parade an assertion of a claim as an argument for that claim. Of course, Craig is a professional philosopher who has carefully studied the arguments for and against the existence of God. So, like others of us who have worked in the field of the philosophy of religion, he is entitled to assert a conclusion that he has reached as a result of his investigations. But on such matters as the existence or non-existence of God, where philosophers disagree so profoundly on the merit of the arguments for or against the existence of God, little headway can be made by simply reciting one's own view on the merits of the arguments for and against. What is needed is the presentation of and support for certain arguments on one side or the other. And, here, it must be said that Craig does present some serious arguments for the existence of God – arguments which he discusses with some care.

Craig's first two arguments for the existence of God seek to show that recent physics concerning the age of the universe and the sorts of initial conditions necessary for the support of human life lead us to infer the existence of a being that caused the universe to come into existence and fine-tuned its initial conditions. Each of these is an important argument in support of an intelligent creator, but neither is sufficient, singly or together, to yield the conclusion that God (an omnipotent, omniscient, perfectly good person) exists, let alone *necessarily* exists.[3] At best, these arguments support the existence of a being of considerable power and knowledge. But, if anything, the character of the creation does nothing to support the idea that its creator, if such there be, is an infinitely good, all-powerful, all knowing being, and may provide evidence that its creator, if such there be, is at best finite in goodness, knowledge and power. For despite all the fine-tuning of the intelligent creator, the universe is often a very wretched place, abounding with pain and suffering. Surely an omnipotent, omniscient, perfectly good creator could have arranged matters such that 6 million Jews did not have to suffer and die in ways that defy human comprehension. And if the cost of the creator's doing so would have involved limiting the freedom of some of the perpetrators of this human savagery, any moral being would have gladly accepted that cost.

Craig's third argument is based on two claims: objective moral values exist; and objective moral values exist only if God exists. Although some atheists think that objective moral values don't exist, many believe in objective moral values as firmly as theists do. Surely, Craig knows that this is so. It is, therefore, question-begging and misleading, at best, for him to simply declare, without even the hint of an argument, that 'On the atheistic view there is nothing really wrong with your raping someone. Thus, without God there is no absolute right and wrong ....'[4] The proposition that morality is objective can have the same status for an atheist and a theist, as does the proposition that logic and mathematics are objective.[5] On such a view, that an innocent person's not suffering eternally is better than an innocent person's suffering eternally is as objectively true as any truth of logic or mathematics. These are necessary truths, not invented by humankind or God. God can no more make that moral truth false than He can make it false that $2 + 2 = 4$. So, by my lights, Craig is plainly mistaken in simply declaring that 'without God there is no absolute right and wrong'.[6] One might argue that God is needed to enforce the observance of morality, or needed to so arrange things that being moral is not in conflict with a person's long-range best interests. But the claim that God is needed for morality to be objective is absurd. Indeed, if morality and logic are objective, God cannot be needed for them to be so.

Craig's fourth argument rests on what he takes to be 'historical facts' about Jesus, such as that he performed miracles and exorcisms, and was believed by his disciples to have been raised from the dead. He thinks, and cites some biblical scholars who think the same, that the Bible stories, although written down many years after the events in question were supposed to have occurred, are historically accurate on such matters. And since it would seem to require a being such as God to bring about a Resurrection from the dead, God must exist.

Do the New Testament stories about the empty tomb, the various sightings of Jesus after his death by crucifixion and the dramatic change in his disciples from despair to hope and confidence provide strong evidence for the Resurrection of Jesus from the dead? And if these stories do provide strong evidence for the Resurrection of Jesus, do they also, therefore, give us good reason to think that God exists? Craig's support for an affirmative answer to the second question is that if Jesus was resurrected from the dead it would have to be a divine miracle, and therefore, an act brought about by God. This seems at least partly right. If Jesus was resurrected from the dead, then it is only reasonable to infer that a supernatural being having great power exists and brought this about, for the Resurrection of a dead person is such an extraordinary event that any non-supernatural explanation has little chance of success. But what of the first question? Do these biblical stories provide strong evidence for the Resurrection of Jesus from the dead? Well, many able biblical scholars, as Craig notes, hold that they do. But here we should remind ourselves, first, that many able biblical scholars already devoutly believed, or were disposed to believe, in the Resurrection of Jesus before they became biblical scholars. This is not to cast doubt on their expertise as scholars. Nor is it to doubt their honesty. It is simply to say that when one has a devout belief in something, and then becomes a scholar in a field (devoted to that something) in which *decisive evidence* is not really available, one's judgements concerning the weight of the evidence may well be influenced to some degree by one's quite natural desire to find evidence that tends to corroborate one's deeply held religious beliefs. And, second, we should remind ourselves what it is for some dead person to be *resurrected* from the dead, as opposed to being brought back to life. When a person is brought back to life, as, according to the Bible, happened to Lazarus, the dead body is resuscitated and made to be alive again. But the resuscitation of a dead person is not the Resurrection of a dead person. Lazarus was brought back to life with a material body that was still subject to decay and death. Historically, Christianity has believed that Jesus was raised from the dead with a 'body' that was truly immortal, not subject to decay and death. It would be one thing to recognize the natural body of someone who has died and been resuscitated. It would be something altogether different to have evidence that a person has come back to life with a resurrected body, a body that cannot be harmed, hurt, damaged or destroyed by any natural process whatever. It takes, I suspect, an act of faith to 'discover' that the biblical stories of the Resurrection of Jesus provide strong evidence that Jesus rose from the grave with an altogether different body from the body he grew up with – a body not subject to any natural processes of corruption. How could some stories written down years after the events they purport to describe provide 'strong evidence' for such an event as that, as opposed to the resuscitation of the natural body of Jesus? Suppose, then, we were to put aside our qualms of the lack of documentary evidence at all close in time to the reported

Resurrection event and were to agree with Craig that the biblical stories provide genuine evidence for an empty tomb, for reports by some of Jesus' followers that Jesus later appeared to them, and for the renewed faith of his disciples some time after his death. Is Craig right in saying that the 'best explanation' of those 'facts' is that, after his death, Jesus somehow acquired a supernatural body – a body unbelievably different from the body with which he grew up and died, a body utterly incapable of aging, harm or destruction of any kind at all? To regard this as the 'best explanation' is to suppose that the 'facts' in question make something utterly extraordinary very likely, something that goes far beyond what those 'facts' even suggest, let alone provide strong evidence for.

One final point about Craig's argument for the existence of God based on the biblical stories of the Resurrection of Jesus is worth noting. If we already know that God exists, we have good reason, I believe, to think that life after death is not only possible but rather likely. For it seems clear that God's good purposes for human beings, whatever they may be, are not realized in this life. But suppose we are trying to determine whether there is a God and are searching for good reasons to think that there is or isn't such a being. We must then ask how likely is it that there is life after death, leaving aside the supposition that God exists? On this question, I think the only plausible answer is that life after death is extremely unlikely, for the best evidence we have shows that the conscious experience of human beings is causally dependent on the existence and proper functioning of the human brain. We know, for example, that when the brain is severely damaged, conscious experiences become severely limited and certain intellectual activities may no longer be possible. Therefore, when the body and the brain decay after death, the most reasonable inference is that the conscious life of the person whose body and brain are destroyed can no longer occur. So, if we leave aside the supposition that God (or some very powerful spiritual being) exists, we must conclude that the total evidence we have overwhelmingly supports the thesis that there is no conscious life at all after the death and destruction of the human body, including the brain. And that will be so regardless of the fact that various people contend that they have received messages from departed spirits or the fact that certain stories in the Bible imply that Lazarus was resuscitated and Jesus was resurrected from the dead. In short, without the supposition that God exists, the evidence against life after death is enormously strong. Indeed, it is so strong that it easily counterbalances whatever weight we might give to the biblical stories of the Resurrection of Jesus. And, for this reason, Craig's argument *for* the existence of God *based* on stories of survival of bodily death is overwhelmed by all the evidence we have that the conscious life of a human being depends on the existence and proper functioning of that human being's brain. My point is this. If we have good reason to think that God exists, then we have good reason to think that life after death is not only possible but likely. And depending on the strength of our reasons to think that God exists, we may be justified in believing in life after death, even though we have good evidence in support of the view that, when the body is destroyed at death, conscious life must cease. But Craig is proposing to go the other way. He is proposing to argue that, since we have good reason to think that there are cases of life after the death of the body, and after the brain is in a state of decay, there is good reason to believe that there is a God. But since, without the supposition that God exists, the evidence against any kind of life after death is so strong, I think we must conclude that his argument is very weak.

Craig's last 'argument' is from the immediate experience of God. He tells us that 'If you are sincerely seeking God, then God will make His existence evident to you'.[7] Of course, if Craig is right, we also have here the basis for a proof of the non-existence of God. All we need is someone who sincerely seeks God, but to whom God's existence is not made evident. Surely, there are many such individuals in human history. Craig, of course, must take such a claim as simply a proof of the pervasiveness of insincerity in seeking God. So, his claim is really question-begging. It amounts to this: if you sincerely seek God, God will make His existence evident to you; but if His existence isn't made evident, that's only evidence that your seeking was insincere!

Flew allows that Craig's experiences 'appear to *him* to be of God', but points out that 'this is a matter in which the subject's honest testimony is not authoritative'.[8] The question, Flew notes, is not whether Craig has an experience which *seems* to him to be of God, it is whether any of us should take Craig's experience to be veridical – a genuine experience of God, as opposed to delusory, caused by something other than God. To this point, which seems the sensible one for Flew to make in response, Craig acknowledges that the key question is: 'is my experience of God veridical?'[9] But he does nothing by way of arguing that it is veridical. Instead, he turns the issue to the question of whether he himself is entitled to believe his experience is veridical.

> But what I want to know is, in the absence of good arguments for atheism, why deny my experience? God is real to me, just as the external world is real. In the absence of good reasons to deny that experience, why am I not rational to go on believing in God?[10]

Again, no one, including Flew, is denying that Craig has an experience that seems to him to be a genuine experience of God. The question is whether it actually is a genuine experience of God, rather than a delusory experience. And Craig here seems to be abandoning the argument from experiences which seem (to those who have them) to be of God. For the only point he makes is that in the absence of good arguments for atheism and good reasons to take his experience to be delusory, *he* is rational to go on believing in God. And this response may explain why he initially introduced his fifth argument from the immediate experience of God by saying that it 'isn't really an *argument* for God's existence'.[11] His view seems to be that, apart from arguments, one can be rational in believing in God on the basis of an experience one takes to be of God. For if one has such an experience, and has no good reasons to think it delusive, and no good reasons to think that God doesn't exist, that experience can make it rational (for the person having it) to believe in God. And about this, I'm inclined to think that Craig is right. Of course, people may differ in terms of whether they have reasons for believing that God does not exist. And

Craig clearly allows here that, for someone who sincerely thinks he has reasons for disbelief, Craig's own experience, which seems to him to actually be of God, would not make it rational for such people to believe. Indeed, it is not even clear that Craig thinks that someone who has reasons neither for nor against the existence of God should accept Craig's experience as evidence for the existence of God. So, I think we do no injustice to Craig if we say that his own experience provides no adequate reason for others to believe in God.

As a general comment, Craig uses his time expeditiously, providing several clear arguments for the existence of some sort of personal creator of the universe. Despite some lapses that I've noted, his presentation is carefully crafted with respect both to logical force and personal appeal. Human beings want more than a being whose existence is necessary to explain the existence and character of the universe. They want a being to whom they can be personally related. So, there is good reason for Craig to offer an 'argument' from the direct experience of God. What is noticeable, however, is the total lack of an argument noting the almost universal character of claims to have experienced the divine – claims that can be found in each of the great religious traditions of the world. There is also no mention of the sacred scriptures of these other religious traditions. Indeed, listening to Craig, one senses that Craig thinks it is only in Jesus and Christianity that God is available to us, and that only the Christian Bible contains the historically reliable documents concerning God's activity in the world. Of course, Craig doesn't directly say this. But the omission of any references to other religious traditions and their scriptures speaks for itself.

Flew

It is unfortunate that Flew gives up so much ground to Craig at the outset by choosing only to argue that the reasons for thinking that there is a God are inadequate. Surely, the enormous amount of apparently pointless suffering in the world provides an important argument for the non-existence of God. There are also notorious difficulties in the notion of a supremely perfect being. For example, if God must be supremely perfect, then each of the superior-making qualities – power, goodness, knowledge, and so on – must have an upper limit, a degree beyond which there can be no greater degree of that superior-making quality. But it is at least doubtful that each of the superior-making qualities God would have to possess has an upper limit. It is unfortunate that Flew chose not to advance these and other arguments in the context of arguing that God does not exist. Since the issue is whether God exists or does not exist, the proponents should offer positive arguments for their respective sides and endeavour to point out weaknesses in their opponents' arguments. Craig vigorously undertakes both tasks, but Flew basically confines his remarks to noting weaknesses in Craig's positive arguments. The result is that, even if Flew is entirely successful, it is an open question whether God exists or not. To fail to provide any arguments for the non-existence of God is simply an invitation to the audience to infer either that there aren't any or that Flew thinks they fail to show that God's existence is very unlikely. And to create that impression in their minds is both to mislead them and to virtually concede the debate to the person who at least gives some arguments, however weak, in behalf of the proposition that God exists.

This is not to say that, in his first address to the audience, Flew fails to make some good points. Indeed, he makes two quite important points. The first is that when we explain one thing by something else, we either must accept the something else as a 'brute fact' – something we don't try to explain – or we must go on to explain it in terms of some third thing, which then becomes our brute, unexplained fact. Flew combines this point with what he thinks is our inability to go outside our universe in the search for explanations, and draws the conclusion that we should take the Big Bang itself as our brute, unexplained fact, at least until the physicists enlarge their theory and propose some explanation of it. But as practical as this suggestion is, it ignores the possibility of finding a fact that is itself necessary and in terms of which the origin of our universe in the Big Bang can be explained. And Craig is suggesting that the fact that God exists with the purposes he has may be such a necessary fact. So, unless Flew shows that there cannot be an explanation of our universe of the sort that Craig proposes, his claim that the series of explanations must always stop with a brute fact, rather than a necessary fact, is, in my judgement, insufficient to refute Craig's first two arguments. Flew does make the more telling point that, even supposing there is a being sufficient to create the universe, we've no good reason to think that the being has the features that Craig believes God to have. For Craig believes that God assigns some of his creatures, perhaps most of them, to eternal torment in hell, and how is that gloomy idea supposed to fit with the idea that God is infinitely loving and just? In fact, Flew argues that this picture of God as inflicting eternal punishment for an offence committed by a human being in a short life is, in his judgement, inconsistent with God's attributes of benevolence and justice. But instead of turning this into a positive argument for the non-existence of God, he only concludes that it shows there are no convincing reasons to believe such a God exists. Perhaps, however, this is just as well. For we need to distinguish between showing that God does not exist and showing that Craig, in company with Christian fundamentalists, has some seemingly inconsistent beliefs about God's loving treatment of his creatures. At best, Flew's remarks show only the latter.

Connected to his point that God, on Craig's view, has consigned many of his creatures to an eternal life of torment in hell, Flew devotes considerable effort to arguing that a long tradition within Christian theology, including such important thinkers as Augustine, Aquinas, Luther and Calvin, embraces a view of human freedom that allows for God to actually move the will of the creature towards certain ends without thereby precluding the creature's freely choosing those ends. And if this is so, Flew notes that an omnipotent God would be able to make people such that they would freely choose to do what he desired. The obvious implication of this view is that, although God could have made us so that we would freely do what is best, thus assuring us a place in heaven, he has made many of us such that we freely do an enormous amount of evil, thus assuring us a place in hell where we shall suffer eternal torment for our misdeeds. (Flew points out that Luther was so disturbed by these ideas that it was only by an extraordinary act of 'faith' that he could believe God to be merciful and just.) Clearly, we have here the makings of an argument from evil for the non-existence of an omnipotent, omniscient, infinitely just and merciful being. For surely it is only rational to believe that such a being could, and would, have moved our wills to freely do the good, thus both avoiding the suffering resulting from our freely doing evil, and markedly increasing the population of heaven.

Actually, what Flew's argument shows is only that it is likely that God is an irresponsible tyrant, bereft of mercy and justice, *if* the view of human free will adopted by Augustine, Aquinas, Luther, Calvin and the like is correct. And Craig is able to escape judging God to be bereft of mercy and justice by adopting, instead, the view of free will advanced by the sixteenth-century Jesuit theologian, Luis De Molina. For, on Molina's view, it is impossible for God to move the human will to *freely* make a certain choice. So, if God gives us free will he cannot determine what choice we freely make. Although this may appear to be an attempt by Craig to dodge the issue raised by Flew, it is not. For quite apart from its implications for God's control over our free choices, there is much to be said for the libertarian conception of freedom advocated by Craig. It has good credentials in its own right, quite apart from its merit of rescuing God from appearing to be an unjust and unmerciful warlord. There remains, however, a somewhat less forceful argument from evil, even on the libertarian conception of freedom. For unless, in creating us, God plays dice with the world, God knows what we would freely do if created and placed in certain situations. And while it may be logically possible that God could do no better than this world with all its horrendous evil, it boggles the mind to think that, among all the possible worlds with free creatures (in Molina's sense), this world is the best that could be created by an omnipotent, omniscient, infinitely good being.

Conclusion

The question period following the formal debate presents a number of interesting questions for the speakers. I'll comment on only one – a question addressed to Craig. Clearly, the background of the question is Craig's contra-causal account of human freedom – an account on which a free choice or action by an agent cannot be a choice or action that has a sufficient causal condition in some prior state of the world. The problem the questioner raises is how Craig can hold this view if he also holds that every event has a cause – the principle he used to show the need for a cause of the Big Bang. This strikes me as a relevant and important question. Craig response is as follows:

> My premise is that everything that begins to exist has a cause. Now, I think that, in the case of actions they do have causes in agents, and it's the same kind of causality that I appeal to as the cause of the Big Bang. You must get back to a personal agent

endowed with free will who is able to bring about new effects without prior determining conditions. That's the whole notion of agent causation.[12]

This is a direct and sensible response. But I suspect the questioner is still puzzled. For a free action – for example, lifting one's arm – clearly is an event that has a beginning. So, it must have a cause. What is the cause, if it is a free action? Craig's answer is that it is the agent. But then there must surely be an event which is *the agent's causing his lifting his arm*. (Or perhaps Craig would say it is 'the agent's causing his arm to rise') But then we have the event which is *the agent's causing his lifting his arm*. And the questioner will note that this event also has a beginning and must, on Craig's principle, have a cause. What then is the cause of this event? Well, it looks like we must posit a still further event: *the agent's causing his causing his arm to rise*. And we are off to the races, an unending series of events each caused by the preceding event in the series. I suspect that it is this issue to which the questioner wanted an answer. Craig needs either to answer this question or to refine his principle so that it does not require, or seem to require, a cause for every action and event that has a beginning.

The debate as a whole strikes me as a good interchange, presenting interesting arguments and thoughts on one of the most basic questions to have emerged in the history of human thought: are we the product of blind chance or is there a divine being who has created us for some purpose?

Notes

1   See p. 19.
2   See p. 27.
3   Craig views his five arguments as cumulative, no one of which is sufficient to establish the existence of a being with the attributes of God. But, as we shall see, the five arguments he gives fail to provide a satisfactory case for the existence of the God of traditional theism.
4   See p. 22.
5   See, for example, George Edward Moore, *Principia Ethica* (Cambridge: Cambridge University Press, 1963).
6   See p. 22.
7   See p. 24.
8   See p. 31.
9   See p. 35.
10 Ibid.
11 See p. 23.
12 See p. 41.

Chapter 5

The Burden of Proof and the Presumption of Theism

William J. Wainwright

William Craig's case for theism is more persuasive, in my opinion, than Antony Flew's rebuttal. Rather than scoring the debate, however, I would like to reflect on its nature.

The Burden of Proof

It is widely assumed that theists bear the burden of proof. According to this assumption, if theists are unable to provide compelling arguments for theism, atheism is the only reasonable option. This assumption appears to govern our exchange. Craig assumes the burden of proof and offers five arguments that he thinks demonstrate God's existence when taken cumulatively. Flew remains unconvinced, providing reasons for thinking that Craig hasn't established his conclusion. But is the assumption correct?

A reason sometimes given for thinking that this assumption is correct is that the burden of proof always rests on the person making a positive existence claim. If you assert that Horus exists, for example, it is reasonable for me to demand evidence, and to disbelieve in Horus's existence if you can't provide it. Cases like these suggest that the burden of proof is on the theist who asserts that God exists, not on the atheist who denies it. Appearances may be deceiving, however. For the atheist, as well as the theist, is implicitly making an existence claim. The theist finds the existence of a world consisting in a set of contingent beings that are grounded in the free activity of a necessary being intrinsically more probable than that of a world consisting only in a set of contingent beings. He therefore believes that the burden of proof is on one who denies that the former is in fact more probable than the latter. Atheists like Flew believe that the existence of a world consisting only in a set of contingent beings is intrinsically more probable than the existence of the theist's world, and that theists therefore bear the burden of showing that the probability of their world is in fact higher than that of the atheist's. On the face of it, both theists *and* atheists are making positive existence claims – that is, both believe in the existence of a world of a certain sort, and both enter the debate with certain intuitions concerning the intrinsic probabilities of the two kinds of world. So *even if* the burden of proof rests on the person making a positive existence claim, it is unclear why it lies more heavily on theists than atheists.

Let us approach the problem from a different angle. Scott Shalkowski suggests that the burden of proof is 'context-sensitive'. 'In the context of our current scientific community', for instance, the burden of proof is borne by one who denies the existence of electrons. And, in general, the burden of proof rests on the person who disputes 'an apparently well-established claim'.[1] Whether the claim is positive or negative is irrelevant.

Suppose this is correct. Does it provide a reason for thinking that theists, rather than atheists, bear the burden of proof? It does not. One might, of course, argue that although theism was *formerly* 'an apparently well-established claim', it no longer is – in that many more doubt or deny it than formerly did, the arguments for theism seem less persuasive to many than they once did, and so on. But note that atheism isn't 'apparently well-established' either, for too many educated and intellectually sophisticated people reject it. So, on the face of it, the atheist bears as heavy a burden of proof as the theist. If theists must do more than undermine the atheist's objections, then atheists must do more than rebut the theist's arguments. If the theist must provide positive reasons for his position, then (*pace* Flew) so too must the atheist. The general point is this. If the burden of proof rests on the one making a controversial claim, then the atheist's burden is no lighter than the theist's. For, in our society at least, atheism is at least as controversial as theism.[2]

Consider yet another approach. Thomas Morris proposes the following principle: if one reasonably believes oneself to be in a good epistemic position relative to P, and has 'no good evidence or any other positive epistemic grounds for thinking that P is true, one should disbelieve P'. Does this principle place a heavier burden of proof on theists than atheists? Two of Morris's additional claims imply that it does not. First, in the absence of a proof or disproof of a metaphysical existence claim, we lack 'good grounds for making any reasonable judgment that we are or that we are not in a good epistemic position relative to the claim'. Second, when the metaphysical claim is 'God exists', and we lack a proof or disproof of it, we can't rule out the possibility that either the noetic effects of sin are blinding us to the force of the evidence for the claim or, alternatively, mechanisms such as wishful thinking are impairing our ability to appreciate the strength of the evidence against it. Since this possibility can't be ruled out, then (if we lack a proof or disproof) we have good reason to doubt that we are in a good epistemic position relative to 'God exists'.[3] So if Morris's considerations are correct, neither theists nor atheists are warranted in asserting their respective claims in the absence of good arguments for them. An atheist who asserts that God doesn't exist bears as heavy a burden of proof as the theist who asserts that he does.

Flew's Presumption of Atheism

But Flew would not (or at least should not) deny what I have said so far. For Flew uses the term 'atheism' in a non-standard way. In his view, atheism is any form of non-belief in theism. As he uses it, the term embraces not only atheism in the standard sense (disbelief in God's existence) but also agnosticism and the view that the theist's claims are 'meaningless'.[4] So when Flew speaks of the 'presumption of atheism', he need not deny that atheists in the standard sense bear as heavy a burden of proof as theists. What he *does* deny is that non-believers bear as onerous a burden as believers. In his view, it is incumbent upon believers to provide compelling arguments for their belief. If they can't, non-belief is the reasonable option.

One may doubt that Flew is always careful to observe his distinction in practice. (It often sounds, in any case, as if he is defending not merely *non-belief* but *disbelief*.) Be this as it may, the important point was made by Blaise Pascal and William James.[5] The distinction between disbelief and non-belief is typically a distinction without any real difference. Refusing to bet on God's existence has the same practical consequences as betting on his non-existence. In either case, one lives as if God does not exist, and so loses the good promised by theism 'if good there be'. Yet if the good is great enough, it seems unreasonable to forgo one's chance of achieving it in the absence of substantial evidence that the probability of achieving it is negligible. If this is correct, then one shouldn't embrace non-belief without possessing substantial reasons for thinking that God does not exist. Consequently, it isn't clear that non-believers bear a lighter burden of proof than believers. It is doubtful, in other words, that the presumption of atheism is stronger than that of theism *even when 'atheism' is used in Flew's sense.*

Before dismissing Flew's presumption, however, let us see how he justifies it.

> To adopt a presumption about the burden of proof is to adopt a policy. And policies have to be assessed by reference to the objectives and the priorities of those for whom they are proposed. Thus the [legal] policy of presuming innocence is rational for all those for whom it is more important that no innocent person should ever be convicted than that no guilty person should ever go free, but irrational for those harboring the opposite priorities .... The objective by reference to which the policy of accepting the presumption of atheism has to be justified is the attainment of validation of knowledge about the existence and activities of God if such knowledge is indeed attainable.[6]

But notice three things. First, Flew seems to assume that *knowledge* about God is more important than true belief about him. (If it isn't, it is unclear why we should adopt a policy that has the attainment of knowledge, rather than true belief, as its object.) Why should we accept this? Plato thought that knowledge was better than (mere) true belief because it is *more secure*. For example, if our moral opinions are grounded in good reasons, we are less likely to abandon them under pressure (sceptical attacks, irrational passions, the lure of self interest and so on). Plato conceded, however, that knowledge and true belief are *equally successful* guides to practice. A person with the correct opinion about the best way to get from Milwaukee to South Bend will get there as quickly as someone who *knows* the way.

Of course, the problem is that, in the absence of knowledge, one has no assurance that one's opinion is correct. Still, it would be foolish to systematically reject opinion when knowledge is unavailable and, in practice, no one does so (not even Flew who guides his life by the opinion 'The gods do not exist'[7]). It may also be foolish not to guide one's life by the opinion 'God exists', if knowledge *about God* is unavailable, since the following might be true:

1   Human beings are capable of sharing in God's own life.
2   A necessary condition of doing so is adopting the proper stance in relation to him.
3   One can't do that, however, unless one has correct beliefs about him.
4   Our intellectual faculties are devices for acquiring as many important truths as possible, and the most important truths are truths about God.

Suppose these propositions are true. Knowing divine truths may be better than simply believing them (as Augustine, Anselm and Aquinas all thought). It is nevertheless better to hold true beliefs about God that are inadequately supported by argument and other positive epistemic grounds than to hold false beliefs about him, or no beliefs at all. For if one's beliefs *are* true, one holds correct beliefs about the most important matters and has met a necessary condition for sharing in an overwhelming good. So if propositions 1 through 4 are true,[8] then, arguably, our primary objective should be *true beliefs* about God, not knowledge. Knowledge about God is one way of achieving it. But if Christianity or other forms of traditional theism are true, it is not the only way, or necessarily the most effective or best. True (and secure) belief in divine things is achieved by conversion, a 'closing with Christ', or a surrender to the message of the Qur'an, that is as much a matter of one's heart as one's head.[9]

The second thing to notice is this. William James claims that there 'are two materially different laws' for conducting our 'intellectual life. We may regard the chase for truth as paramount, and the avoidance of error as secondary; or we may, on the other hand, treat the avoidance of error as more imperative and let truth take its chance.'[10] I suggest that Flew's second assumption is that we are more likely to attain true beliefs about God if our belief-forming practices are guided by the maxim 'Avoid error' rather than by the maxim 'Seek truth'. In this respect, Flew's policy is like the legal policy with which he compares it. Anglo-American judicial policies are shaped by our fear of error (about guilt). To avoid it, we are willing to pay the price of sometimes (perhaps often) missing the truth.[11] This policy is quite reasonable in criminal cases. But is it reasonable in *all* cases and, in particular, in those in which the possession of the right beliefs may be a necessary condition of enjoying an infinite good? William James, at least, thinks that it isn't.

Finally, notice that Flew's judicial analogy, and his own practice, suggest that he is making a third assumption: formal debate is the best way of determining the truth about controversial matters.[12] This is not entirely implausible, and philosophical practice supports it. In the Platonic dialogues, opinions are broached and subjected to philosophical scrutiny in the hope that the truth will emerge through a process of questioning and answering. The medieval practice of examining philosophical and theological theses in public debates is reflected in the structure of Aquinas's *Summa Theologiae*. Modern philosophers proceed in the same fashion. Someone advances a thesis, offers arguments for it, and then responds to the criticism of other philosophers. The thesis that best survives criticism is then regarded as the closest approximation to the truth currently available.

But are formal debates the most effective way of ensuring that one has the truth *about God*? Shalkowski argues that they may not be. In the first place, it isn't clear why we should assume (as Flew appears to) that a proposition is rationally believed only if the person believing it can win a debate over its truth in which she takes the affirmative side.[13] Is one's belief in the reality of physical objects – for example, rational only if one (or, in any case *some*one) can win a debate with philosophical sceptics? Not obviously. In the second place, 'only something entertained as propositional evidence is of use in a debate', and that skews things since evidence can be non-propositional.[14] For example, at one point, Craig appeals to his own conversion experience. Flew dismisses this, arguing that Craig's experiential evidence has no force unless he can make a propositional case for his experience's veridicality. However, what Flew needs to show is that his dismissal of Craig's experiences isn't as unreasonable as a dismissal of ordinary perceptual reports on the grounds that compelling arguments for sense perception's veridicality haven't been given.[15]

But even if properly conducted public debate *is* the most effective way of establishing the truth of 'God exists' and other controversial matters, it isn't clear why the *theist* must bear the burden of proof. As Shalkowski observes, the affirmative side in a debate *does* bear the burden of proof. But the affirmative side is simply the one that initiates the discussion by making an assertion ('God exists', for instance, or 'God does not exist') and providing reasons for it 'that the negative side [then] tries to undermine by showing that there is no need to change the status quo'. Why, though, 'should *theism* be [regarded as] the side that starts the debate?'[16] Craig did take the initiative in the Madison debate, but the debate could have been structured quite differently. If *Flew* had initiated the discussion by asserting that God does not exist and offering reasons for his assertion, it would have been only incumbent upon Craig to undermine Flew's case. Flew's burden would have been heavier and Craig's lighter. Why assume, then, that the dispute between theists and atheists (in the standard sense) must be framed as a debate in which *theists* take the initiative and bear the burden of proof? An answer isn't easily forthcoming. Nor is the situation altered when 'atheism' is defined in Flew's broad sense, not as the position that God does not exist, but as the claim that there are no sufficient reasons for believing that he does. If Flew were to take the initiative instead of Craig (and Craig has no more obligation to take it than Flew does), then it would be incumbent upon Flew to support his position by providing reasons for it (for example, critiques of the various grounds that have been offered for God's existence), and only incumbent upon Craig to undermine them. Those of us who are unpersuaded by the standard critiques suspect that this will be a comparatively easy duty to discharge.

Let us suppose, however, that the burden of proof does rest on Craig's shoulders. Why think that he hasn't met it? Because he hasn't convinced Flew and other atheists that theism is true? Because, in other words, *they* don't find the evidence for theism that Craig adduces as persuasive as he does?[17] But this is an unreasonable standard to impose on Craig or anyone else, for no interesting philosophical arguments for controversial conclusions are compelling in the sense that all who understand them accept them. Indeed, Flew's own arguments for the conclusion that the evidence Craig offers is insufficient to establish God's existence fail to meet this standard, for Craig and many other good philosophers aren't persuaded by them.

So what standards *should* we expect arguments to meet? George Mavrodes has called attention to the fact that good arguments are 'person-relative' since a good argument for A is an argument employing premises that A knows or rationally believes, and what A knows or rationally believes may differ from what B knows or rationally believes.[18] But good arguments are also person-relative in a more interesting sense. For A and B may both know or rationally believe *the same premises*, and yet A appreciates their force, or sees their bearing on the conclusion, while B does not. When that happens, A's knowledge (or stock of rational beliefs) is extended by the argument and B's isn't. As a result, the argument is a *good* argument for A but not for B.

What accounts for differences of this kind? Where intelligence, training and information are equal, they are largely explained by dissimilarities in what James called our 'passional nature' – our temperament, hopes, fears, passions, aversions, intimations, and the like. Blaise Pascal, John Henry Newman and William James think that a person's 'heart' or 'passional nature' affects her assessments of complicated bodies of evidence for disputed propositions. For example, the theist's assessments of evidence for God's existence may be inflected by her love of God or by her desire or need for God. (And note that *if theism is true*,[19] these dispositions may *enhance* the operation of one's cognitive faculties.) By contrast, the atheist's assessments may be affected by his fear of being duped, by his failure to appreciate the splendour or importance of the good at stake, or by his hostility towards religion. My point, however, is not that all atheists' readings of the evidence are infected by attitudes like these. Nor would I deny that some theists' readings of the evidence are partly vitiated by blindness to the force of real difficulties, hostility toward their critics or a complacent triumphalism. My point, rather, is that *all* readings of complicated bodies of evidence for existentially important theses are *unavoidably* inflected by passional factors of *some* kind or other.

So the fact that Craig finds the evidence for God's existence compelling, while atheists like Flew don't, isn't decisive. It must also be shown that Flew's reading of the evidence is better, or more rational, than Craig's. And to show *that*, one must show that the passions and interests affecting Flew's reading are epistemically more benign than those affecting the readings of Craig and his fellow theists.[20]

The Presumption of Theism

Let me conclude with a controversial suggestion. Since a belief in a 'higher universe'[21] is natural, the presumption is *in favour of religious conviction*.[22] The concept of a 'natural belief' is Hume's. Natural beliefs first, belong to naive common sense (that is, aren't produced by sophisticated reflection); second, lack rational justification (or, at the least, are comparatively unaffected by sophisticated challenges); third, must be believed if we are to act successfully; and, fourth, are held universally. Natural beliefs include our beliefs in an external world, in other minds and in the uniformity of nature.[23] A great deal of evidence supports the thesis that belief in a higher universe, too, is natural in Hume's sense. One of the most impressive pieces of evidence is the 'virtual universality throughout human life of ideas and practices that are recognizably religious',[24] and their surprising survival in the Soviet Union and communist China. There is also some evidence that autism and frontal lobe damage cause people to lose their capacity for religious belief, suggesting that this capacity is part of our normal psychological equipment.[25] If, in addition, Christianity or some other form of traditional theism is true, then humanity's natural religiosity is implanted by the God who created us, and attests to the reality of the 'higher universe'. In any case, it seems to me that James is right: disbelief requires the suppression of natural religious instincts. If (as James also thought), it is reasonable to trust our faculties and natural instincts in the absence of compelling reasons for not doing so, the presumption is in *favour* of religious belief. The burden of proof is thus on Flew, not Craig.

There is no more a presumption of atheism than a presumption of solipsism or of disbelief in the external world. It would be absurd to claim that the burden of proof is on those who believe in other minds or an external world, or to insist that they don't know or rationally believe these things unless they can produce arguments for their beliefs that would compel the assent of sceptics. I submit that it is also misguided to insist that the burden of proof rests on the shoulders of the religious believer. The difficulty of repelling sceptical challenges to our common-sense beliefs in other minds or the reality of the external world – *in a non-question-begging manner* – suggests that a presumption of solipsism or of disbelief in the external world would be at least as difficult to counter as Flew's presumption of atheism. Most of us undoubtedly do believe that the case for 'Other minds exist' or 'The external world is real' is stronger than that for their denials. I strongly suspect, however, that we are more impressed by the former than the latter because we have a strong disposition to believe in the reality of other minds and the external world, and no disposition to believe in their denials. If what I said in the preceding paragraph is correct, most of us also have a strong disposition to interpret the world religiously.

But my case mustn't be overstated, for there are disanalogies. A 'presumption of solipsism', for example, sounds odder than 'a presumption of atheism'. Why? It seems odd to speak of a presumption of solipsism because:

1   our experience *seems* to present us with other minds;
2   there are no compelling reasons for thinking that our experience is deceptive; and
3   our disposition to believe in other minds is virtually irresistible.

Our belief in a higher universe is a bit different, however. First, most religious experiences aren't as psychologically compelling as our apparent experiences of other minds (although some are), and some people don't have them. Second, the only reason for thinking that other minds don't exist is the failure to demonstrate that they do. (There does, on the other hand, appear to be *positive* evidence, of the higher universe's non-existence – namely, the pervasiveness of evil and suffering.) Third, the disposition to believe in a higher universe is weaker, or more easily suppressed, than our disposition to believe in other minds. So there *are* disanalogies. What is unclear, though, is their philosophical relevance,[26] or why they should cast the burden of proof on the theist. (The second disanalogy *may* impose a burden upon the theist of explaining why apparent counterevidence such as evil doesn't falsify theism. But this isn't the same burden that Flew would impose on her, and is more easily met.[27])

Conclusion

So where are we? Craig has produced five proofs of God's existence and responded to Flew's objections. I have not argued that Craig's proofs are probative or that his responses to Flew are successful (although, in my opinion, he gets the better of the debate.) I *have* argued that it is not only unclear that theists bear a heavier burden of proof than their opponents, but there is also reason to think that it rests with the atheist. If it does, then any failure on the part of theists to establish their position by providing universally compelling arguments for it is not a reason for disbelief.[28]

Notes

1   Scott Shalkowski, 'Atheological Apologetics', *American Philosophical Quarterly*, 26 January 1989 p. 6.
2   Whether this is true of the secular academy is doubtful. But it is also doubtful that the secular academy is representative of society as a whole, or even of the intelligent, educated and thoughtful part of it. Furthermore, the atheism of many academics is as unthinking as the theism of some theists.
3   Thomas V. Morris, 'Agnosticism', *Analysis*, 45 (October 1985), pp. 219–24. P.J. McGrath argues that Morris's principle countenances agnosticism with respect to 'tribal deities, elves ... leprechauns' or Cartesian demons, and that this is absurd. In his view we disbelieve in these things because there is no positive evidence for them – period. (See Patrick J. McGrath, 'Atheism or Agnosticism', *Analysis*, 47 (January 1987) pp. 54–57.) This seems mistaken. We rule out the existence of tribal deities, elves and leprechauns because (1) we implicitly assume that their existence is antecedently very unlikely and/or because (2) we (implicitly) assume that if elves, for example, did exist, we would have better evidence for their existence than we do – that is, we implicitly assume that we are in a good epistemic position relative to the proposition 'Elves exist'. The absence of positive evidence isn't the whole story.

Similarly, our disbelief in Cartesian demons is grounded in our well-founded(?) resistance to scepticism, as well as in the absence of evidence.

4 Antony Flew, 'The Presumption of Atheism', in Philip Quinn and Charles Taliaferro, (eds), *A Companion to the Philosophy of Religion* (Oxford: Blackwell, 1997).

5 In Blaise Pascal, *Pensées* (New York: Modern Library, 1941); and William James 'The Will to Believe', in idem, *The Will to Believe and Other Essays in Popular Philosophy* (New York: Dover, 1956), respectively.

6 Flew, 'The Presumption of Atheism', p. 411.

7 I am taking Flew at his word when he professes not to know whether or not the world has a first cause or not. If he doesn't, he doesn't know that the 'gods' don't exist.

8 And we don't know that they are false.

9 Whether this, too, can be called knowledge is a moot point. It is not, however, what Plato, or Aquinas, or Flew means by 'knowledge' since the propositions believed don't have the evidence of 'first principles' and aren't established by 'demonstration'.

10 James, 'The Will to Believe', p. 18.

11 Or at least ignoring it.

12 The debate can be internal, of course, with the investigator assuming the roles of both advocate and critic.

13 That is, in which she undertakes to establish its truth.

14 Shalkowski, 'Atheological Apologetics', pp. 3–5.

15 And it is doubtful that they could be. William Alston, for example, has argued that any sound argument for the reliability of sense perception will turn out to be circular. See, for example, William Alston, 'Epistemic Circularity', *Philosophy and Phenomenological Research*, 47 (1986), pp. 1–30.

16 Shalkowski, 'Atheological Apologetics', pp. 3–5, my emphasis.

17 Some remarks of Flew suggest that he is operating with this standard. For example, on page 26 above Flew claims that Craig's argument for a first cause is flawed because not all 'rational chaps' would be persuaded by it.

18 See, for example, George I. Mavrodes, *Belief in God* (New York: Random House, 1970), ch. 2, and his more recent 'On the Very Strongest Arguments,' in Eugene Thomas Long (ed.), *Prospects for Natural Theology* (Washington, DC: The Catholic University of America Press, 1992).

19 And we can't simply assume that it is false without begging the question.

20 For more on this point, see William Wainwright, *Reason and the Heart* (Ithaca, NY: Cornell University Press, 1995).

21 'A more spiritual universe from which it ["the visible world"] draws its chief significance', 'a wider self through which saving experiences come', 'a larger power friendly to [us] and to [our] ideals'. See William James, *Varieties of Religious Experience* (New York: Modern Library, c. 1902), pp. 475, 505 and 515.

22 For a related suggested, see Charles Taliaferro, *Contemporary Philosophy of Religion* (Malden, MA: Blackwell, 1998), pp. 255–64.

23 John C.A. Gaskin, 'God, Hume, and Natural Belief', *Philosophy*, 49 (1974), pp. 281–94.

24 John Hick, *An Interpretation of Religion* (New Haven, CT: Yale University Press, 1989), p. 21.

25 See Ellen Kappy Suckiel, *Heaven's Champion: William James's Philosophy of Religion* (Notre Dame, IN: University of Notre Dame Press, 1996), pp. 66–68. What apparently happens is that the neurological damage causes an inability to

experience feelings of 'religious awe and wonder,' and other affective responses necessary for the formation of vital religious beliefs.

26   Or more accurately, the philosophical relevance of the first and third disanalogy. These disanalogies help explain why atheism is psychologically possible for some people while solipsism is not. What isn't clear is that they provide good reasons for being more suspicious of beliefs in a higher universe than of our belief in other minds. However, the second disanalogy does provide a good reason for being more suspicious of the former than the latter. Of course, traditional theists think that this suspicion can be met. Craig, for example, appeals to Molinism to rebut Flew's argument from evil.

27   This might be challenged, but it seems obvious to me that it is easier to defuse the problem of evil by providing reasons why the existence of apparently pointless suffering isn't conclusive than to produce universally compelling arguments for theism (arguments compelling the assent of even such die hard atheists as Flew).

28   To avoid misunderstanding, let me emphasize that while I don't think that theists can provide universally compelling arguments for their position, I believe that they can provide good arguments for it. If there is a presumption of theism, however, they needn't even do that.

Chapter 6

Comments on the Craig–Flew Debate

Michael Martin

The publication of the transcripts of the oral debate between Craig and Flew in this volume gives us the opportunity to distance ourselves from the rhetoric and spectacle inherent in the occasion and concentrate on the soundness of the arguments used by the participants. Skilled oral debaters impress their audiences by their rhetorical proficiency, their delivery, their personality and even their appearance. With the bare transcript before one, these irrelevancies are eliminated and the strengths of the contrasting positions can more easily be ascertained. This distancing is especially important in assessing the Craig–Flew debate on the existence of God. Craig is a professional debater known far and wide for his skills in oral disputation and it would hardly be surprising if he were judged the victor in this debate prior to abstracting the argument from rhetoric, presentation and personalities.

Overview of the Debate

In the 18 February 1998 oral debate on the existence of God at the University of Wisconsin between William Lane Craig, a famous Christian apologist, and Antony Flew, a distinguished atheistic British philosopher, Craig presented five arguments for believing in God. In his first argument, Craig maintained that the universe is caused by an immaterial, timeless, changeless, spaceless, beginningless, uncaused personal Creator. In his second argument, he argued that, since only a small range of physical constants are compatible with life, life was probably created rather than being a result of chance. His third argument purported to show that God is the source of moral objective value. His fourth argument maintained that the Resurrection of Jesus must be explained in theistic terms. His final argument held that personal experience gives us a God who can be immediately known.

In his opening statement, Craig challenged Flew to give reasons for believing that God does not exist and professed scepticism that Flew would succeed. But Flew, in his opening statement, rejected Craig's gambit by saying that, instead of giving reasons for not believing in God, he would show that there is no good reason to believe. Craig is too bold, Flew said, in supposing that humans can have knowledge of matters outside the universe. Then, in his closing remarks Flew reiterated that his intention had not been to give reasons for non-belief in God. It had simply been to argue that our knowledge is limited to the universe and cannot extend beyond it.[1] It is not clear whether Flew's actual practice was completely consistent with his intention, for some of his arguments suggest that he was trying to show that God does not exist. Thus, for example, in a long exchange with Craig over whether human freedom is compatible with divine power, Flew appears to have been arguing that the doctrine of eternal punishment is incompatible with God's existence: that God could bring it about that human beings with free will are good and, consequently, that no punishment – let alone eternal punishment – is necessary. Hence, Flew seems to have been maintaining that the concept of God assumed by Craig is logically incoherent and therefore that God could not exist. In what follows I will, however, ignore any of Flew's arguments which can be construed as being for the non-existence of God on the grounds that they are lapses from his original intention and will concentrate on the two following questions. Has Flew shown that Craig's reasons are inadequate for belief in God? If not, can Craig's reasons be shown to be inadequate? I will be concerned only with Craig's first, third and fifth arguments since his second and fourth arguments are discussed by Keith Parsons in Chapter 8.

The Origin of the Universe

Craig's first reason for believing in God is based on the *kalam* cosmological argument which he formulates as follows:

1   Whatever begins to exist has a cause.
2   The universe began to exist.
3   Therefore the universe has a cause.

Since time and space commenced with the beginning of the universe, Craig infers that the cause of the universe must be timeless and spaceless. Moreover, because change takes place in time and matter is in space, Craig deduces that the cause of the universe must be changeless and immaterial. Furthermore, Craig argues that this cause must be personal.

Flew's critique of this argument can be understood as follows. First, he accepts premise 2 as being based on the latest scientific cosmological evidence. Second, he accepts premise 1 only with qualification. He points out that premise 1 is not a truth of logic but a statement that is based on empirical evidence. We only have reason to suppose that it holds *within* our universe. Flew maintains that it is not inconceivable that the universe began without a cause. Third, he argues that any explanation is ultimately in terms of some brute fact – something that remains unexplained in the light of our present knowledge. God in the theistic world-view remains unexplained and thus is a brute fact. The implication seems to be that there is no difference in principle between the beginning of the universe being uncaused and God being uncaused. Fourth, Flew points out that there are not just two alternatives: either God created the universe or the universe is uncaused.

With a little elaboration, these criticisms undermine Craig's argument. Craig's acceptance of premise 1 is not based on empirical evidence but on what Craig calls the 'metaphysical intuition' that nothing comes from nothing. But metaphysical intuitions have been notoriously unreliable. Everything from the principle of no action at a distance to microdeterminism has been intuited to be true only later to be discarded. Furthermore, it is by no means obvious that, once one knows exactly what is involved in accepting premise 1, one will agree with Craig's intuitions. Craig implies that his metaphysical intuitions are universally shared by all rational people and that anyone who disagrees is a crank or worse. He neglects to mention that some eminent cosmologists, including Steven Hawking, have proposed theories in which the universe has no cause.[2]

Flew is certainly correct that, on empirical grounds, the scope of premise 1 should be restricted to the confines of our universe. However, the restrictive scope of premise 1 is at least partly conceptual. On our ordinary concept of cause, a cause is prior in time to the effect. Since, according to current cosmology, time is created with the universe, the universe could not be caused. We literally do not know what we are talking about when we refer to a non-temporal cause of the universe. Craig's case would not be improved if some causes were simultaneous with their effects. Although I know of no plausible examples of simultaneous causality, if a cause did occur simultaneously with the effect, the cause would still be *in* time.

Craig insists that the cause of the universe is a choice. But, on our ordinary concept of choice, a choice is temporally prior to what it causes. On Craig's theory the choice that causes the universe is *outside* of time and space. To be sceptical, as Flew is, of this extension of our ordinary causal concepts to causes – especially choices as causes – *outside* of time and space, and to effects *in* time and space, seems to me to be eminently reasonable.

However, let us suppose that some sense can be made of non-temporal causality. Flew also raises the brute fact objection. Craig professes that he cannot understand how the universe, along with time and space, could not have a cause and be simply a brute fact – something that is unexplained. But Craig professes no difficulty in understanding how a timeless and spaceless cause such as God can be a brute fact. It is unclear why, once we accept the intelligibility of non-temporal and non-spatial causation, the temporal and spatial nature of something should make a difference.

In short, using his metaphysical intuition Craig rejects:

1 Some things that begin have no cause.

But using his metaphysical intuition Craig accepts:

2 Some non-temporal causes have no cause.

Needless to say, for anyone who does not share Craig's intuitions, the difference between 1 and 2 seems arbitrary and without rational justification.

Flew mentions that there are more than the two alternatives assumed by Craig: God created the universe and the universe has no cause. He considers the possibility that the universe was created by a powerful torturer – an evil being. It is important to see that Craig's argument that an all-good God could permit eternal torture, even if successful, does not eliminate this possibility. Flew might have mentioned other alternatives. For example, the cause of the universe might be the actions of many gods, or of a single god who is finite in power and knowledge, or of a non-personal force or non-personal forces. Although Craig attempts to eliminate some of these alternatives, he does not try to eliminate all of them. For example, everything Craig says is compatible with polytheism or with a finite god. The cause of the universe might be the result of the choices of many gods or the choice of a god with limited powers. However, even if we suppose that the possibilities of polytheism and a finite god could be eliminated, Craig would still not have proven that God exists, since nothing has been shown about God's moral attributes. Whether Craig is successful in doing this in his third argument remains to be seen.

One alternative Craig does try to eliminate is that of a non-personal force or non-personal forces as a cause of the universe. He argues:

> If the cause were an impersonal set of necessary and sufficient conditions, then the cause could never exist without the effect. If the causes was timelessly present, then the effect would be timelessly present as well. The only way for the cause to be timeless and for the effect to begin to exist in time is for there to be a personal agent who freely chooses to create an effect in time without any prior determining conditions.[3]

Let's assume that we can make sense of a choice not being in time and space. Craig says that if a cause were timelessly present, the effect would be too. But God's choice to create the universe is not in time. Consequently, the choice *is* timelessly present. Recall that, according to Craig, God is changeless. He does not decide at a particular time for, if he did, he would not be changeless. In this respect, God's choice is no different from an impersonal set of necessary and sufficient conditions. If Craig's argument eliminates an impersonal force as a cause, it also eliminates the choice of a personal creator as a cause.

In short, Flew's arguments provide excellent reasons to be sceptical of Craig's argument from the origin of the universe.

Objective Morality

Craig's third reason for believing in God is based on the following argument:

1 If God does not exist, objective values do not exist.
2 Objective values do exist.
3 Therefore, God exists.

Commenting very briefly on this argument at the end of the debate, Flew denied that he is committed to ethical relativism. Citing Hume with approval, he argued that the language of morality commits one to an objective moral point of view and rejected the inference from objective moral judgements to God's approval.

What Flew said is correct as far as it goes; however, it could go further. The first thing that must be pointed out is that the soundness of this argument is crucial to Craig's overall position. For even if his first argument from the origin of the universe were successful, Craig would not have shown that an all-good God exists. The second thing to note is that Craig gave no good reason at all to accept premises 1 and 2. Indeed, the only thing he did to establish premise 1 was to cite authorities – Russell, Michael Ruse, Nietzsche – who believe premise 1. However, Craig did not even do this for premise 2. Here he simply asserted that premise 2 is true, saying that we all know this 'deep down'.[4]

It is important to see that Craig was selective in his choice of authorities. Not all theists claim that atheistic morality is subjective. For example, Richard Swinburne, who is perhaps the most famous contemporary Christian philosopher, argues that many moral statements are true independent of God's commands. Swinburne says, 'Genocide and torturing children are wrong and would remain so whatever commands any person issued.'[5] Furthermore, he believes that although it is true that if God had issued commands on a topic, these commands would be morally relevant to this topic, he assumes that it is possible to settle moral disputes concerning this topic objectively if God does not exist. Craig also neglected to mention ethical philosophers such as Roderick Firth, Richard Boyd, Peter Railton and David O. Brink who have given objective accounts of morality that are compatible with atheism.

Indeed to support premise 1 Craig would have to refute the following argument:

1 In order to show that atheistic morality necessarily is subjective, it must be shown that all attempts to ground objective morality on a non-theistic basis fail.
2 But it has not been shown that all attempts to ground objective morality on a non-theistic basis fail.
3 Hence, it has not been shown that atheistic morality is necessarily subjective.

Here Craig has his work cut out. There have been many attempts to show that morality can have an objective basis that is independent of religion[6] and, to my knowledge, these attempts have not been refuted.

In his writing, as in this debate with Flew, Craig assumes that theism *can* provide an objective basis for morality. Is he correct? How can he claim that objective morality is compatible with theism and not with atheism? The problem goes back to the Euthyphro dilemma. In order to illustrate the problem I will consider the immorality of rape – one of the prime examples Craig has used to illustrate the failure of atheistic morality and the superiority of theistic morality. According to Craig, the judgement of the objective wrongness of rape is possible with theism but not with atheism.

The Euthyphro dilemma can be stated as follows: does God condemn something because it is wrong or is it wrong because God condemns it? On the first alternative, what is wrong is based on God's condemnation and exists independently of God. On the second alternative, what is wrong is arbitrary, dependent on God's will. Consider rape as a special case of something that is wrong. It might be supposed that God has various reasons for thinking rape is wrong: it violates the victim's rights, it traumatizes the victim, it undermines the fabric of society and so on. All of these are wrong-making properties. However, if these wrong-making properties provide objective grounds for God's thinking that rape is wrong, then they provide objective grounds for others thinking this as well. Moreover, these reasons would hold even if God did not exist. For example, rape would still traumatize the victim and rape would still undermine the fabric of society. But then, atheists could provide objective grounds for condemning rape – the same grounds used by God.

Let us suppose now that rape is wrong because God condemns it. In this case, God has no reasons for His condemnation. His condemnation makes rape wrong, and it would not be wrong if God did not condemn it. Indeed, not raping someone would be wrong if God condemned not raping. However, this hardly provides objective grounds for condemning rape: whether rape is right or wrong would be based on God's arbitrary condemnation. On this interpretation, if atheists can provide no objective grounds for condemning rape, they are no worse off than theists.

Thus, we have a special case of the Euthyphro dilemma: either rape is condemned by God because it is wrong or it is wrong because it is condemned by God. The first horn of the dilemma entails that objective morality is possible without God. The second horn entails that objective morality is impossible with theism. In his debate with Flew, Craig made no attempt to address this dilemma and I am not aware that he has done so in his written work, either. Moreover, the attempt by some theists to avoid the dilemma by basing morality on the necessary attributes of God's character rather than directly on his commands is futile: appealing to God's character only postpones the problem since the dilemma can be reformulated in terms of His character.[7]

According to Craig in the question and answer session of the debate, the objective wrongness is known via intuition or via God's command as revealed in the Bible. But intuition is a weak reed on which to base objective morality since intuitions differ and there is no way of reconciling the conflicts. Biblical revelation also has its problems. Craig must assume that God condemns rape and that His condemnation can be supported from reading the Bible. In addition, does he assume that God condemns rape on the same grounds on which it is condemned in contemporary society? The biblical position is complicated and does not always support the common view that rape is wrong because it harms the victim. To be sure, one can find rape condemned in the Bible but one can also find passages in which God seems to be tacitly approving of rape, as well as passages in which rape is condemned but without regard for the victim's welfare.[8]

First of all, in some passages God seems tacitly to sanction rape. In the Old Testament Moses encourages his men to use captured virgins for their own sexual pleasure – that is, to rape them. After urging his men to kill the male captives and also the female captives who are not virgins, he says: 'But all the young girls who have not known man by lying with him, keep alive for yourselves.'[9] God then explicitly rewards Moses by urging him to distribute the spoils. He does not rebuke Moses or his men.[10]

Second, when rape is condemned in the Old Testament the woman's rights and her psychological welfare are ignored. For example:

> If a man meets a virgin who is not betrothed, and seizes her and lies with her, and they are found, then the man who lay with her shall give fifty shekels of silver to the father, and she shall be his wife because he had violated her, and he may not put her away all of his days.[11]

Here the victim of rape is treated as the property of the father. Since the rapist has despoiled the father's property he must pay a bridal fee. The women apparently has no say in the matter and is forced to marry the person who raped her. Notice also that if they are not discovered, no negative judgement is forthcoming. The implicit message seems to be that if a man rapes an unbetrothed virgin, he should be sure not to get caught.

In the case of the rape of a betrothed virgin in a city, the Bible says that both the rapist and the victim should be stoned to death: the rapist because he violated his neighbour's wife and the victim because she did not cry for help.[12] Again the assumption is that the rapist despoiled the property of another man. The welfare of the victim does not seem to matter. Moreover, it is assumed that a rape victim could, in all cases, cry for help and that, if she did, she would be heard and rescued. Both these dubious assumptions are insensitive to the contextual aspects of rape.

On the other hand, according to the Bible, the situation is completely different if the rape occurs in 'open country'. Here the rapist should be killed, not the victim. The reason given is that if a woman cried for help in open country, she would not be heard. Consequently, she could not be blamed for allowing the rape to occur. No mention is made about the psychological harm to the victim. No condemnation is made of a rapist in open country, let alone in a city, who does not get caught.

The only place I know in the Bible where any sensitivity is shown to the victim of rape is in the story of David's son Amnon who rapes his half-sister Tamar and then rejects her. This story describes Tamar's immediate grief in some detail and her brother, Absalom, revenges her rape by killing Amnon. As Gerald Larue has described it: 'The death of Amnon put the Israelite justice in balance, so to speak, but the pain experienced by the woman was not considered worthy of further record.'[13]

In short, Craig would be hard-pressed to justify his judgement that rape is always considered wrong – let alone on the grounds morally sensitive people think it is – by relying on biblical revelation.

The Immediate Experience of God

The fifth and final reason Craig gives for believing in God is the immediate experience of God. This reason plays a small role in the debate, as it should. By

Craig's own admission, such appeal is not based on argument. However, since a debate by definition is based on argument, one is hard-pressed to understand why this appeal is made at all.

In response to Craig's appeal to the immediate experience of God, Flew correctly pointed out that having such experience does not mean that the experience is veridical. Craig's answer to this was that, in the absence of good arguments for atheism, he is justified in taking his experience as veridical. Although Flew does not respond to this point, it would have been easy enough for him to have done so. Flew might have said that one of the primary problems in Craig's appealing to his own religious experience is that religious believers in non-Christian traditions have different religious experiences – ones that often conflict with the religious experiences of Christians. It is obvious that conflicting religious experiences cannot all be veridical. Yet Craig gives no reason whatsoever to suppose that Christian religious experience is veridical and that other religious experiences are not. Furthermore, religious experiences do not seem to differ in their epistemic status from experiences of ghosts, fairies and little green aliens. Why should we suppose that Craig's experience of God is veridical and that Betty Hill's experience of being kidnapped by aliens is not?

Another aspect of Craig's appeal to religious experience is explicit in his written work, although only hinted at in the debate. In his written work Craig had argued that everyone has an experience of the Christian God although many people reject it. Consequently, no one has an excuse for not believing in Christianity even if they are presented with unsound arguments for God's existence. Since belief is a sufficient and necessary for salvation, damnation is based on the perversity of human beings in rejecting the experience of God.[14] In the debate, this point was muted and changed slightly. There Craig said that, for those who listen, God becomes an immediate reality in their lives. The clear implication was that someone who does not experience God has not listened and her non-belief is her fault. Here Craig seems to assume that anyone who sincerely tries *could* have such a direct experience of God.

Implicit in Craig's words there lurks the following argument:

1 If God exists, then if non-believer X sincerely tries to experience God, non-believer X experiences God.
2 Non-believer X did not experience God.
3 God exists.
4 Non-believer X did not sincerely try to experience God.

However, what reason do we have to suppose that premise 1 is true? There is no *a priori* reason to suppose that God would reveal himself to everyone who tried to experience him; moreover, religious believers often refer to the hidden and mysterious nature of God. However, let us suppose that premise 1 is true. What reason do we have to suppose that premise 3 is true? Since Craig's appeal to religious experience cannot provide such a reason, the burden falls on Craig's other arguments.

Moreover, Flew could 'reverse' the above argument and use it against Craig, thus cancelling out the force of the original argument:

1   If God exists, then if non-believer X sincerely tries to experience God, non-believer X experiences God.
2   Non-believer X did not experience God.
3'   Non-believer X sincerely tries to experience God.
4'   God does not exist.

Notice that premises 1 and 2 are the same in both arguments. Of course, Craig would not accept premise 3. But why not? Whether someone's belief is sincere is, in principle, an empirical question and can be evaluated by behavioural and verbal evidence. Surely, there is excellent evidence of this kind that some non-believers have sincerely tried and failed to experience God. In fact, for some non-believers, this failure is one of their reasons for their non-belief. Indeed, evidence for premise 3' is much more reliable and widely accepted than evidence for premise 3. There are literally thousands of non-believers who appear to have sincerely tried to have a religious experience but have failed. To reject this evidence one would have to suppose the most outlandish hypothesis: that all these people are lying or self-deluded.

In short, Craig's appeal to his religious experience fails to come to terms with the main objection of this appeal – conflicting non-Christian religious experiences. His argument from sincerity assumes dubious premises and is capable of easy reversal.

Conclusion

The upshot of my analysis is that, whatever the respective rhetorical powers of Craig and Flew may be, with regard to the three arguments under review Flew had by far the strongest philosophical position in the debate. With a little elaboration Flew's arguments against Craig's first reason – the origin of the universe argument – completely refute Craig's position. Flew's brief comments on Craig's third reason from objective values go part of the way to showing Craig's error. More could easily have been said, however. Once said, the problems of theological ethics become manifest. Craig's final reason – an appeal to his religious experience – was correctly, if briefly, countered by Flew. Craig's reply to this counter can easily be answered and an argument implicit in it not only can be refuted but can also be reversed and used against Craig.

Notes

1   In other words, it appears that Flew decided to defend negative atheism – the view that there are no good reasons for believing in God's existence – and not positive atheism – the view that there are reasons to disbelieve in God. For this distinction see Michael Martin, *Atheism: A Philosophical Justification* (Philadelphia, PA: Temple University Press, 1990).
2   Quentin Smith, 'Why Steven Hawking's Cosmology Precludes a Creator', *Philo*, 1 (1998), pp. 75–94.

3 See p. 20.
4 See p. 22.
5 Richard Swinburne, *The Coherence of Theism* (Oxford: Oxford University Press, 1977), p. 204.
6 See, for example, Roderick Firth, 'Ethical Absolutism and the Ideal Observer', in Wilfrid Sellars and John Hospers (eds), *Readings in Ethical Theory*, 2nd edn (Englewood Cliffs, NJ: Prentice-Hall, Inc., 1970), Richard Boyd, 'How To Be a Moral Realist', and Peter Railton, 'Moral Realism', in S. Darwall, A. Gibbard and P. Railton (eds), *Moral Discourse and Practice* (Oxford: Oxford University Press, 1997), David O. Brink, *Moral Realism and The Foundations of Ethics* (Cambridge: Cambridge University Press, 1989), pp. 37–39, 197–203.
7 See Michael Martin, 'Atheism, Christian Theism, and Rape,' 23 July 1997, available on the Internet at: http://www.infidels.org/library/modern/michael_martin/rape.html.
8 I am indebted in what follows to Gerald Larue, *Sex and the Bible* (Buffalo, NY: Prometheus Books, 1983). ch, 16.
9 Numbers 31:18.
10 Numbers 31:25–27.
11 Deuteronomy 22:28–29.
12 Deuteronomy 22:23–25.
13 Larue, *Sex and the Bible* p. 104.
14 See Michael Martin, 'Craig's Holy Spirit Epistemology', 15 April 1998, available on the Internet at: http://www.infidels.org/library/modern/michael_martin/holy_spirit.html.

Chapter 7

Theism, Atheism and Cosmology

Keith Yandell

Preface

Five arguments for God's existence figure in William Craig's contribution to his debate with Antony Flew. His premises are:

1 The physical universe had a beginning.
2 The appearance of life and consciousness in the world was incredibly unlikely.
3 There is a genuine distinction between right and wrong.
4 The traditions of the empty tomb of Jesus and of his post-resurrection appearances are reliable, and the origin of the Church requires explanation.
5 There are theistic religious experiences.

From these premises, Craig infers that it is more reasonable than not to believe that God exists. At one point or another, Flew has something to say about why he does not find any of the inferences compelling.

Experience of God and Resurrection-Relevant Traditions

Concerning two of these arguments I shall have almost nothing to say here. The appeal to at-least-apparent experiences of God as evidence that God exists is important in itself but receives very little careful attention in the debate. There isn't enough discussion to merit much comment. Craig, in effect, suggests that if it seems to him that he experiences God, then this is some evidence that he does. Flew, in effect, distinguishes between having an experience whose content represents God and having an experience of God. Each point is relevant by way of being the barest beginning of a discussion of the issues, which are not pursued further. Central to the dispute is whether apparent experiences of God are subject–consciousness–object in structure, independent of whether they actually are experiences of God. The alternative is that, if they are not experiences of God, they should be thought of as merely subject-content in structure, analogous to feeling pain. As I've said what I have to say concerning religious experience as evidence for God's existence in *The Epistemology of Religious Experience*,[1] I'll not pursue the matter here.

The discussion of the empty tomb and post-resurrection appearances, and the matter of explaining the origin of the Church, is brief. The data is sufficiently complex and the relevant considerations are sufficiently numerous as to require far more attention than the debate gives to them or than I can give here. The importance of oral (and possibly written) sources in 'filling in' the 30 years to which Flew refers between the death of Jesus and the relevant New Testament passages, and the reliable role of memory in largely oral societies, is not mentioned. The appeal to agreement among New Testament scholars without discussion of its depth and basis remains unhelpful.

Morality and Design

Concerning two of the other arguments, I will be brief. Craig and Flew agree that there is a genuine distinction between right and wrong. This entails, for example, that there are true propositions of the sort (I) *It is morally wrong to torture people for pleasure* and (II) *It is morally obligatory to respect persons who have not so acted as to forfeit their desert of respect* which cannot be properly analysed as merely expressing people's individual or collective feelings or preferences. They would be true even if no one believed them or if everyone believed their contradictories. My problem with Craig's inference to the existence of God is this. If propositions of the sort represented by (I) and (II) are true – as I grant that they are – then they are necessarily true. There are no possible conditions under which torture for pleasure is right, and no possible conditions under which it is not right to respect a person who has not so acted as to forfeit desert of respect. If (I) and (II) are true at all, then they are, as they say, true in all possible worlds. But while one can explain why one should think that a proposition is necessarily true, there is no such thing as explaining that a necessary truth is true rather than false. Its being false is not a possibility, and hence not a possibility that an explanation could be required to rule out. Hence no reference to God's existence or God's will is required in order to explain the truth of a proposition such as (I) or (II). If one thinks that God has logically necessary existence, one can hold that the content of true moral propositions provides part of the content of God's thoughts – thoughts that it is logically impossible that God lack. But there is nothing in Craig's argument to support the claim that God has logically necessary existence and it is nothing like obvious that a theist should accept that view.[2]

The argument based on the extremely high improbability of life or consciousness arising in a world whose initial conditions are as current physics suggests is complex and interesting. I admit to being suspicious about the relevant probability calculations. Granted, they are not so-called *a priori* probabilities – alleged probabilities of logically contingent propositions, given tautological evidence only. I see no reason to believe in any such thing. Rather, they are probabilities concerning the arising of conditions reasonably believed to be required in order for life and consciousness to arise, given specific initial conditions and specific laws. Before I would be willing to accept the sort of argument from low probabilities that Craig offers, I'd want some good reason to think that the same range of data could not, from a defensible perspective, be as reasonably seen quite differently, and (perhaps due to limits of time) this issue is not investigated.

Peter Van Inwagen recently argued, against the cosmological argument, that there is just one possible universe in which there is nothing that exists logically contingently and many universes in which there is something or other that exists logically contingently.[3] Hence the probability that there exists something that exists logically contingently is overwhelmingly high and the answer to the question *Why is there something rather than nothing?* is something like *It is incredibly probable that there should be something*. A different, and I'd have thought more proper, way of considering the relevant probabilities is this. One logical possibility is that there exists something that exists logically contingently; express this by *E*. Another logical possibility is that there does not exist something that exists logically contingently; express this by *not-E*. If one is to assign a probability to each of these logical possibilities (it isn't clear that one either must or should) then one should assign each the same probability, namely .5. There are of course many sorts of things the existence of which will make *E* true, but suppose, for simplicity, that there are just three – the existence of frogs, logs or bogs. Let these be represented, respectively, by *EF*, *EL*, and *EB*. Then *EF*, *EL*, and *EB* should each be assigned one-third of .5. In fact, of course, the probability of any particular proposition being true whose truth will entail *E*'s truth will be very low – provided that the whole enterprise of such probability assignments is sensible in the first place. One result is that the cosmological argument escapes Van Inwagen's objection.

Whatever the justice of this critique of Van Inwagen's suggestion, it illustrates the idea of a *probability-shifting consideration*. How the probabilities lie, and what can be concluded from them, can be significantly affected in a given case by whether or not there are probability-shifting considerations relative to that case. If some have claimed that the chances of life and consciousness arising in a universe with the initial conditions and laws we have reason to think present in our universe are incredibly low, others have claimed that this is not so. The idea of 'multiple universes' (presumably not to be so understood as to be an oxymoron) is central to one such attempt. A careful consideration of whether there is a plausible probability-shifting consideration relative to the likelihood of life and consciousness arising in our world is a necessary condition of reasonably accepting the force of Craig's appeal to probability considerations. The debate, understandably, did not provide this consideration.[4]

What remains is the argument that receives the fullest attention in the debate – namely, Craig's claim that the physical universe has a beginning and, if so, then it has a cause.

Craig's Version of the Cosmological Argument

On what I take to be an eminently defensible view, there are two sorts of things. There are things that exist whose non-existence is logically impossible. Such items provide the truth-conditions of logically necessary truths. They are not things that might not have been. Let us call these *necessary beings*. There are also things whose non-existence is not logically impossible. They do exist, but they might not have existed. Let us call these *non-necessary beings*.

One cannot explain the existence of necessary beings. To explain the existence of something is to explain the fact that, among two alternatives – its existing and its not existing – it is the alternative of its existing that obtains. Regarding necessary beings, there is no alternative of their not existing that might have obtained.

At least two questions arise as to there being things that might never have been. One concerns the explanation of their existing rather than their not existing, since their not existing was a possible alternative. The other concerns why they are ordered in the way in which they are. Craig deals with both sorts of consideration.

There will be non-necessary beings only if there is some sort of stuff or other that does exist but might not have.[5] Insofar as this stuff is physical, the task of saying what sort of stuff it is typically falls under one or another physical science. For simplicity, without prejudice to biology and biochemistry and the like, let us suppose that physics is the fundamental science in terms of telling us what sort of physical stuff exists.

Physics tells us, Craig contends, that the sort of physical stuff that exists has existed only for a limited period of time. In particular, he notes, Big Bang physics tells us that it has existed for a time extended backwards an impressive, but finite, distance. This, he adds, is one source of the claim that physical stuff has existed only for a finite past time. Another source is reflection on the notion of infinity. There cannot be, he assures us, anything that is actually infinite, and so there cannot have been an infinite amount of past time in which physical stuff existed.

Physics, then, and reflection on the notion of infinity combine to tell us that physical stuff has existed only for a finite past time. But then, Craig reasons, there was a time at which physical stuff came to exist, not having existed before that time. If we appeal to the Big Bang, at least as Craig seems to understand it, time and physical stuff began together.

Since Craig also holds that God is temporal and that human persons can exist independent of their bodies, not to mention the possibility of unembodied angels who are in time, it seems possible on his overall conception that time pre-existed physical stuff. This raises a question concerning how much support his overall view receives from physical cosmology. He does not view time as simply a fourth dimension in which physical stuff exists. Strictly, his argument is that what we can call 'physical time' – time conceived as a fourth dimension, or the like – began when the physical universe took something like its present shape (when the laws that hold now began to hold). Without his claim that there cannot be an actually infinite past, he could hold that time had no beginning but physical stuff began some 15 billion years or so ago. Even with no infinite past, it is possible that time began before matter did.

Craig assumes without argument that the beginning of the universe and the beginning of time coincide, although his overall argument does not strictly require that claim. Perhaps the existence of physical stuff and there being such a thing as time co-occurred, but perhaps not. Either way, Craig claims, given Big Bang theory, there was some time T at which physical stuff first existed, and T was some finite backwards temporal distance from the present.

The coming into existence of physical stuff, Craig continues, is the coming to be of some non-necessary being. Such beginnings are possibly explicable and so have an explanation. Explanations of such things are not as plentiful as blackberries. They seem to be limited to one explanation – namely, the activity of a non-physical being with sufficient power to make it the case that there comes to be physical stuff. The alleged alternative explanations that the coming-to-be of physical stuff was by chance or that it simply popped into existence are not explanations, but denials that there is any explanation of there coming to be physical stuff. So one either embraces theism or one admits to holding that the coming-to-be of physical stuff has no explanation. The latter position, Craig concludes, is less reasonable than the former and hence, relative at least to the coming-to-be of physical stuff, theism is more reasonable than atheism or agnosticism. This gives us, I take it, a fair statement of the general structure and content of Craig's cosmological argument for theism insofar as it rests on Big Bang considerations and reflections concerning what can be explained and what requires explanation.

There is also the claim that there cannot be an actual infinite, and hence past time is not infinite. But, Craig reasons, if God or the physical universe were everlasting, then past time would be everlasting, and what is everlasting is infinite. Hence neither can be everlasting. So the physical universe had a beginning. A physical universe cannot just causelessly come to be. Its existence is explicable and so has an explanation, and creation by a God whose own existence in principle cannot be explained provides that explanation.

What should be said about this overall argument? There is the appeal to Big Bang physics and the appeal to reflections concerning infinity. Both, as we shall see, face some severe problems.

Flew in Response to Craig's Cosmological Argument

Flew does not propose to prove that God does not exist. He endeavours only to show that nothing Craig says shows that God does exist. He begins by expressing what might be called a scientistic agnosticism, although the scientism and the agnosticism pull in different directions. The agnosticism claims that while we can know things that occur 'within' the physical universe, we cannot know anything about the universe as a whole. The idea seems to be that an *event* smaller than universal in scale can come within our ken, as can a *thing* smaller than the universe itself. But such events as *there coming to be physical stuff*, or such a (pseudo?) thing as *the physical universe*, cannot be objects of knowledge. The scientism insists that what can be known regarding the physical universe is known through science alone.

Flew's explicit claims are that:

(a) No one knows, or can know, where (if anywhere) the physical universe came from.
(b) All explanations end in brute facts.
(c) It is possible that the physical universe just 'popped into existence'.
(d) Where physics stops, there all knowledge of the physical universe stops.

No argument is presented for any of (a)–(d). Let's consider them in turn. Claim (a) expresses Flew's agnosticism, with which he both begins and ends his contribution to the debate. It denies, for example, that one can have better reason than not to believe in an intelligent cause of either the existence or the order of physical stuff. That is, of course, a matter central to the debate and asserting (a) defines Flew's position without doing anything to establish that position.

Claim (b), relative to the issues at hand, says that whenever one explains the existence of one sort of thing, one does so by reference to another sort of thing, and both sorts of thing must be things that might never have existed and whose existence is possibly explicable. It reflects Flew's agreement with a dictum of David Hume to the effect that whatever we can conceive the existence of, we can conceive the non-existence of, with the added claim that whatever we can conceive the non-existence of we can conceive of as being caused to exist.[6] These ideas are the background for the claim that one never reaches anything whose existence is in principle inexplicable, so there is no inherent stopping point for explaining the existence of anything. Thus stopping with the existence of physical stuff is perfectly reasonable, particularly if that is where physics stops.

Claim (b) is a metaphysical claim, not an epistemological claim. It is a claim about what there is, not a claim about what we happen to know. Flew claims to know that there are only non-necessary beings, and that among these none is such that its existence is logically impossible to explain. Thus there can be no abstract objects, and no God such that, if God exists, it is logically impossible that God be caused to exist or depend for existence on anything. Claim (b) is not to be confused with the banal claim that when we run out of information, we stop explaining. Claim (b) is, of course, highly controversial, but no argument on its behalf is provided.

Claim (c) says that it is logically possible that there was a time T at which physical stuff came to exist, that there was no physical stuff prior to T, and that at T nothing caused there to come to be physical stuff. That this sort of thing never seems to happen 'within' the universe is said to be no reason that it could not, so to speak, happen to the universe itself.

Claim (c) is false if some relevant version of the principle of sufficient reason is true. Suppose, for example, it is true that:

(P) *If there are non-necessary things whose existence it is possible to explain, then the explanation of this fact is that they are caused to exist by something whose existence it is not possible to explain, which has the powers necessary to produce them.*

Let us say that *something whose existence it is not possible to explain, which has the powers necessary to produce non-necessary things whose existence it is possible to explain* is a *necessarily independent cause*. The existence of a necessarily independent cause is not, in Flew's sense, a brute fact. A brute fact, in Flew's sense, is something that exists, whose existence is in principle explicable, but such that either we don't know its explanation or such that its existence happens to have no explanation. A necessarily independent cause would be something that exists, whose existence it is logically impossible to explain. Flew assumes, without argument, that nothing along the lines of (P) is true.

Claim (d) says that, whatever we come to know regarding the explanation of there being a physical universe, we will learn from physics. This itself, of course, isn't something we could learn from physics. Physics doesn't include any claim to the effect that we can only learn from physics the explanation of there being physical stuff. Any explanation in physics – at least if 'physics' is strictly construed – will take the existence of some sort of physical stuff as given. But, in order to derive claim (d) from this, one needs a further claim to the effect that all it is logically possible to discover relative to the explanation of there being physical stuff must come only by reference to physics. Then it follows, of course, that there isn't going to be any explanation of the fact that there is physical stuff. But claims of the form *It is logically possible to discover the explanation of there being physical stuff only by X* are philosophical claims. Claim (d) is simply part of Flew's own philosophical perspective, itself in need of argument. The actual content of physics *per se* is inherently neutral to whether or not it is true. The reference to physics, strictly construed or *per se*, is required because contemporary physical cosmology appears to include ineluctably philosophical claims and disputes – claims and disputes that happen to violate Flew's own epistemological strictures. We return to this topic shortly.

What claims (a)–(d) do, then, is define a partial theory of knowledge relevant to claims about the coming-to-be of physical stuff. This theory is competitive to Craig's perspective. Whether it is rationally preferable to Craig's perspective, or at least as reasonable to accept as Craig's perspective, is not something that Flew addresses. Flew's own perspective, as we shall see, faces severe problems of its own.

Craig's Use of Big Bang Physics

One issue concerns Craig's use of physics – in particular, the Big Bang theory. I waive the question as to whether the theory itself is correct; we will suppose that it is. One problem that arises concerns the nature of physics itself. One conception of physics goes as follows. Any physical theory has a certain structure. It takes certain things as given and, given them, explains other things. Among the things it takes for granted is the existence of some sort of physical stuff. So no physical theory can explain the fact that there exists non-necessarily existing physical stuff;[7] that is something that must be taken for granted in all our reasoning in physics. A physical theory can tell us that the sort of physical stuff that now exists has only been around for a limited amount of time. It can tell us that the sort of physical stuff that preceded the sort of physical stuff now available was very different from current physical stuff. It can tell us that we don't know what sort of physical stuff preceded the current brand and even add that we, for certain reasons, are not going to be able find out what sort of physical stuff it was. But, simply as physical theory, it cannot explain there coming to be any physical stuff at all. That there is some such stuff must, as we've said, be taken for granted in all our reasoning in physics.[8]

One thing that follows from this conception of physics is that to seek in physics for an account of creation – of there coming to be physical stuff that is not made out of previous physical stuff – is a hopeless enterprise. This is so, even though science writers love to talk about physics as a source of information about creation.[9] A Big Bang theory can tell us something of 'the beginning of the universe' if we mean by that something along the lines of (a) 'how there came to be the sort of physical stuff there is now, given a prior different sort of physical stuff', but not if we mean (b) 'how there came to be any physical stuff at all, or any stuff at all from which what we call physical stuff came.' (It would, of course, be cheating simply to define 'physical stuff' as 'physical stuff of the sort there is now'.) Only because 'the beginning of the universe' can be seen as ambiguous between (a) and (b) can one claim to have found evidence in Big Bang physics for 'the beginning of the universe'. If the difference between prior physical stuff (or stuff of some sort) and current physical stuff is great, as Big Bang theory says it is, the conflation of (a) to (b) is facilitated. It is (b) that would be, strictly, a beginning of the universe. The idea that physics tells us about the finitely temporal past beginning of the universe is simply a mistake. It is necessarily silent about (b). Thus Craig's apparently cosmological argument is, on this view, really another version of a design argument.

One can put the point differently. Suppose one insists that the Big Bang theory be read as telling us how there came to be anything at all, or at least as explaining the process by which, so to speak, things went from there not being anything physical to there being something physical. That this is the right way to read the Big Bang theory, as opposed to reading it as telling us how there came to be the sort of physical stuff there now is – as explaining the process by which things went from there being something we aren't at all clear about to there being the sort of stuff contemporary cosmology talks about – is at least as much a metaphysical claim as it is a claim in physical cosmology. It is the sort of claim regarding which the question 'Is the matter on which it takes sides one of physical cosmology or metaphysics?' is properly answered 'Yes' – the matter in question lives in a conceptual neighbourhood common to physical cosmology and philosophy.[10]

What Craig says about physical theory illustrates both of the readings of Big Bang theory just mentioned. Cosmologists, as Craig notes, talk about the universe (physical stuff being organized as we know it) coming from a 'singularity' which is described in terms of a condition in which there aren't any causal laws, of being an 'edge' of the space–time universe, as being without space or time, and as being an incredibly dense point from which all matter exploded.[11] The Big Bang is described as an event (or whatever) that created space, time, and matter.[12]

Whether all of this actually requires a revision of the notion that physics explains there being physical stuff by reference to there being earlier physical (or whatever) stuff is not clear. It is clear that *if* no revision is required, then physics will have to take some physical (or whatever) stuff for granted, and hence as unexplained. It is clear that *if* revision is required, physics is assuming something in the neighbourhood of creation *ex nihilo* minus a Creator, and the views that live in this neighbourhood, whether plausible or not, are metaphysical views.

Craig's argument reads the Big Bang theory as entailing that time has a beginning, and proceeds on the assumption that the existence of time rides piggyback on the beginning of physical stuff. This fits ill with the view that God's thoughts and human souls are also in time, although neither divine thoughts nor human souls are physical. One could hold that time *as it relates to physics* begins with the Big Bang but that time itself exists independent of matter. Craig's view about God's thoughts and human souls, we have noted, comports with that account. But his view that were God everlasting then past time would be infinite, whereas past time cannot be infinite, leads him to claim that time must have a beginning. Perhaps it is only for convenience of argument that he takes the Big Bang to define that beginning; if an actual infinite is impossible but entailed by past time being everlasting, then time must have begun sometime.

Suppose that we follow Craig in taking the Big Bang as concerned with the coming to be of anything at all, God excepted. Craig's proposal is that the creation must be done by an eternal being. The idea is that an eternal being creates a universe that is not eternal; God has the idea of a non-eternal universe and makes it the case that reality corresponds to idea. The divine idea, and the divine intention to create, are eternal. How do we get to the non-eternal universe? Creation includes creation of time, and the idea of a non-eternal universe, in Craig's view, includes the idea of a beginning of time. How are we to understand that temporal reference? Further, Craig believes that there are immaterial minds. These are not in space-time but they are in time. So can the creation of the universe be the creation of space-time, but not the creation of the time in which immaterial minds are located? How is this latter time to be understood? Or is there one time which is both the time of space-time and the time in which minds and even God, post-creation, exists? How does that work?

There are, then, some highly complex issues related to Craig's cosmological argument (if it is, strictly speaking, cosmological rather than teleological). Central among them is whether a physical cosmology that tell us about a beginning of space, time and matter that is preceded by no stuff at all really is what we have in contemporary physical cosmology. Other issues have to do with how Craig construes time (in the sense of 'time' in which it applies to God and human minds or souls) and space-time. The argument's overall success depends on how these issues turn out.

Craig on Infinity

The other consideration to which Craig appeals concerns a reason to suppose that the physical universe has a beginning. His claim is that it is logically impossible that there be an actual infinite. The relevant issues are complex and, of course, debate concerning them has a long history. I will try here to be fair and brief without entering unduly into a discussion of that history. Craig's conclusion is that due to the nature of infinity, *if there is a physical universe then it has a beginning* is a *necessary* truth; the claim is that it is logically impossible that there be a *beginningless* physical universe. His argument goes like this:

1   There is a physical universe.
2   If there is a physical universe, then either it has a beginning or not.
3   If the physical universe does not have a beginning, then it exists infinitely into the past.
4   It is logically impossible that anything exists infinitely into the past.
5   The physical universe has a beginning (*from 3,4*).
6   Whatever has a beginning has a cause.
7   The universe has a cause (*from 5,6*).

The key idea in this argument lies behind the claim (4) that it is logically impossible that anything exists infinitely into the past. The idea is that there cannot be an actual infinite.

There can be a potentially infinite series, but not an actually infinite series. This raises the obvious question: why not? Craig's argument here is puzzling. An *actually infinite series* is contrasted to a *potentially infinite series*; but (one would think) if there cannot be an X, there can't be anything that is potentially an X. As it turns out, the notion of a potentially infinite series is the idea of a series to which one more can always be added, and this, strictly speaking, is not the idea of a potentially infinite series at all. It is just the closest thing there could be to an infinite series that those who suppose an (actual) infinite series to be logically impossible are willing to countenance. Talk of a potentially infinite series is a red herring.

Why, then, can't there be an actually infinite series? One would have thought that there actually are an infinite number of necessary truths about, say, the whole positive integers. If one supposes that there are such truths, and the states of affairs that correspond to them, one thinks that there are numbers, or sets, or Forms, or ideas in the mind of God, or whatever exists, to ground these truths. (Conventionalist accounts of mathematical truths leave their necessity unaccounted for.) There is no good reason to think that this sort of view is logically inconsistent, and it entails that there is an actually infinite series. If, then, Craig's alleged inconsistency is supposed to arise between *being actual* and *being infinite*, it doesn't arise at all.

Let's put the point another way. Consider the plainly true claim:

(I3)   The series of whole positive integers is infinitely long.

Consider also two readings of (I3):

(I3a)   The series of whole positive integers is such that for any integer N there an integer one higher than N.
(I3b)   The series of whole positive integers is such that it is a completed series of actual members and there are an infinity of such members.

For historical reasons, the (I3a) reading is often said to express the notion of a 'potentially infinite' series – a singularly unfortunate locution that expresses the rough idea that, no matter how far you have gone in counting by use of integers, you can go further. One who accepts the truth of (I3b), and holds that numbers themselves are the truth-makers for it, is a realist about numbers; she thinks that what makes (I3) true is the existence of the things that (I3) is true of – the number one, the number two and so on.[13] She construes these items as abstract objects, existing human-mind-independently and non-spatially. Her position is perfectly consistent.

Craig can retreat to the view that a temporal series, or at least a series of physical items, cannot be infinite. Aquinas thought that, so far as philosophical reflection goes, the physical universe might have had a beginning and it might not have had a beginning – philosophical reflection does not tell us which.[14] Such Hindu monotheists as Ramanuja and Madhva held that the physical universe has always existed, enjoying the sort of beginningless existence that Craig believes to be logically impossible. Craig can simply hold that, whatever is the case regarding (say) an actually infinite series of abstracta, there cannot be an actually infinite series of things that are not abstracta. The suggestion that, although while the idea of an infinite series involves no contradiction, there being such a series is logically impossible, is itself logically inconsistent. If the idea of an X is not inconsistent, then there being an X cannot be logically impossible.[15] Thus, if an actually infinite series of abstracta is a logical possibility, then the notion of an actually infinite series is not a contradiction, and the inconsistency needed by Craig must arise between *being temporal* and *being infinite* or between *being physical* and *being infinite,* or the like. Aquinas, Ramanuja and Madhva must therefore all be wrong in supposing that God could beginninglessly create a physical world. Why?

Here is one answer. Suppose that the physical universe is beginningless. In this case, it has existed for an infinite amount of time. There is now a physical universe, and nothing can traverse an infinite amount of time. But in order for there now to be a physical universe that is beginningless, it would have to have traversed an infinite amount of time. So the physical universe cannot be beginningless.

The argument appeals to at least two ideas. One is that if you start out with a finite series, you cannot build it up into an infinite one by constantly adding to it. This isn't relevant to the idea of a beginningless universe – that idea does not entail a universe in the process of gaining infinity as it chugs along through time. The other idea is that, if it were beginningless, it would never have reached now. But why think that?

Suppose one argues as follows: to say that the universe is beginningless is to say that, for any past time T, the universe existed at T, and at T-1 as well. For any such time T you mention, there is a finite distance between T and now. So the universe could have chugged along from T until now. There is hence no past time such that it is impossible for the universe to chug along from that time until now. What the idea of the universe being beginningless entails is that, for any past time T, the universe actually has chugged along from it until now. Since that is not impossible, it is not impossible that the universe is beginningless. What, exactly, in Craig's argument shows that this line of reasoning is inconsistent?

Perhaps one can put the idea like this: the idea that the universe is beginningless, as characterized above, is consistent. Hence it entails no inconsistent ideas. Thus either the universe being beginningless does not entail that its past is infinite or, if it does entail that, then it is not logically impossible that its past is infinite. What, exactly, in Craig's argument shows that his line of reasoning is inconsistent? The sum of the matter is that, so far as I can see, it would be perfectly possible for God to make it beginninglessly the case that there was physical stuff.

God's Existence as not a Brute Fact

Craig takes it as a necessary truth that necessarily, if God exists, then God neither depends for existence on something else nor is God's existence a brute fact. A fact F is brute if and only if it is indeed a fact, it is logically possible that it has an explanation, and it is false that it has an explanation. The idea is that God cannot be dependent and hence cannot be caused. That God cannot be a brute fact is another way of saying what systematic theologians often say by way of ascribing aseity to God.

Parenthetically, it does not follow that there cannot exist anything that exists independent of God, although if God is omnipotent presumably anything that exists and *can* depend on God does depend on God. A minority of theistic thinkers have held that there are abstract objects, that these items exist necessarily and hence depend on nothing else for their existence, and that they are not identical to thoughts in God's mind or otherwise identical to some aspect of the divine nature. Craig himself takes this view to somehow limit God's sovereignty or to be otherwise inappropriate to God's metaphysical status. I confess to not seeing why the idea that something exists that could not depend on anything for existence and so does not depend on God for its existence is somehow theistically problematic. Granted, it goes against what some call the intuitions of some theists. So far as I can see, this simply means that some theists have convictions that they cannot justify by appeal to anything deeper in the structure of their thought such that there being necessarily existing abstract objects that exist independent of God violate these convictions.[16] Certainly abstract objects are not going to get in the way of divine providence. They are not conscious or self-conscious and cannot act.

Returning to the main argument, Craig's line of reasoning also requires that the physical universe is dependent. Atheists typically agree that there are possible worlds in which no physical universe exists – that the physical universe does not possess a logically necessary existence. Craig holds, along with most theists, that the physical world not only does not exist necessarily but that it depends for its existence on God. This dependence, Jewish and Christian and Islamic monotheists add, is not a matter of the physical universe depending for its existence on God at the moment of its coming to be, and then existing on its own. It is a matter of the physical universe depending for its existence on God sustaining it for as long as it does exist. Craig's argument requires, then, that one accept the following claims:

(1)   It is logically possible that the physical universe not to have existed.
(2)   It is possible that its existence be explained and
         Thus
(3)   There is an explanation of its existence.

This is at the core of the disagreement regarding the cosmological argument; the atheist asserts that the physical universe is a brute fact. She insists that, even if claims (1) and (2) are true, claim (3) does not follow.

Craig's argument needs the line of reasoning captured by:

(A) Both (1) and (2) are true, and (3) follows from (1) and (2)
or
(A*) *Necessarily, if it is logically possible that X not exist and logically possible that X's existence be explained, then there actually is an explanation of X's existence, or something in the near conceptual neighbourhood.*

A cosmological argument can be offered that uses only (1), (2) and (A), or (A*). That version, it should be noted, makes none of the controversial claims regarding the possibility of a durational (or any other sort of) infinite series. If it is successful at all, it is successful regarding the existence of the physical universe at each moment, not merely at its first moment or at some past moment. It makes clear what the core difference regarding cosmological issues is between theist and atheist. Further, Craig's version requires that this trimmer cosmological argument be correct in its insistence that what exists and can have an explanation does have one.

The argument also requires that God's existence cannot be a brute fact. This claim can be defended by claiming that

(i)   God exists is a logically necessary truth
or
(ii)   Necessarily, if God exists then God is essentially omnipotent, omniscient and morally perfect and this, plus the claim that God exists, entails that God depends on nothing other than God for God's existence
or

(iii)   Necessarily, if God exists then God is metaphysically perfect and, necessarily, nothing that is metaphysically perfect can depend for its existence on anything else, and these claims, together with the claim that God exists, entail that God depends on nothing else for existence

or

(iv)   Necessarily, if God exists then God is essentially omnipotent and omniscient and necessarily, if God exists and is temporal and is ever morally perfect then God is always morally perfect, plus the claim that God exists and is sometime morally perfect entail that God never depends for existence on anything else. So if God exists, God does not depend on anything else. If God were to be caused to exist, then God would depend for existence on something else. So God is not caused to exist.

The general idea is to offer a conditional proof for the conclusion that, if God exists, then God is not dependent for existence on anything else. The proof assumes that God exists, derives from that assumption and the appropriate set of necessary truths that God is not dependent and so not caused, and ends up with the conditional *If God exists, then God is not caused to exist* – that is, if God exists, that God exists is not caused. There are obviously some complex and interesting issues here, but this is not the place to discuss them. (I note that even if there are things on whose existence God necessarily depends, so long as these are necessarily existing items on which it is not possible that God not depends, this will not ultimately interfere with a successful cosmological argument.)

Flew's Critique of Craig's Cosmological Argument

Flew's agnosticism and his scientism lead him to reject this trimmer version of the cosmological argument that rests on the rejection of brute facts. Interestingly, his agnosticism and his scientism pull in opposite directions. The physical universe is *all the physical stuff there is, considered together*. Things within the physical universe are *some physical stuff, but not all*. Flew's agnosticism says that we can know about things within the physical universe but not about the physical universe as a whole. We can, for example, know that even very big things within the universe come into being only if they have causes, but in principle we cannot know this about the universe itself. His scientism commits him to the view that all we can know, either about *all the physical stuff there is, considered together* or about *some physical stuff, but not all* is what physics tells us, and what it tells us is properly believed. But physics tells us things about *all the physical stuff there is, considered together*, including the claim that it was all produced, in the forms it now takes, in a Big Bang. Flew's agnosticism should prevent him from believing any such thing.

Flew joins Craig in not clearly distinguishing between all the physical stuff there is, considered together coming to be the sort of physical stuff that we now encounter and there coming to be any physical stuff, of whatever sort. Only the latter event being caused is, strictly speaking, creation; the former event would be a matter of physical stuff changing form. Flew's scientism precludes dealing with there coming to be any physical stuff, of whatever sort since, as we have noted, that is (on the narrower understanding of physics described above) not a possible object of physical explanation. But the scientism is simply fiated, not argued for, and irrational to accept on its own terms.

There could be results in physics that raised the question Flew takes to be unanswerable. One could have scientific evidence that there was once a time when no material stuff existed. Suppose we discovered that there are exactly two sorts of fundamental material particle, Azads and Bebubs. Everything physical, except Azads and Bebubs, are made up only of them. Their nature is such that they survive by irreversibly expending unreplenishable energy at a constant rate. Azads, we discover, will expend their energy in 15 billion years; Bebubs do so in 25 billion years. Then, one day, we find that there are no more Azads and infer that the universe is 15 billion years old. There is no trace of the Azads; we have pictures and memories of them but they themselves have simply vanished. We then infer that, in 10 billion years, Bebubs too will vanish and there will be no more physical universe. Given this scenario, we could claim that (a) 15 billion and one years ago, no Azads existed. We could add that (b) 10 billion and one years hence, there will be no material stuff. We might, of course, be wrong. Azads might leave traces that we cannot detect. There might be a series of one Azad/Bebub world after another in everlasting oscillation. But we might be right, and a proper festooning of our scenario could make it plain that, were we to be in that situation, we would be irrational not to accept (a) and (b).

This scenario would raise the question as to what explanation could be given of there being Azads and Bebubs. The question would be perfectly intelligible, and no explanation-in-physics could answer it. Both Flew's agnosticism and his scientism would lead him to suppose it impossible that there be any answer. But if the question is intelligible, one needs at least an argument that no answer can be given.[17] That God created Azads and Bebubs would, of course, explain there being such things, and it is hard to see what else would.

Flew's Compatibilist Assumption

Flew's quotations from Aquinas, Luther and Calvin reflect a compatibilist view of human freedom which Craig rejects. I agree with Flew that if one is a compatibilist, then one is hard-pressed to see why God would not simply determine things so as to rule out wrong choices and their consequences. I also agree with Craig that if one rejects compatibilism and holds that if persons are free in any morally significant sense then libertarianism is true, then one will take Christianity to include the claim that God created libertarianly free persons – moral agents capable of choosing wrongly and determining their own character traits. Flew's argument (more carefully, a more fully articulated successor thereof) is powerful indeed against the claims *Determinism, compatibilism, and theism are all true* and *Compatibilism and theism are true.*

The moral I draw is that, since theism is true, determinism and compatibilism are not true.[18]

Flew and Hell

In something of an aside, Flew claims that Christian monotheism and the doctrine of hell are logically incompatible. His argument makes essential appeal to the claim that no action could be worthy of endless punishment.[19] Craig's reply is that a person who continues forever to reject God's love is properly forever separated from God, and that perhaps irrevocably rejecting divine love would be worthy of endless punishment. One could develop Flew's argument a bit further by contending that a loving God would not create anyone who would be better off not ever having existed and that anyone who was irrevocably in hell would be better off never having existed. This last claim seems to me entirely gratuitous.[20]

The Trimmer Cosmological Argument Again

One can offer a cosmological argument that remains neutral regarding whether the universe has a beginning. In that sense, it is trimmer than Craig's version – it does not require a controversial metaphysical assumption. Further, while for the purposes of debate Craig offered a simple three-step statement of his argument, he too must face the objection that if everything has a cause, God must. Further still, on his view, there is a first time at which God exists, and if *If there is a first time at which X exists, then X begins to exist* is true, then *God begins to exist* is true on his view. This is so even though, on his view, God exists independent of the existence of time. By the time Craig deals with these other issues, each crucial to his argument, we are a long way from the simple three steps of the debate. Thus no apology is made for the fact that the 'trimmer' version of the argument requires a presentation in more than three steps. Both this version and Craig's require that the existence of non-necessary things whose existence is possibly explicable requires explanation, but this version holds that this is so whether there ever first came to be non-necessary things or not. The argument goes as follows.

Definitions

D1   P is a *logically contingent* proposition = neither P nor not-P is self-contradictory; P is a *logically necessary* proposition = not-P is self-contradictory.

D2   P is an existential proposition = P entails a proposition of the form *X exists*.

D3   It is logically possible that P's truth be explained = there is some proposition Q such that *Q's truth explains P's truth* is not self-contradictory.[21]

Note that first, if it is logically possible that the existence of something be explained, then it is logically possible that it *not* exist, and, second, if it is logically possible that the truth of a proposition be explained, it is logically possible that it *not* be true.

Argument

1   If it is logically possible that the truth of a logically contingent existential proposition be explained, then there actually is an explanation of its truth (whether we know what it is or not).

2   *There exist things whose existence it is logically possible to explain* is a true logically contingent existential proposition.

3   There is an explanation of the truth of *There exist things whose existence it is logically possible to explain, (from 1,2)*.

4   The truth of *There exist things whose existence it is logically possible to explain* cannot be explained by there being things whose existence it is logically possible to explain (the existence of *those* things is just what is to be explained).

5   That a logically contingent existence proposition is true can only be explained by some other existential proposition being true.

6   If an existential proposition does not concern something whose existence it is logically possible to explain, it concerns something whose existence is logically impossible to explain.

7   The truth of *There exist things whose existence it is logically possible to explain* can only be explained by a true existential proposition concerning something whose existence it is logically impossible to explain.

8   Some existence proposition concerning something whose existence it is logically impossible to explain, and whose existence can explain the existence of things whose existence it is logically possible to explain, is true.

9   If some existential proposition concerning something whose existence it is logically impossible to explain, and whose existence can explain the existence of things whose existence it is logically possible to explain, is true, then something exists whose existence it is logically impossible to explain and whose existence can explain the existence of things whose existence it is logically possible to explain.

10   Something exists whose existence it is logically impossible to explain and whose existence can explain the existence of things whose existence it is logically possible to explain.

Without detailing the rest of the argument, its gist is that the only sorts of thing whose existence it is logically impossible explain are abstract objects and God, and abstract objects lack causal powers and so are not able to make it the case that there are things that might not have existed.

As noted, this argument is neutral regarding whether or not the physical universe had a beginning in time; it does not matter to it whether the physical world exists beginninglessly or not. There being a cosmological argument for the existence of God does not depend on the physical universe having had a beginning.[22]

Conclusion: A Somewhat Different Strategy

There is a different strategy that is worth mentioning. Whether viewed as a distinction in kind, or as a matter of degree, there is a distinction between theoretical propositions and observational reports. *A Big Bang occurred* illustrates the former class and *The meter reads 6.2* exemplifies the latter. Theoretical propositions are reasonably accepted if they explain things that are hard to explain, are not falsified by counterexample, and do at least as well explanatorily as their competitors. Observational propositions are reasonably accepted if one observes that what they say exists and has particular observable properties actually does exist and has those properties.

Taken in its robust monotheistic sense, *God exists* has this feature: if it is true, its truth explains there being something rather than nothing, there being a world that is accessible to theoretical and practical reason, and there being moral agents. (The list is illustrative, not exhaustive.) It is thus a theoretical claim. (No amount of talk of one not wanting an inferred God or distaste for theory in theology alters what is the case regarding the features that belong necessarily to the proposition *God exists*.)

It is also the case that, cross-culturally and over long periods of time, people have reported experiences which, if veridical, are properly described as experiences of God. These are best thought of not as experiences from whose occurrence one can infer that God exists, but as experiences of God. When one sees a collie or a bus, one's knowledge that there is a collie or a bus is perceptual, not inferential; it is likewise for experiences of God. Thus *God exists* has another feature: it is sometimes an observational report.

A single proposition, then, can play both a theoretical and an observational-report role. If it does, it can be reasonably believed both on the grounds of its explanatory power and on the grounds of its observational evidence. *God exists* plays this sort of dual theoretical–observational role. A full investigation of its grounds will consider both roles.

I suggest that Craig's conclusion is best defended, even within the constraints of a debate, by explicitly considering *God exists* as both theoretical and observational, and by reference to its explanatory power and its observational grounds. As to competing explanations, if one grants that there being physical stuff is explicable and that what is explicable has an explanation, one is forced to acknowledge that there is something whose existence is not possibly explicable with the power to bring it about that there is physical stuff. The existence of abstract objects is not possibly explicable, but such items lack the causal power to produce physical stuff. The notion of a being whose existence is not possibly explicable with the power to make it the case that there is physical stuff is the notion of a being relevantly like God – an argument that there exists such a being is a step towards an overall argument for theism.

Notes

1 Keith Yandell, *The Epistemology of Religious Experience* (Cambridge: Cambridge University Press, 1993).

2 For some reason to think that a Christian ought not to think that God has logically necessary existence, see Keith Yandell, 'Ontological Arguments, Metaphysical Identity, and the Trinity', *Philosophia Christi*, Series 2, 1:1 (1999), pp. 83–101.

3 Peter van Inwagen, 'Why Is there Anything at All?', Proceedings of the Aristotelian Society (1996).

4 See William Lane Craig's website for his discussions of these issues: http://www.leaderu.com/offices/billcraig/index.html.

5 I use 'stuff' here *very* generally. For example, *there being self-conscious agents, there being prime numbers* and *there being roasted peanuts* will involve *there being stuff.*

6 There are obvious problems with these contentions. Given them, for example, no existential statement can be necessarily true. But 'There are more than seven primes' seems both necessary and existential. If it is either a necessary truth that God exists, or a necessary truth that if God exists then God is not dependent on anything else, then an explanation of there being possibly caused things that might not have existed by reference to God's creating them does not end by reference to a brute fact. At least, 'If God exists, then there is nothing on which God depends for existence' seems to be a necessary truth – not by fiat, but by reflection on the properties God necessarily has, if God exists.

7 I take it to be a necessary truth that, for any physical stuff S, it is logically possible that S never have existed. In possible world talk, there are possible worlds in which nothing physical exists.

8 This conception of physics is fairly standard; for exposition and sources, see Scott Sturgeon, 'Physicalism and Overdetermination', *Mind*, 107 (1998), pp. 411–32, and works therein cited. Of course, as Craig would point out, and as we note shortly, cosmology as part of physics may significantly alter the nature of the beast.

9 About, that is, not creation as 'what was created', but as 'the creation of stuff'.

10 The development of cosmology as a part of physics challenges the notion of physics as simply an empirical discipline. Fred Hoyle postulated hydrogen atoms coming into existence without any cause as part of his anti-Big-Bang view (he is said to be responsible for the term 'Big Bang' which he meant as a term of abuse) – a sort of something coming from nothing without the aid of a Creator.

11 See John D. Barrow, *The World Within the World* (Oxford: Clarendon Press, 1988); and William Lane Craig and Quentin Smith, *Theism, Atheism, and Big Bang Cosmology* (Oxford: Clarendon Press, 1993).

12 See Barrow, *The World Within a World*, pp. 226–33; and John Bosleigh, *Stephen Hawking's Universe* (New York: Avon Books, 1989), p. 7. When cosmologists seek to discover what happened before 'a billion trillionth of a second after the Big Bang' when perhaps 'all the forces and laws of nature were unified' do they seek to explain later physical stuff by reference to earlier stuff? Some cosmologists happily speak of 'creation from nothing' and insist that this is an idea inherent in Big Bang cosmology. Perhaps talk of space-time coming into being motivates such talk, although there already being a dense point of matter that explodes does not sound like 'nothing'.

13 Or some other sort of abstract object or divine idea whose existence renders (I3) true.

14 Aquinas also thought that Genesis, properly read, teaches that the physical universe had a beginning.

15   There is the further argument: 'There are abstract objects' is, if true, then necessarily true. So if it is possibly true, it is necessarily true. If the idea of there being abstract objects is logically consistent, then it is possibly true. Hence if it is possible that there are abstract objects, then there are. It is possible that there are abstract objects. So there are. If there are any abstracta, there is an infinity of them. So there is an infinity of them.

16   If I could, I'd restrict the term 'intuition' to things like seeing that 'No proposition of the form P and not-P is true' and recognizing that 'A or B, and not-A; so B' is a valid argument form. This would differ greatly from its current use in which it means something very like 'what seems true to someone although they don't know how to argue for it' and applies to both of two or more views that contradict, or are contrary to, one another.

17   It is no defect in this argument that physics does not actually tell us about Azads and Bebubs. Scientific reflections concerning what would happen under (unactualized) ideal conditions are perfectly legitimate, as are reflections in philosophy about what a philosophical thesis entails about what would be true were something the case that probably is not. Consider, for example, an ethical theory that tells us that, if we have the chance, we should torture to death everyone under 63 years of age. Is it a defence of this theory that we probably won't have the chance?

18   I have argued for these matters in 'God and Other Agents in Indian Philosophy', *Faith and Philosophy* (vol. 16, no. 4, 344–561 (October, 1999)) and 'God, Freedom, and Creation in Cross-cultural Perspective: Augustine, Aquinas, Ramanuja, and Madhva', *Proceedings of the Twentieth World Congress of Philosophy*, vol. 4, 147–68.

19   Craig commendably did not argue here that actually infinite punishment is logically impossible, so the punishment in question could only be potentially infinite.

20   For some relevant reflections, see Keith Yandell, 'The Doctrine of Hell and Moral Philosophy', *Religious Studies*, October 1991, pp. 1–16.

21   Strictly, is not broadly logically necessarily false.

22   This argument, and the line of reasoning noted in the Conclusion, are discussed further in Keith Yandell, *The Philosophy of Religion* (London: Routledge, 1999).

Chapter 8

The Universe is Probable;
The Resurrection is Not

Keith M. Parsons

As my title implies, the purpose of this essay is to criticize two of the arguments presented by William Lane Craig in his debate with Antony Flew: the argument that sees evidence of a divine Designer in the 'fine-tuning' of the fundamental constants of nature and in the historical argument for the Resurrection of Jesus of Nazareth.[1] I chose these because I personally regard them as the two most appealing and plausible of the theistic arguments. Nevertheless, I shall contend that both arguments are complete failures that do not provide any objective evidence for the existence of God or the truth of Christianity.[2] Since space is limited, I turn directly to my critique.

The Fine-tuning Argument

Craig offers this argument in his debate with Flew:

> During the last thirty years scientists have discovered that the existence of intelligent life depends on a delicate and complex balance of initial conditions simply given in the Big Bang itself. We now know that life-*prohibiting* universes are vastly more probable than any life-*permitting* universe like ours. How much more probable? Well, the answer is that the chances that the universe should be life-permitting are so infinitesimal as to be incomprehensible and incalculable. For example, Stephen Hawking has estimated that if the rate of the universe's expansion one second after the Big Bang had been smaller by even one part in a hundred thousand million million, the universe would have recollapsed into a hot fireball .... There are around 50 such quantities and constants present in the Big Bang which must be fine-tuned in this way if the universe is to permit life. And it's not just each quantity which must be finely tuned. Their ratios to one another must also be exquisitely fine-tuned. So improbability is multiplied by improbability by improbability, until our minds are reeling with incomprehensible numbers.[3]

Further, Craig claims that there is no physical reason, no law, which would determine the values of these constants. He summarizes his argument as follows:

1 The fine-tuning of the initial conditions of the universe is due to either law, chance or design.

2   It is not due to either law or chance.
3   Therefore, it is due to design.[4]

Let us call this argument FT1 (fine-tuning 1). It is the second premise of FT1 that I dispute.

The second premise can be expressed as the conjunction of two subpremises:

2a   The fine-tuning of the initial conditions of the universe is not due to law.
2b   The fine-tuning of the initial conditions of the universe is not due to chance.

Let us first consider 2b. In support of 2b Craig argues that it is inconceivable that the fundamental constants could have their values by chance. He argues that life-prohibiting universes are vastly more probable than life-permitting ones. What justifies that claim? First, we need to clarify just what the claim is. Since there is only one actual universe, what it must mean is that of all the *possible* universes, the number that are life-prohibiting *vastly* (say, googolplex to one) outnumber those that are life-permitting. Therefore, the chance that the *actual* one would be life-permitting is infinitesimal.

Immediately we run into a problem. What sense can we make of a claim about the chances of the actualization of *possible* universes? What possible construal can we place on such concepts as 'chance' or 'probability' in such an *outré* context?[5] Further, on any such construal, something has a definite degree of probability only *given* something else. The chance of 'heads' is 50 per cent *given* that we have tossed a fair coin. As is alleged of universes, probabilities do not pop into existence *ex nihilo*. They are meaningful only in the context of background information. For instance, a 50 per cent chance of rain tomorrow is 50 per cent *given* a vast amount of meteorological data and theory.

Therefore, when we ask for the probability that a given constant has a particular value, we are asking for the probability of that value given … what? As Robin Le Poidevin pointedly asks, against what possible background could we judge, say, that it was extremely improbable that the charge on the electron would be 1.602×10^{-19} coulomb?[6] The laws of physics cannot constitute the background since they will either be irrelevant to the charge on the proton or will entail precisely the charge it has. Problems abound when we try to apply probabilistic concepts to the actualization of possible worlds. I summarize these below:[7]

1   In all of our usual assessments of probabilities – from the rolling of dice to the behaviour of quanta – we presuppose some empirical basis for such judgements. However, we necessarily have no experience whatsoever of unactualized universes (as they are not there to be experienced) and hence no grounds for assigning degrees of probability for the actualization of possible universes. In other words, insofar as the fine-tuning argument

prescinds from *every* physical reality, the 'probabilities' it invokes are completely *a priori*.

2   Fine-tuning claims seem to suppose, along with the classical construal of probability, that probability is a matter of the ratio of favourable cases to the total number of *equally possible* cases. This implies that the principle of indifference is applicable to possible universes – that is, that we should assume that each possible universe is equally likely to be actualized. However, the principle of indifference notoriously leads to outright inconsistency.[8] We therefore need an argument justifying the application of the principle of indifference in this context.

3   Ordinarily, as when we are assessing the probability of a certain roll of a dice or the decay of a particular isotope, we assume that the events we are evaluating are well-defined physical processes. The actualization of possible universes is certainly not physical and hardly well-defined. *What* are we judging the probability of here?[9]

Defenders of fine-tuning arguments might dismiss the above objections as quibbles that fail to come to grips with the extreme disproportion of life-permitting to life-prohibiting possible universes. They might dig in their heels and declare that it is just intuitively clear that, given this vast disproportion, the chances of getting a life-permitting universe are infinitesimal.

But is there such a disproportion? If we suppose that the fundamental constants can take *any* rational value within a given range (which the fine-tuners seem to suppose), and if there is *any* variability in the values possible for life-permitting universes, there will be an *infinite* number of life-permitting universes! The reason is simply that between any two rational numbers there exists an infinite number of other rational numbers. Thus, if the charge on the electron in life-permitting universes can vary between, say, $1.6020001 \times 10^{-19}$ coulomb and $1.6020002 \times 10^{-19}$ coulomb, there will be an infinite number of such possible charges since there is an infinite number of rational numbers between 1.6020001 and 1.6020002.

Maybe, though, I have so far misrepresented Craig's argument. Maybe the argument does not turn on deriving a probability for the actualization of possible universes (although I think Craig's wording is often ambiguous on this point). Maybe the argument appeals to *ex hypothesi* random processes – the spontaneous symmetry-breaking processes postulated by the grand unified theories cosmologists currently entertain.[10] Perhaps the physical constants that 'crystallized out' of the primordial symmetry *could* have randomly assumed any of a stupendously large set of equiprobable values, only an infinitesimal subset of which are life-permitting. In this case, fine-tuners argue that, except on the hypothesis of an Intelligence which rigged the cosmic lottery, the chances of getting life-permitting values out of the Big Bang would be effectively nil.

Perhaps then, Craig's fine-tuning argument should be reconstrued. Let us call this argument FT2 (fine-tuning 2):

1' Our most plausible current cosmological theories postulate in the very early universe a process of symmetry-breaking in which the values of the fundamental constants were randomly selected from a vast number of equiprobable possible values.
2' Of these equiprobable possible values, only a very tiny subset permits life.
3' Therefore, unless a divine designer interfered with those primordial processes, the probability of getting life-permitting values was effectively nil.

Therefore, since we have a life-permitting universe, there very probably exists a divine designer.

However, premise 1' may be incorrectly stated. As I understand Alan Guth's explication of the postulated random symmetry-breaking, the possibilities for the values of the fundamental constants are not merely *vast*, but *infinite*.[11] Paul Davies, whom Craig often quotes with approval, recognizes that, if there is an *infinity* of possible values, the odds of getting *any* particular value is the same – that is, zero.[12] Davies admits that this is a *reductio ad absurdum* of the whole fine-tuning argument.[13]

Premise 2' could also be challenged. Physicist Victor Stenger has devised a programme called 'MonkeyGod' that alters the values of four fundamental constants and computes the results for various factors.[14] These are factors, like the binding energy of the hydrogen atom and the lifetime and mass of main-sequence stars, that bear on the possibility that *some* form of life can develop in a universe. Based on these results, he argues that the scientists who originally discussed the 'anthropic coincidences' may have been far too pessimistic in their estimates of the range of constant values that permit life.[15]

The most serious problems with FT2 relate to the divine designer hypothesis mentioned in premise 3'. As Quentin Smith has argued, the fine-tuning argument would confirm the existence of a completely evil Designer just as much as a good one.[16] Just as a good designer would wish to create intelligent life so that there could be moral good, so an evil designer would want moral evil and sentient beings to torment. It also would confirm an indefinitely large number of other possible hypotheses postulating a being (or beings) capable of designing universes – a race of superintelligent aliens inhabiting another universe or dimension, perhaps.

Further, all hypotheses postulating supernatural designers face what Paul Edwards called the '*modus operandi* problem'.[17] Such designer hypotheses give us no clue about how the Designer supposedly operated to achieve the fine-tuning. We have no plausible models for creation *ex nihilo*; acts of creation experienced by humans provide no analogy.[18] Whatever deficiencies current cosmological theories might have in accounting for the constant values, at least those theories are *intelligible* (to Ph.D physicists, anyway). A 'hypothesis' postulating incomprehensible processes effected in an unknowable way by a transcendent designer clearly does not *explain* at all. It is only a marker for our ignorance – a placeholder for an explanation we hope someday to get.

Obviously, if we can find naturalistic hypotheses compatible with known physics that explain the 'specialness' of the constant values in our universe, these should be preferred over designer hypotheses. Two such hypotheses have been proposed:

(A) A number of cosmologists (for example, Martin Rees and Andrei Linde) speculate that our visible universe may be only one among a vast number of sub-universes constituting a mega-universe. Within each sub-universe the values of the constants is determined randomly. However, the number of these sub-universes is so vast that it is a mathematical certainty that some of them will be life-permitting. In short, the appearance of 'fine-tuning' in our sub-universe may be due to the (unsurprising) fact that we could evolve only in one of those sub-universes in which the conditions happened to be right.

(B) Lee Smolin has recently developed a scenario in which the universe reproduces and evolves in a way analogous to biological evolution. In this scenario selection effects operate to produce universes such as ours where life is possible. Though highly speculative, Smolin's scenario is testable and constrained by current scientific theory.[19]

Finally, as the continuing search for a Theory of Everything (TOE) shows, we simply do not know whether the values of the constants are truly fundamental, or whether they might be explicable in terms of deeper law. One of the things that a successful TOE could do is to predict the values of the constants.[20] This means that one claim denied by Craig in his premise 2 – that the constants were determined by law – could well be true.

In the debate with Flew, Craig rejects this last possibility by claiming that the values of the constants were truly *initial* conditions and as such cannot be explained by law.[21] But again, for the atheist, truly *initial* conditions, truly *ultimate* physical facts, will simply be brute facts neither having *nor needing* an explanation. The only way in which Craig could argue this point with the atheist would be to claim that the initial conditions themselves were improbable. However, this would return to the claim, discredited above, that some types of possible universe are more likely to exist than others.

I conclude that Craig has not adequately supported either of the subpremises 2a and 2b of his original argument, FT1. Concerning 2b, the claim that the values of the fundamental constants cannot be due to chance, if this is interpreted as making a claim about the improbability of the actualization of a type of possible universe, no meaning can be given to that claim. Concerning 2a, the claim that the fundamental constants are determined by law, Craig has not shown that a successful TOE cannot achieve this. On the other hand, if the claim is the one in FT2 – that life-permitting constant values are very unlikely to emerge from the random symmetry-breaking postulated in the very early universe – that argument fails too. Mega-universe and selection-effect scenarios incorporate such random processes in a larger scheme that makes life-permitting universes highly probable. Further, divine design is a non-starter as an explanatory hypothesis. Thus, FT1 and FT2 both fail, and Craig has not shown that the universe is 'finely tuned' for life.

The Resurrection of Jesus

At one time Flew was famous for arguing that religious claims are unfalsifiable.[22] St Paul would have disagreed; he lays it on the line:

> If there be no Resurrection, then Christ was not raised; and if Christ was not raised, then our gospel is null and void, and so is your faith; and we turn out to be lying witnesses for God, because we bore witness that he raised Christ to life, whereas, if the dead are not raised, he did not raise him. For if the dead are not raised, it follows that Christ was not raised; and if Christ was not raised, your faith has nothing in it ....[23]

Nobody could ask for fairer than that. I shall argue that it is eminently reasonable to disbelieve in the Resurrection and so it is equally reasonable to reject the Christian Gospel as null and void.

Craig defends the Resurrection as the best explanation of what he calls three 'established facts':

> *Fact 1. On the Sunday following his crucifixion Jesus' tomb was found empty by a group of his women followers ....*
> *Fact 2. On separate occasions different individuals and groups saw appearances of Jesus alive after his death ....*
> *Fact 3. The original disciples suddenly came to believe in the Resurrection of Jesus despite having every predisposition to the contrary ....*[24]

I shall argue that not all these alleged facts should be regarded as 'established' and that those that are point to explanations other than Resurrection.[25] Since he had little space to develop his arguments for the Resurrection in his debate with Flew, I shall also draw upon Craig's arguments in his book *Reasonable Faith*.

The claim that a group of Jesus' women followers discovered his empty tomb assumes that they would have known where Jesus was buried, but this is doubtful. Acts 13:29 states that Jesus was buried by those Jews who had asked Pilate to execute him – that is, representatives of the Sanhedrin. This implies, in contradiction to the Gospel burial stories, that Jesus' body was disposed of in the hasty and dishonourable way appropriate for a condemned criminal – probably unceremoniously dumped in an obscure grave. Noted New Testament scholar Reginald Fuller regards the Acts account as older and more reliable than the story in Mark.[26]

Mark 15:47 says that Mary of Magdala and Mary the mother of Joseph saw the tomb where Jesus was laid. But this claim is tied in to the Joseph of Arimathea story, which is dubious at best. However, Craig defends the authenticity of the Joseph of Arimathea story:

> It seems very unlikely that Christian tradition would invent a story of Jesus' honorable burial by his enemies, or even that it would invent Joseph of Arimathea, give him a name, place him on the Sanhedrin, and say he was responsible for Jesus' burial if this were not true. The members of the Sanhedrin were too well-known to

allow either fictitious persons to be placed on it or false stories to be spread about one of its actual members' being responsible for Jesus' burial. Therefore, it seems very likely that Joseph was the actual, historical person who buried Jesus in the tomb.[27]

On the contrary, the early Christians' embarrassment at the failure of the disciples to care for Jesus' body could easily have led to the invention of a secret friend on the Sanhedrin who would do the proper honours.[28] In fact, as Fuller notes, we can watch the Joseph of Arimathea legend grow in the Gospels.[29] In Mark 15:43, the earliest source, he is just a 'respected member of the Council, a man who looked forward to the kingdom of God'. In Luke 25:51 he is described as '. . . a member of the Council, a good, upright man, who had dissented from their policy and the action they had taken'. In Matthew 27:57 he has become '. . . a man of means, . . . [who] had himself become a disciple of Jesus'. In John 19:38 he is described as '. . . a disciple of Jesus, but a secret disciple for fear of the Jews . . . .' Thus, in the Gospels, Joseph goes from a good and pious Jew, to one who actively dissented from the Sanhedrin's policy, to an actual follower of Jesus, to a secret disciple. Clearly, we have a growing legend.

Fuller, who is otherwise quite sceptical of the Gospel burial stories, admits that the story of Mary Magdalene discovering an empty tomb is very early, standing right at the beginning of the tradition (he regards Mark's addition of 'Mary, the Mother of James' and 'Salome' to the group that discovered the empty tomb as a later modification of the original pericope).[30] Let us suppose, then, that there was a particular woman, Mary Magdalene, who not too long after the crucifixion reported to the disciples that she had visited Jesus' tomb and found it empty. Who was Mary Magdalene? Jesus is said to have cast seven devils out of her. This hardly implies a stable or reliable personality and may in fact suggest mental illness.[31] The report of a single person, distraught and of dubious reliability, is clearly a very frail reed on which to base anything.

Michael Martin ably summarizes the grounds for doubting the empty tomb story:

> It is difficult to take seriously the alleged fact of the empty tomb given: the inconsistencies in the stories, the lack of contemporary eyewitnesses, the unclarity of who exactly the eyewitnesses were, the lack of knowledge of the reliability of the eyewitnesses, the failure of the early Christian writers to mention the empty tomb, the failure of the tomb story to be confirmed in Jewish or pagan sources.[32]

To this I would add that we have no evidence that the earliest Christians venerated the site of Jesus' tomb.[33] No place could have been more sacred for the earliest Christians than the very spot where the Resurrection supposedly had occurred. They certainly would have honoured the site if they had known where it was.

Finally, even if the tomb *had* been found empty, this fact, by itself, would have been a profound humiliation for the disciples:

If there had been a tomb and the tomb had been found empty, it would have meant only that one more insult had been delivered to the leader of the tiny Jesus movement. The disciples, whoever they were, would have concluded that not even the dead body of this Jesus had been spared degradation. No Easter faith would have resulted from an empty tomb. Therefore no such tradition could have been primary. It was but a story incorporated later into the narrative.[34]

In other words, the discovery of the empty tomb, by itself, would only have caused deeper humiliation and despair. This is shown in the Gospel of John where Mary Magdalene is depicted as discovering Jesus' empty tomb and crying in anguish 'They have taken my Lord away, and I do not know where they have laid him'.[35] The empty tomb becomes evidence of Resurrection rather than desecration only if added to the accounts of the encounters with the risen Jesus. Let us now turn to those accounts.

Craig and other apologists put great store in the formula recited by Paul in I Corinthians 15:3–8 where Paul lists various alleged witnesses of the risen Jesus: Cephas (Simon Peter), 'the twelve', over 500 at once, James the brother of Jesus, all of the apostles, and finally Paul himself. This passage is important because: first, it is very early; second, it names or refers to numerous alleged witnesses of the risen Jesus; and, third, it gives Paul's own testimony, the only undisputed first-person report of an encounter with the risen Jesus in the entire New Testament.

First, the early date of the formula is irrelevant. Contrary to what apologists have often claimed, legends can, and do, spread almost immediately and despite the opposition of eyewitnesses.[36] Second, as for the list of 'witnesses', we do not know whether these people were reliable or how Paul obtained his information about them.[37] Did Paul interview these alleged witnesses himself, or did he get the information second- or thirdhand? The '500' witnesses are especially dubious since neither the Gospels nor Acts knows anything about such a remarkable event.[38] Further, Paul leaves it unclear whether the appearances were physical or visionary; the Greek text is entirely ambiguous on this point.[39] Finally, although it would have been to his advantage to give such information, Paul does not mention the empty tomb, nor does he give a place or date for the Resurrection.

What, then, about Paul's own testimony? If we believed every 'eyewitness' testimony to miracles, we would be credulous indeed. So, is Paul particularly credible? On the contrary, he himself tells us that he experienced ecstatic visions, a fact that he assumed would enhance his credibility among the early Christians. In II Corinthians 12 Paul says he was 'caught up as far as the third heaven' (verse 2) and not knowing whether he was 'in the body or out of it' (verse 2, repeated in verse 3). He reports he was 'caught up into paradise' (verse 4) and that he 'heard words so secret that no human lips may repeat them' (verse 4). Clearly, this is an account of a mystical vision. Why not conclude that Paul's experience of the risen Christ was of the same kind?[40]

What, then, about the Gospel accounts of the appearances of the risen Jesus to the disciples? All except the most conservative scholars agree that Mark, the earliest Gospel, originally ended with verse 16:8 and included no account of appearances to the disciples. As G.A. Wells notes, these stories as recounted in the other synoptics are full of inconsistencies:

> Matthew, following hints by Mark, sites in Galilee the one appearance to them that he records: the risen one has instructed the women at the empty tomb to tell the disciples to go to Galilee in order to see him (28:10). They do this, and his appearance to them there concludes the gospel. In Luke, however, he appears to them on Easter day in Jerusalem and nearby on the Emmaus road (eighty miles from Galilee) and tells them to stay in the city 'until ye be clothed with power from on high' (24:49. Acts 2:1–4 represents this as happening on Pentecost, some fifty days later). They obey, and were 'continually in the temple' (24:53). Luke has very pointedly changed what is said in Mark so as to site these appearances in the city.[41]

So, the accounts of to whom, when, and where the risen Jesus supposedly appeared are badly garbled. John K. Naland notes that the geographical and chronological contradictions in the Gospel stories preclude a coherent account of the post-crucifixion appearances.[42] He cogently states the grounds for doubting that the disciples experienced a literal (that is, non-visionary) appearance of the resurrected Jesus:

> While the original disciples were regarded as being the official witnesses to Jesus' post-Crucifixion reality, we cannot find in the New Testament a consistent picture of the official event (or events) to which they bore witness. One might think that, if the risen Jesus had actually appeared on a specific date, at a specific place, to a specific group of people, the memory of that unique and pivotal event would have been burned into the very soul of the early Christian church .... Why, then, have we not inherited a single, orderly account of the post-Crucifixion appearances of Jesus?[43]

If, as apologists insist, Paul and the Gospel writers wrote in consultation with the original eyewitnesses, *why* are the accounts so inconsistent?

For the sake of argument, though, let us suppose that, shortly after the crucifixion, some of the disciples did have experiences they took to be encounters with the risen Christ. How do we interpret those experiences?

Apologists reject the possibility that these experiences were hallucinations.[44] Should they? The article 'Hallucinations' in the *Encyclopedia of Psychology* says that one-eighth to two-thirds of the psychologically *normal* population experiences waking hallucinations.[45] Causes of hallucinations in normal people include social isolation and rejection and severe reactive depression. Soon after the crucifixion, the disciples were very likely to be suffering a strong sense of rejection, isolation and depression, so it is not at all unlikely that several of them experienced vivid hallucinations of Jesus at that time. After a careful study of the post-crucifixion appearances of Jesus in his book *What Really Happened to Jesus*, Gerd Lüdemann concludes that all these experiences can be explained as visions. I find his treatment wholly convincing and simply recommend it to the reader.

What, then, of Craig's final argument – that the disciples were strongly predisposed *not* to believe in the Resurrection? Craig's argument is that Jewish thought about the Resurrection viewed it as an event that would take place at the apocalyptic close of history, not as an event *in* history.[46] Further, the understanding was that there would be a Resurrection of *all* righteous people, not the raising of a single individual.[47] Jewish theology did have the concept of 'translation' – the bodily assumption of individuals into heaven,[48] therefore, even if the disciples had experienced post-crucifixion hallucinations of Jesus, they would have envisioned him as translated into heaven rather than as returning to the physical world.[49]

Consider a passage from a standard textbook:

> [Christianity] ... shared with much of Judaism the hopes for the New Age that God had promised through the prophets and seers. But it differed from the rest of Judaism in one crucial point: It was convinced that the New Age had already begun to dawn. More specifically, it believed that God had acted in Jesus of Nazareth to inaugurate the New Age, and that the community itself was the nucleus of the People of the New Age. The basis for this conviction was the belief that God had raised Jesus from the dead.[50]

That is, early Christians believed that they *were* at the closing of history and that the Resurrection of Jesus *was* an eschatological event that ushered in the New Age, the coming of the Kingdom. Further, Jesus' Resurrection was not conceived as an event separate from the general Resurrection, but as merely the first Resurrection preceding and prefiguring the others. This is why Paul refers to Jesus as the 'first fruits of the harvest of the dead'.[51] Paul continues: 'As in Adam all men die, so in Christ all will be brought to life; but each in his own proper place: Christ the first fruits, and afterwards, at his coming, those who belong to Christ.'[52]

In all honesty, I just do not see an unbridgeable conceptual hiatus between traditional Jewish concepts of Resurrection and those of the early Church. According to the Gospels, Jesus' preaching was full of heretical and apocalyptic elements. Such preaching, combined with post-crucifixion visions of Jesus certainly seem adequate to bring about a 'paradigm shift' in the disciples' concepts of the Resurrection. If Craig insists that the conceptual shift was so great that it would have required supernatural intervention, I must ask him to indicate some criteria. At what point do concepts become so alien that it would take divine intervention to make someone shift from one to the other?

Conclusion

In summary, Craig's three arguments fail to provide any good evidence for the Resurrection. Either his 'established facts' are not established, or they are quite compatible with other explanations. He has not shown that it is unreasonable to reject the Resurrection of Jesus and consequently to reject the Christian Gospel as null and void. I conclude that he has not shown that the universe is improbable and that the Resurrection of Jesus was not.[53]

Notes

1 I would like to thank Stan Wallace for inviting me to participate in this discussion. I had my own debate with Doctor Craig in Dallas in June of 1998. Unlike some other interlocutors I have encountered, he met my arguments with argument, rather than invective. It is therefore a pleasure to address these remarks to him.

2 When I say that these arguments provide no objective evidence for theism, I am presupposing the sort of circumstantial objectivity recently articulated by Nicholas Rescher in *Objectivity: The Obligations of Impersonal Reasoning* (Notre Dame, IN: Notre Dame University Press, 1997), p. 8. On this view, objectivity consists not in attaining a God's eye view (which is impossible) but in making the appropriate judgements in one's particular epistemic circumstances. As an atheist and a proponent of materialistic naturalism, given my epistemic circumstances, I have every right to demand very good arguments for theism. (Likewise, a Christian would have the right to demand very good arguments for atheism.) It was therefore completely wrongheaded for one critic to castigate me for demanding 'compelling' evidence for theism. See J.P. Moreland, 'Atheism and Leaky Buckets: The Christian Rope Pulls Tighter', in J.P. Moreland and K. Nielsen (eds), *Does God Exist?* (Nashville, TN: Thomas Nelson, 1990), p. 239.

3 See pp. 20–21.

4 See p. 21.

5 In an earlier critique of J.P. Moreland's version of the fine-tuning argument (Keith Parsons, 'Is there a Case for Christian Theism?', in Moreland and Nielsen, *Does God Exist?*), I also desired to know what meaning was given to 'probable' in the context of the actualization of possible universes. My request was contemptuously dismissed and I was accused of something called 'methodism':

> Parsons' objection fits a pattern: because we cannot formulate here precise and all-embracing criteria prior to our argument, we cannot know anything at all about design and its role in arguing about atheism and theism. But this is epistemological methodism again .... (Moreland, 'Atheism and Leaky Buckets', p. 227)

Whatever evils 'methodism' is supposed to embody (and better methodism than Methodism, in my book!), the dismissive attitude towards my request is utterly inappropriate. If the context were anything like ordinary circumstances in which something is judged extremely unlikely – like the simultaneous jamming of all ten rifles in a firing squad – I would happily waive my demand. But the context is an extremely bizarre one postulating occult processes (the actualization of possible universes) which, by definition, utterly transcend any possible experience. When probabilistic concepts are applied to arcane metaphysical claims, clearly we have the right to ask the Kantian question of whether such concepts have legitimate application there.

Moreland's other reactions to my criticisms are also badly confused. For inexplicable reasons he fulminates against my framing the discussion in terms of probabilities ('Atheism and Leaky Buckets', p. 226). In the very next two sentences he asserts:

> The real point of my design argument is twofold. First, certain phenomena (for example, the nature of cosmic constants) are highly unlikely, surprising, and without explanation if they resulted without originating in a mind, because they

bear features that apparently point to a mind responsible for their existence. ('Atheism and Leaky Buckets', p. 226)

So, according to Moreland, the values of the cosmic constants should be regarded as 'highly unlikely' and 'surprising' but not improbable. I have no idea what he could mean.

As for the claim that ultimate physical facts have no explanation if we do not postulate an originating mind, this is precisely what naturalism asserts. If the fundamental constants are regarded as ultimate, irreducible, brute physical facts – not explicable in terms of more basic physical facts, like those postulated in multiple-universe cosmogonies – then naturalism regards those constants as neither having nor needing an explanation. This is a grammatical point: brute facts are neither probable nor improbable; they just are. To argue that it is 'highly unlikely' and 'surprising' that the ultimate physical facts should be these, puts us right back where we started – trying to make sense of assigning probabilities to the actualization of possible universes. In fact, Moreland makes my point for me:

> The world-view of Christian theism makes the occurrence of life likely as part of its overall hypothesis. The concurrence of the particular factors necessary for the emergence of life with those predicted by Christian theism is to be compared with the emergence of those factors necessary for life against the backdrop of the atheist hypothesis, which does not make any particular arrangement more likely than any other ('Atheism and Leaky Buckets', p. 226).

Precisely! Evidence E confirms hypothesis H more than hypothesis H_1 only if $p(E/H) > p(E/H_1)$. Where E is the values of the fundamental constants, T is theism, and N is naturalism, E confirms T more than N only if $p(E/T) > p(E/N)$. But if, as naturalism insists, no value at all can be given for $p(E/N)$, then it just cannot be said that E confirms T more than N because it just cannot be said that $p(E/T) > p(E/N)$. Nothing that Moreland says undermines this reasoning.

6   R. Le Poidevin, *Arguing for Atheism: An Introduction to the Philosophy of Religion* (London: Routledge, 1996), pp. 49–50.

7   These remarks are based on George Schlesinger's excellent discussion of these points; see George Schlesinger, *Metaphysics* (Oxford: Blackwell, 1983), pp. 73–74.

8   W. Salmon and J. Earman, 'The Confirmation of Scientific Hypotheses', in W. Salmon *et al.*, *Introduction to the Philosophy of Science* (Englewood Cliffs, NJ: Prentice Hall, 1992), pp. 75–76.

9   It might be argued that Schlesinger's objections presuppose an objective construal of probability. For instance, the third objection supposes that probability applies to physical situations whereas the subjective and personalist interpretations see probability as a measure of the degree of conviction with which a belief is held. However, it seems to me that the probabilities presented in fine-tuning arguments are offered as objective probabilities. When Craig says that it is extremely unlikely that the fundamental constants could have their values by chance, I do not think he intends merely to announce his degree of conviction.

10 For a clear account of these arcane matters see Alan Guth, *The Inflationary Universe* (Reading, MA: Addison-Wesley, 1997), pp. 136–45.

11 Ibid., p. 141.

12 Paul Davies, *The Mind of God: The Scientific Basis for a Rational World* (New York: Simon & Schuster, 1992), pp. 204–5.

13   Ibid., p. 205.

14   Victor J. Stenger, 'Cosmomythology: Is the Universe Fine-Tuned to Produce Us?', available online at: http://www.phys.hawaii.edu/vjs/www/cosmyth.txt), pp. 6–10.

15   Ibid., p. 8.

16   Quentin Smith, 'The Anthropic Coincidences, Evil and the Disconfirmation of Theism', *Religious Studies*, 1992, 28, pp. 347–50.

17   Paul Edwards, *Reincarnation: A Critical Examination* (Buffalo, NY: Prometheus Books, 1996), pp. 301–3.

18   Theodore M. Drange, 'The Fine-Tuning Argument (1998)', available online at: http://www.infidels.org/library/modern/theodore_drange/tuning.html, p. 2.

Theists often appeal to human agency as an analogy to divine acts of creation. In particular, basic actions, like blinking or clenching a fist, which we just do without doing anything else first, are taken as analogous to God's creative acts. However, there are deep problems with such an alleged analogy. First, God is often conceived as existing timelessly, and all of our human experience of agent causation is temporal. What it would mean to act atemporally is deeply mysterious. Second, actions are explained in terms of reasons and purposes; underlying physical (for example, neurophysiological) processes are not invoked in such explanations. Yet it is precisely such a physical *modus operandi* that we would like to have in many contexts. For instance, evolutionary theory provides much understanding of how, for example, birds came about. The creationist 'explanation' is this: God says 'fiat aves!' and POOF! the air is full of birds. Whatever creationist claims might tell us about God's purposes in creating birds (or universes), they are clearly gravely deficient in giving us a *modus operandi*.

19   Davies criticizes these scenarios in his book *The Mind of God*. He complains that the mega-universe scenarios only permit a selection among physically possible states of the world and cannot explain the laws that define physical possibility (ibid., p. 219). Similarly, for Smolin's evolving universe scenario, Davies charges that it leaves unexplained the laws that permit the postulated linkage between biological and cosmological evolution (ibid., p. 222). But neither Davies nor anyone else has yet shown why it would be improbable that the most basic laws that hold in our universe (or mega-universe) do obtain. Again, if a set of laws is *ex hypothesi* truly fundamental – that is, not the result of even more basic physical laws or processes, atheism can conceive of no probability, high or low, that such laws would hold.

20   M. Rees, *Before the Beginning: Our Universe and Others* (Reading, MA: Addison-Wesley, 1997).

Even a successful TOE might not predict the values of all the constants. Even if we possessed a Final Theory that gave us all the laws of nature, it could well be that many features of the universe will result from random symmetry-breaking processes; see J.D. Barrow, *Theories of Everything: The Quest for Ultimate Explanation* (Oxford: Clarendon Press, 1991), p. 131. The point is that, until we have such a TOE, we just do not know which (if any) values of the constants are due to underlying law and which (if any) are due to random symmetry-breaking processes.

Barrow also examines an interesting scenario, postulating baby universes, connected by 'wormholes', that might allow us to predict the probable values of the constants; see J.D. Barrow, *The Origin of the Universe* (New York: Basic Books, 1994), pp. 102–13, 115–28). However, Barrow admits that these scenarios cannot predict the values of the non-zero constants such as the mass or charge of the electron (ibid., pp. 120–1).

21 See p. 30.
22 Antony Flew, 'Theology and Falsification', in Antony Flew and A. MacIntyre (eds), *New Essays in Philosophical Theology* (New York: Macmillan, 1955).
23 I Corinthians 15: 13–17. New Oxford Annotated Bible.
24 See p. 23.
25 A thorough treatment of this issue would begin with the Humean task of showing that the Resurrection is initially improbable. This is especially important since some writers have badly muddied the waters; see, for example, Moreland, 'Atheism and Leaky Buckets', pp. 231–32. However, space is very limited here and Michael Martin has recently argued very cogently that the prior probability of the Resurrection must be low even for Christians; see Michael Martin, 'Why the Resurrection is Initially Improbable', *Philo*, 1:1 (Spring/Summer 1998), pp. 63–73. In this discussion I shall presume that Martin has already made the case for the initial improbability of the Resurrection.
26 Reginald Horace Fuller, *The Formation of the Resurrection Narratives* (New York: Macmillan, 1971), pp. 54–55; Gerd Lüdemann, another leading NT scholar, agrees. See Gerd Lüdemann, *What Really Happened to Jesus?*, trans. John Bowden (Louisville, KY: Westminster/John Knox Press, 1995), p. 23.
27 William Lane Craig, *Reasonable Faith: Christian Truth and Apologetics* (Wheaton, IL: Crossway Books, 1994), p. 273.
28 Lüdemann, *What Really Happened to Jesus?*, p. 21.
29 Fuller, *The Formation of the Resurrection Narratives*, p. 55.
30 Ibid., p. 56
31 Michael Martin, *The Case Against Christianity* (Philadelphia: Temple University Press, 1991), p. 103.
32 Ibid., p. 89.
33 Lüdemann, *What Really Happened to Jesus*, p. 24.
34 J.S. Spong, *Resurrection: Myth or Reality?* (San Francisco: Harper Collins, 1995), p. 228.
35 John 20:13.
36 It is easy to show that legends can and do arise and spread very quickly after a remarkable person's death, despite the opposition of eyewitnesses. A remarkable piece of scholarship, James Moore, *The Darwin Legend* (Grand Rapids, MI: Baker Books, 1994), examines the growth of the famous 'Darwin deathbed' legend. Charles Darwin died on 19 April 1882. Almost immediately stories began to circulate suggesting that Darwin, the agnostic and author of the godless theory of evolution, had repudiated his theories and confessed his faith in a dramatic deathbed conversion. Moore shows that these stories spread quickly despite the emphatic denials of the Darwin family. He includes evidence that within one week of Darwin's burial in Westminster Abbey, a Welsh minister preached a sermon alleging a deathbed conversion.
37 Martin, *The Case Against Christianity*, p. 83.
38 Craig, *Reasonable Faith*, p. 282, defends the historicity of the appearance to the 500. He notes that Paul specifically mentions that most of these persons are still alive, implying that sceptics could still interview them. However, this claim may have been part of a memorized formula or credo, not implying a firsthand acquaintance with surviving members of the original group.
        Even if Paul did know firsthand that there had been a crowd of approximately 500 that had undergone some sort of strange experience, we simply do not know enough even to conjecture about what really happened. Without more information we simply do not know what members of that crowd claim to have seen or how

qualified they were to make such claims. Also, odd things happen when people get together in crowds. The human herd instinct is very strong. Experienced rabble-rousers – like Mark Antony in Shakespeare's *Julius Caesar* – are quite aware that people in crowds are even more gullible than they are individually and that it is easy to whip them in to a murderous (or credulous) frenzy. It is quite easy to imagine a crowd of 500 coming to believe that they had seen the risen Jesus when no such thing had occurred.

39 Apologists have claimed that the Greek verb *horao* employed by Paul in I Corinthians: 5–8 always refers to physical sight and not visions. However, Paul himself, in Colossians 2:18 uses the same verb to denigrate false visions. Also, as Fuller, *The Formation of the Resurrection Narratives*, p. 30, says: 'The appearances [in I Corinthians 15: 5–8)] are characterized by the verb *ophthe* [the aorist passive form of *horao*] literally "was seen ...." but when used with the dative, "appeared"'. Fuller notes that this verb is used in the Septuagint to describe theophanies and the appearance of angels. Lüdemann agrees, but also points out that the word is used in the Septuagint with cases of physical seeing; see Lüdemann, *What Really Happened to Jesus?*, p. 82. So the word seems to be utterly unspecific and indeterminate between denoting physical seeing and 'seeing' with the eye of the mind or spirit.

40 Craig, *Reasonable Faith*, p. 286, insists that Paul does make a distinction between the appearances of the risen Jesus, which are physical, and visions of him which, though veridical and caused by God, occur purely within the mind. He says the distinction is 'conceptual (if not linguistic)', which seems to concede that Paul's language is ambiguous and therefore that the distinction is not explicit (p. 286). Further, Paul specifically says in I Corinthians 15:50 that '... flesh and blood can never possess the kingdom of God ...'. He says this in the context of arguing that the spiritual body (which the resurrected Christ possessed) is utterly different from the physical body.

Craig, ibid., pp. 285–6 argues that Paul conceived the resurrected body as physical and that, when Paul describes such a body as 'spiritual', he does not mean 'made out of spirit' but 'dominated by or oriented towards the Spirit'. However, this interpretation simply seems at odds with Paul's words and purpose:

> If there is such a thing as an animal body, there is also a spiritual body. It is in this sense that Scripture says 'The first man, Adam, became an animate being,' whereas the last Adam has become a life-giving spirit. Observe, the spiritual does not come first; the animal body comes first, and then the spiritual. The first man was made 'of the dust of the earth': the second man is from heaven (I Corinthians 15: 44–47).

The plain emphasis of the passage is on the reiterated distinction between the animal and the spiritual or the earthly and the heavenly. Paul's aim is to address the doubts of the Corinthians about bodily Resurrection. As the commentators in the Oxford Study Edition of *The New English Bible* put it:

> The Corinthians seem to have balked at the idea of bodily Resurrection. Paul agrees that the flesh has no part in the kingdom (v. 50), arguing that there are many kinds of bodies and that Christians will receive bodies made not of flesh, but of spirit. (*The New English Bible*, ed. Samuel Sandmel, [New York: Oxford University Press, 1976], p. 216).

Clearly, in such a context it is most implausible to suggest that Paul only meant by 'spiritual' a body 'dominated by or oriented towards the Spirit'. Had he only meant that the resurrected body was 'spiritual' in that weak sense, he would have failed even to address the Corinthians' concerns and made inexplicable his reiterated emphatic contrasts.

41   George Albert Wells, *Who Was Jesus? A Critique of the New Testament Record* (La Salle, IL: Open Court, 1989), p. 100.

42   J.K. Naland, 'The First Easter: Evidence for the Resurrection Evaluated', *Free Inquiry*, 3:2 (Spring 1988), p. 17.

43   Ibid., pp. 18–19.

44   Peter Kreeft and Ronald K. Tacelli, *Handbook of Christian Apologetics* (Downer's Grove, IL: InterVarsity Press, 1994), pp. 186–88, offer 14 (!) arguments against the hallucination theory. Craig, more modestly, only offers four; see *Reasonable Faith*, pp. 287–8. In part, Craig claims that the hallucination theory cannot account for the physicality of the appearances or the fact that they occurred to more than one person at a time. However, as the recent 'alien abduction' craze shows, the alleged abductees consistently reported how real the experiences seemed to them. As Susan Blackmore reports, abductees often claim to have been taken from public places, in the presence of witnesses, and even in groups; see Susan Blackmore, 'Abducted by Aliens or Sleep Paralysis?', *Skeptical Inquiry* (May–June 1998), pp. 23–28, 24. Further, the visions seen by thousands at Fatima, Portugal in 1917 show that mass hallucinations do occur.

45   H.V. Hall, 'Hallucinations', in R. Corsini (ed.), *Encyclopedia of Psychology*, 2nd edn (New York: John Wiley, 1994), p. 101.

46   Craig, *Reasonable Faith*, p. 290.

47   Ibid., p. 291.

48   Ibid., p. 292.

49   Ibid., p. 293.

50   H. Kee, F. Young and K. Froehlich, *Understanding the New Testament* (Englewood Cliffs, NJ: Prentice-Hall, 1965), pp. 52–53.

51   I Corinthians 15:20.

52   I Corinthians 15:22–3.

53   I would like to thank Michael Martin and Victor Stenger for reading drafts of this essay and for their valuable suggestions.

Chapter 9

Infinity and Explanation, Damnation and Empiricism

David Yandell

While there were many issues of philosophical importance raised in this debate, a number of questions went unanswered or even unasked (perhaps due to time constraints). I wish to raise a few of these and to offer some further discussion concerning problematic claims made by each of the participants. I conclude with an appraisal of the debate.

Questions for Craig

There are several points at which one might question Craig's position. For example, it isn't obvious that the historical issues concerning the Resurrection of Jesus are as straightforward as he suggests; responsible critical scholarship is divided over what to make of the evidence that Craig cites. I will focus, though, on three main issues in his version of the cosmological argument: his views concerning infinity, his attempt to derive the claim that the cause of the universe is an eternal person, and the adequacy of his appeal to God as the ultimate explanation of the existence of the universe.

One question deserving more attention is whether there can be an actual infinite. Craig rejects this as impossible, claiming that the paradoxes surrounding the infinite leave infinity as an idea only – one that cannot correspond to an actual existent. The paradox that Craig cites is the difficulty of answering the question 'What is infinity minus infinity?'. On the basis of the impossibility of the actually infinite, Craig's version of the cosmological argument rests.

Several problems suggest themselves concerning Craig's rejection of the actual infinite and its employment in the cosmological argument. First, if conceptual inconsistencies or contradictions plague the idea of infinity, as Craig's appeal to paradox suggests, then it would seem that we have no coherent idea of infinity – a conclusion much stronger than the one that Craig wants. At least, Craig owes us an explanation of what it is to have an idea that has coherent content but the instantiation of which automatically produces a genuine (that is, irresolvable) paradox. In the absence of such an explanation, Craig apparently finds himself offering an argument that entails that we can have no idea of infinity.

Second, Craig needs to offer an account of how belief in the existence of God – presumably actually infinite in power and knowledge – is compatible with his rejection of the possibility of actual infinites. Craig must either somehow restrict his rejection of the actual infinite to the physical realm (which seems impossible given that the argument for its impossibility is a purely conceptual, mathematical one) or deny that the divine attributes involve any actual infinites. This latter option is unappealing, since God's knowing all of the truths of addition, for instance, requires that God have an actually infinite number of true beliefs.

Third, let us examine Craig's example of a paradox concerning infinity to see whether it is a genuine paradox. Craig asks, 'For example, what is infinity minus infinity? Well, mathematically you get self-contradictory answers.'[1]

But is this a genuine paradox? Are there particular cases where the subtraction of an infinite set from another infinite set generates contradictory results? It is true that one can get an infinite set, a finite set, or a null set as the result of subtracting one infinite set from another. Subtracting the even positive integers from the set of positive integers leaves an infinite set, the odd positive integers. Subtracting all the positive integers greater than 40 from the set of positive integers leaves a finite (40-membered) set. Subtracting all the positive integers from the set of positive integers leaves one with the null set. But none of these subtractions could possibly lead to any conclusion other than each leads to. This alleged contradictory feature of the infinite seems not to generate any actual contradictions. At least, Craig owes us an explanation of what the contradiction is in subtracting the infinite from the infinite.

In any case, it is unclear from what Craig says here that there cannot be actual infinites. In fact, I suspect, the issue is sufficiently disputable that Craig is resting a controversial conclusion (that God exists) on an even more controversial premise. He may, however, be able to avoid this entire issue. The persistence of the universe is just as much in need of explanation as its initial existence. Given the contingency and causal dependence of physical (and finite mental, if this is a separate category) events, that the world continues to exist at any given moment cries out for explanation of a kind not provided by appeal to prior states of the physical (and finite mental) universe. That the universe existed a moment ago is equally compatible with its persisting now and its failing to persist now, so past existence alone is not a sufficient explanation of its persistence. This seems a safer basis for a cosmological argument (as philosophers as far back at least as Descartes have noted) than a controversial claim about the nature of infinity.

A second point at which I wish to take issue with Craig concerns his attempt to show that the universe is caused by the free choice of a timeless person. The basis for this claim is that the ultimate cause of the beginning of the spatio-temporal universe must not itself be in time, and must not be the product of a further cause, and so:

> ... this cause must be an uncaused, timeless, changeless and immaterial being of unimaginable power which created the universe. Moreover ... it must also be

personal. For how else could a timeless cause give rise to a temporal effect like the universe?[2]

A timeless impersonal cause, Craig argues, would produce a timeless effect, since the effect's sufficient conditions would be timelessly fulfilled.

Again, several worries arise. The concept of a changeless person is one in need of explication and defence. A changeless being would either have no emotions, passions or desires or would have whichever of these it had changelessly. Whether such a being could be described as a 'person' is doubtful. The claim that a timeless, changeless person was temporarily incarnate seems, at least, to produce a number of paradoxical implications (for example, that a changeless being was at one time unembodied and at another time embodied). Further, if God does not have reasons prior to, or simultaneous with, God's choices, it seems that the choices would be arbitrary, but both 'prior to' and 'simultaneous with' are relations shared only by temporal entities. This sort of arbitrariness seems incompatible with the willing being that of a perfectly wise being. Even leaving these issues aside, it isn't at all clear that an atemporal personal choice could have the effect of creating time, since the willing itself would be eternal (assuming for argument's sake that an event can be eternal) and there would not be any temporal frame in terms of which its content could be temporally indexed. How, then, could the willing be sufficiently determinant to bring about the existence of the universe without bringing it about eternally? That is, God's willing that the universe come into existence would not itself occur at any time t (where t is the moment that the universe begins existing) and the content of the willing could not include that it be realized at time t since there is no preexisting frame of reference for t. What, then, on Craig's account, could make it the case that the universe come into existence at t?

Finally, I wish to turn to the issue of the explanatory ultimateness of God. Craig asserts that God is 'beginningless' and 'uncaused' and so God's existence does not require explanation. However, it seems possible to imagine a world in which God fails to exist – an empty universe, for example – and, if this is right, the question 'What makes it the case that God exists?' is an intelligible one. One can respond that, at each moment, God's willing that God persist is a sufficient cause for God's continued existence (plausibly enough, since God is omnipotent on Craig's view). Moreover, as Craig notes, God's existence has no beginning, so the question 'How did God come into existence?' is not one that needs answering. There is a general question concerning God's existence that appears to be intelligible – namely, 'Why does God exist at all?' or 'Why is there a God?' If this question amounts to more than asking for each given moment of God's existence why God exists at that moment, then there is an ultimate question concerning God whose answer may be 'It is just a brute fact'. If so, there is a way in which theistic explanation is essentially incomplete, just as there is a way in which non-theistic explanation is essentially incomplete. However, there will be far fewer brute facts for a theist to appeal to, since, on a Flew-style view, the initial existence and the persistence of the universe at every subsequent moment are all brute facts.

There are two ways of responding to this objection – claiming that God's existence is necessary or denying that 'Why is there a God?' adds anything to the conjunction of 'why is there a God at *t*?' for each time *t*. The first of these responses requires the derivation of a contradiction from the claim that an empty world could obtain. It is also worth noting that a demonstration of it would entail not only that 'God does not exist' is a contradiction but also that 'God exists contingently' is a contradiction. I do not see the contradiction in either of these claims; Craig does not discuss this issue. The second response requires a demonstration of the reducibility of the general question to the series of temporally specific questions. I am not sure whether this reduction is possible; Craig does not discuss this issue, either.

Questions for Flew

There are likewise a number of points meriting attention in Flew's comments. For example, it is not clear why he thinks that theists must hold that God everlastingly tortures those who do not believe in God simply on the basis of their non-belief (or that God ever tortures anyone for any reason). I will sketch the evidence that this is not the view put forward in the Christian scriptures. In any case, these objections bear on certain doctrines of salvation and certain conceptions of hell, but they are not pertinent to the question of whether God exists. One might also take issue with the apparent compatibilism in Flew's idea that God could 'make people such that they would freely choose to do what He desired'.[3]

Plantinga has famously sketched the problems for an account on which God makes people so that they freely choose a certain way.[4] I wish, instead, to focus on Flew's positions regarding metaphysical inquiry and concerning the range of our experience and of our ability to conceive of non-material persons generally and God in particular.

Flew holds that theism includes the view that the price of non-belief in God is eternal suffering. I presume that he takes this to be a tenet of Christian theism, since this is the kind of theism from which he draws his views on other issues. This raises the question whether it is a doctrine central to Christian theism that damnation is brought about by non-belief in God. I will briefly sketch some evidence that this is not the view put forward in various strains within the Christian scriptures. I will focus on the New Testament, although one could, I believe, make similar cases based on the Hebrew scriptures and on the intertestamental material. I will examine relevant evidence from several textual strains in the Gospels and from the Pauline letters in turn.[5]

Before turning to this examination, I wish to note what I am *not* doing. I am not examining those passages that describe the conditions (either subjective or objective) for salvation. What I wish to lay out is not the Christian scriptural account of how one avoids damnation but rather the account of how one comes to deserve damnation in the first place. It is perfectly coherent to claim that condemnation is not based on a lack of belief in God but that such belief is, in some way, relevant to unmerited exemption from condemnation (although mere cognitive assent is not what the New Testament or traditional Christian authors have had in mind in speaking of the faith that they believed to be relevant to salvation).

The Gospel of Mark has little to say about hell and damnation. Jesus is reported as saying that 'whoever blasphemes against the Holy Spirit can never have forgiveness'.[6] From the context, this seems to involve calling the works of the Holy Spirit works of the devil. The main mention of hell in the Gospel of Mark is the famously hyperbolic instruction to cut off or tear out one's hand, foot, or eye if it causes one to 'stumble', since being maimed, lame or blind in the kingdom of God is better than being whole and 'thrown into hell'.[7] The writer of the Gospel does not say here what stumbling consists in, but he has cited Jesus (a couple of chapters earlier) as giving a list of the 'evil things' that 'defile a person' (make a person unclean, and hence separated from God): 'evil intentions': 'fornication, theft, murder, adultery, avarice, wickedness, deceit, licentiousness, envy, slander, pride, folly'.[8] In the Gospel of Mark, then, it seems to be sin that leads one to be defiled and so thrown into hell.

A similar view can be found in the 'Q' material (that common to the Gospels of Matthew and Luke but absent from the Gospel of Mark) in the parable about the servants left in charge by their master to distribute food to the other servants. The wicked servant takes advantage of the master's absence and 'begins to beat his fellow servants, and eat and drink with drunkards'. This will lead the master, upon his return, to 'cut him in pieces and put him with the hypocrites, where there will be weeping and gnashing of teeth' (the Gospel of Matthew's favourite way of describing hell).[9] Here, sinful conduct and neglect of duty are the occasions for condemnation.

In the material unique to the Gospel of Matthew, there is a series of parables predicting the separation of the righteous from those doomed to hell at 'the end of the age'. The Gospel writer has Jesus say, in explaining the parable of the weeds, 'The Son of Man will send forth His angels, and they will gather out of His kingdom all stumbling blocks and those who commit lawlessness, and will cast them into the furnace of fire; in that place there shall be weeping and gnashing of teeth'.[10] Again, in the explication of the parable of the fish, the writer has Jesus say that 'The angels will come out and separate the evil from the righteous and throw them into the furnace of fire, where there will be weeping and gnashing of teeth'.[11] Here again, it is commission of acts violating the law (presumably, the law of Moses) and being evil that lead to hell fire. Several more particular sins receive mention as putting one in danger of damnation as well: insulting one's brother out of anger,[12] failing to forgive one's brother as God has forgiven one,[13] and keeping others from the kingdom of God, hypocrisy (feigning righteousness while being full of lawlessness), and persecution of those sent by Jesus.[14] Once again, in these passages it is consistently unlawful or sinful conduct that brings damnation.

In the material unique to Luke's Gospel, there is not a great deal of discussion of the basis of condemnation. However, Jesus is presented as telling his audience that all Galileans and all those living in Jerusalem are sinners and so will perish unless they repent.[15] Here again, sinfulness (without repentance), not lack of belief, is the ground for destruction. Doing evil is similarly the basis for judgement in the Gospel of John, where Jesus is reported as saying that 'the hour is coming when all who are in their graves will hear his [the Son of Man's] voice and will come out – those who have done good, to the Resurrection of life, and those who have done evil, to the Resurrection of condemnation'.[16]

Paul does not often speak directly of hell, but it is clear in his writings too that evildoing is the basis of condemnation. In the Letter to the Romans, Paul speaks explicitly about God's judgement. Judging others hypocritically, with a 'hard and impenitent heart', is:

> ... storing up wrath for yourself on the day of wrath, when God's righteous judgment will be revealed. For he will repay according to each one's deeds: to those who by patiently doing good seek for glory and honor and immortality, he will give eternal life; while for those who are self-seeking and who obey not the truth but wickedness, there will be wrath and fury. There will be anguish and distress for everyone who does evil ....[17]

On Paul's view, 'the wages of sin is death'.[18] This theme is present in Paul's other writings as well, as when Paul asks the members of the church at Corinth, 'Do you not know that wrongdoers will not inherit the kingdom of God? Do not be deceived!'.[19] There follows a list of sins that constitute the wrongdoing in question (see the similar list, along with the identical warning that 'those who do such things will not inherit the kingdom of God' at Galatians 5:19–21). There are other passages in the New Testament that repeat this theme, but by now it should be clear that it is a general view among at least the writers of the Gospels and Paul that the occasion for damnation is sin. Of course there are also many passages that suggest that death and destruction await those who do not faithfully accept God's grace, or the good news or Gospel of Jesus. However, in light of the passages just cited, these should be read as saying (I contend) that such grace is the path away from suffering and death *already merited in virtue of one's having done evil*. At any rate, Flew has given us no reason to reject this well-attested view of the basis for condemnation, and so his repeated comments to the effect that God tortures unbelievers for their lack of belief are unwarranted.

On more safely philosophical ground, I wish to raise several issues regarding Flew's views about the extent of human knowledge. Flew denies that our knowledge can extend to claims about the universe as a whole, since all of our experience is of things within the universe. He tells us that 'we are, all of us, creatures whose entire knowledge and experience has been of the universe'[20] and that 'my very fundamental contention is that one shouldn't be expected to know things outside the universe'.[21] Of course, these claims themselves are claims about the universe as a whole – namely, negative claims about what can be known regarding it. Flew appears to be in danger of offering an epistemically self-defeating view regarding what we can know about the universe as a whole: that is, his own view could not be known if what it says were true.

Perhaps Flew can avoid this problem, however, by claiming that we can know the truth of metaclaims (claims about claims) about the universe as a whole, but we cannot know the truth of first-order claims (claims directly about things) about the universe as a whole. The problem with this response is that Flew endorses the first-order conclusions of physics regarding the origin of the universe as a whole. It is only where physics stops that our first-order inquiry must end, as he implies in his rhetorical question, 'And if physics stops there, isn't that the end of human knowledge?'.[22] Flew should hope that there is no close relation between the end of physical inquiry and the bounds of human knowledge, since his own metaclaims are certainly not deliverances of the sciences, which are simply not in the business of offering normative epistemological or methodological claims for philosophy of the sort that we have seen Flew invoke in arguing against the legitimacy of Craig's cosmological inquiry.

In any event, Flew's position seems to be that some metaclaims (namely those ruling out metaphysical first-order claims regarding the universe as a whole) and some first-order claims (namely the deliverances of physical cosmology) are legitimate. It is only first-order claims that go beyond physics that are illegitimate. For example, metaphysical principles about the necessity for a first cause of the sort Craig invokes are ruled out. This seems an ad hoc restriction, designed solely for the purpose of ruling Craig's sort of inquiry out of bounds. However, Flew will no doubt insist that the metaphysical principles that Craig employs are illegitimate because they are not grounded in experience, while the conclusions of physical cosmology are so grounded. In reply, Craig might well insist that his metaphysical principles are known through conceptual experience. If Flew responds that there is no such experience and insists that all principles be experientially grounded, then he will have to concede that his own metaclaims will be unjustified, since they are scarcely the sort of claims that follow from sense-experience. So, either there is genuine conceptual experience, which may ground either Flew's metaclaims or Craig's metaphysical principles, or there is not, in which case both sets of assertions will be without experiential justification.

Flew similarly rejects claims about bodiless persons on the grounds that such beings are beyond the range of experience. He flatly asserts that persons are material: 'I think that conscious experiences are experiences of a material thing, namely a personal material object, because they are experiences of a human being (or, in some cases, of animals).'[23] Further, he claims that there is a conceptual problem with the idea of a person lacking a body. He reports that *bodiless person* is 'a notion I find very difficult to understand anyway, as all the people I know are creatures of flesh and blood'.[24] The difficulty lies in the content of the idea, not in the conceiver's understanding, Flew explains. 'Why do I have difficulty with the idea of an incorporeal person? Well, if I was asked to explain the meaning of the word "person" to someone who didn't know the meaning, I'd point around the place here.'[25] Apparently, then, Flew is committed to something like the following: all persons are material objects and we cannot conceive of a person without a body because of how we define 'person'. The idea seems to be that whatever criteria we use in ostending (picking out) exemplars for our definition are essential to the kind being defined.

At least a couple of problems arise from this account. First, it is plainly true that we can imagine, understand and conceive of persons without bodies. Science fiction and horror stories abound with such imaginings. Adherents of several of the world's major religions hold that there are such bodiless persons. Idealist and some dualist philosophers, as well as materialists who hold that materialism about persons is contingently true, all hold either that there are, or that there could be, such persons. Any account claiming that understanding such a notion is impossible is faced with overwhelming empirical evidence to the contrary. Of course, it is possible that all of those mentioned have missed some incoherence in their concept or have failed to inspect their own ideas closely enough to detect the absence of such a notion, but it is extraordinarily unlikely, and Flew gives us no reason to suppose it is so. Further, Flew's account begs the question against non-materialists by asserting that we have no experience of non-material persons. The non-materialist may well regard introspection as precisely experience of a person who is not essentially embodied. Flew offers us no reason to think that this is not so. Finally, Flew's apparent position that criteria used in ostensively defining a term are essential to the kind defined falls prey to counterexamples. I may use four-leggedness as a criterion for picking out exemplary horses in ostensively defining 'horse', but this does not imply that a three-legged equine is not a horse, let alone that the notion of a three-legged horse is unintelligible. To summarize, then, Flew asserts without adequate grounds that persons are material and that there is some problem with understanding what a bodiless person is. However, so far as Flew has shown, these objections do not count against Craig's position.

One final point on which I wish to take issue with Flew concerns the evidential status of religious experience. Flew notes that there are two senses of 'experience', one implying that there is a mind-independently existing object of the experience (as when one reports experiencing a cow that is actually before one) and the other not so implying (as when one reports a hallucinatory experience). Religious experiences, he asserts, are of the latter sort. 'Now it seems to me that for people to say that they've had experience of either the Christian God or Shiva the Destroyer or any other god, it is as Thomas Hobbes said, "To say He hath spoken to him in a dream, is no more than to say he dreamed that God spake to him ... "'.[26] While, he concedes, the subject of an experience is authoritative in saying what the content of the experience is, that subject is not authoritative with respect to whether the object of the experience exists. Unfortunately, Flew does not tell us why we are to regard religious experience as akin to hallucination. Perhaps it is because one can be mistaken about the object of a religious experience. However, this is also true of sensory experience (even when it is of cows or something equally large and homely). In any event, Flew offers no argument for the rejection of religious experience as evidence for religious belief. He offers no standard met by experiences where he takes the testimony of the experiencer as reliable that is not also met by testimony concerning religious experience. The closest he comes to doing so is to offer his view that cow experiences are of cows but .... However, the implied standard – only rely on the testimony of experiencers when they have really had an experience of something – will only be of use against claimed experiences of God if one begs the question of whether they are genuine.

A Brief Evaluation of the Debate

It seems to me that Craig has made a cumulative case of some weight. However, he has not dealt here with some important issues concerning the cosmological argument that he offers us, and I have raised a number of questions regarding the claim that the free choice of an eternal person is a coherent notion that helps us to explain how time could have begun. Still, these seem to me to leave in place several abductively weighty considerations in favour of the rationality of belief in God: a revised version of his cosmological argument, his argument from design, a more modest version of his historical argument, and his argument from experience of God. Flew, on the other hand, (as Craig points out) has offered three main arguments: that free bad choices made by human beings are incompatible with God's omnipotence, that God's loving nature is incompatible with his torturing the damned for all eternity, and that the notion of a bodiless person is in some way disreputable. Craig has presented a strong case against the first of these (and general arguments against the compatibilism that Flew assumes are readily available). The second argument is not germane to the issue of whether belief in God is rational, but rather to questions about what doctrines of hell and of salvation and damnation one ought to endorse. For the third, I have tried to show some problems. In summary, none of Flew's arguments seems to me to bear much weight as reasons to think belief in God irrational. Staying strictly with the merits of the cases as presented here, belief in God is more rational that disbelief. This, of course, leaves open what the conclusion would be with different cases mounted on behalf of the two sides.

Notes

1 See p. 19.
2 See p. 20.
3 See p. 32. But Craig has already presented a libertarian alternative. (Moreover, Kant and Van Inwagen, for example, have shown the problems inherent in compatibilism. See Immanuel Kant, *Critique of Practical Reason* in many translations from *Kants gesammelte Schriften* (Berlin: Prussian Academy, 1900–42), volume V, pp. 94–100, and Peter Van Inwagen, 'The Incompatibility of Free Will and Determinism', *Philosophical Studies*, 27 (1975), pp. 185–99.
4 Alvin Plantinga, *God, Freedom, and Evil* (Grand Rapids, Mich.: Eerdmans, 1977; reprinted from New York: Harper & Row, 1974), pp. 29–55.
5 Peter Toon, *Heaven and Hell: A Biblical and Theological Overview* (Nashville, TN: Thomas Nelson, 1986).
6 Mark 3:29; paralleled at Matthew 12:31–32, Luke 12:10 Except where otherwise noted, scriptural references are to the New Revised Standard Version (NRSV).
7 Mark 9:43–48; Matthew 5:29–30, 18:8–9.

8   Mark 7:20–23; Matthew 15:10–11.
9   Matthew 24:48–51; Luke 12:45–46.
10 Matthew 13:40–48. Because the NRSV translation here is very loose, I quote here from the New American Standard Bible (NASB). I am indebted to Paul Moser for discussion of the Greek text of this passage.
11 Matthew 13:49.
12 Matthew 5:22.
13 Matthew 18:23–35.
14 Matthew 23:13–36.
15 Luke 13:1–5.
16 John 5:28–29.
17 Romans 2:5–9.
18 Romans 6:23.
19 1 Corinthians 6:9.
20 See p. 24.
21 See p. 26.
22 See p. 25.
23 See p. 31.
24 See p. 26.
25 See p. 31.
26 Ibid.

Chapter 10

Craig's Case for God's Existence

Paul Draper

In his debate with Antony Flew, William Lane Craig presents five reasons for thinking that God exists. The first four of these are arguments. Craig infers God's existence from the alleged facts that: (i) the universe had a beginning; (ii) the universe exhibits complex order; (iii) moral values are objective; and (iv) Jesus rose from the dead. Craig's fifth reason appeals to the immediate experience of God, which he believes is available to anyone who sincerely seeks God. I do not find any of Craig's five reasons convincing. In what follows I will explain why.

Independent Reasons in a Cumulative Case

Before considering Craig's five reasons individually, an examination of the cumulative nature of his case will be useful. In his opening speech Craig states both that his reasons are 'independent of one another' and that together 'they constitute a powerful cumulative case' for God's existence.[1] In his first rebuttal, he clarifies these statements. He uses Copleston's definition of God as 'a supreme personal being distinct from the world and the creator of the world'.[2] Let's call such a God a 'Copleston-God'. Thus, when he says that each of his five reasons for God's existence are independent, I take it he means that each is by itself a good reason to believe that a 'Copleston-God' exists. And when he says that his case is cumulative, part of what he means, I suspect, is that, because his five reasons are independent, they will, taken together, justify a much higher degree of certainty about God's existence than would be warranted by any one of them.

There is, however, a more interesting sense in which his case is cumulative. Craig claims that, in addition to establishing the existence of a Copleston-God, his five reasons give many other attributes of God. This is important because one can believe that a Copleston-God exists without being a theist. (One could, for example, be a deist.) No God is the God of some theistic religion unless he or she is worthy of the sort of worship practised in that religion. Thus, to make a good case for theism, Craig needs to do more than prove that a supreme supernatural person created the world. He must also show that this creator possesses the additional attribute of holiness (which includes moral perfection) as well as any other attributes required to be worthy of theistic worship.

Notice that building 'supreme' into the definition of 'God' doesn't do much since 'supreme' just means 'superior to other beings'. And, given the known competition (human beings, other primates, dolphins, whales, and so on), that's not a very high standard for a deity. St Anselm and many contemporary philosophical theologians believe that God is not just supreme, but perfect; not just the greatest of all beings, but the greatest of all (logically) possible beings. If perfection is required for worthiness of traditional theistic worship, then no person would qualify for the title 'God' as that title is used by traditional theists unless that person were perfect. If this is right, then to show that a traditional theistic God exists, one would need to show that the creator has, not just enough power to create our universe, but as much power as it is possible to have, not just enough knowledge to fine-tune our universe for life, but as much knowledge as it is possible to have, and so on. One would also have to show that the creator possesses all absolute perfections (or the best possible combination of absolute perfections), including any perfections that no human being can comprehend. It's obvious, I take it, that Craig's five reasons fall far short of showing that a perfect being exists. Perhaps, however, perfection is not required for worthiness of theistic worship. For the purposes of this chapter I will assume that any Copleston-God who is also holy is worthy of theistic worship and so is a theistic God – whether or not that being is also perfect.

What other attributes of God does Craig believe his five reasons establish? The first reason is supposed to show that God is immaterial, timeless, changeless, spaceless, beginningless, uncaused and extremely powerful. He wants the second to prove not just a personal creator, but an intelligent designer of the universe. I assume he would want to add that such a designer would need to have vast amounts of knowledge. The third reason is supposed to 'give us a source of moral value and all goodness'[3] (this is the closest Craig comes to arguing for God's holiness). The fourth adds 'a God who is active in history in the person of Jesus'.[4] And the fifth 'a God who can be immediately known and experienced'.[5] Given the fourth argument and given that the religious experiences to which Craig appeals in his fifth reason include distinctively Christian experiences, it is reasonably clear Craig wants his five reasons to cumulatively establish, not just theism, but Christian theism. Thus, three questions need to be asked about his reasons. First, do they individually or collectively establish the existence of a Copleston-God? Second, do they establish the existence of a theistic God – a Copleston-God who is worthy of theistic worship? And, third, do they establish the existence of a Christian God – a theistic God who became incarnate in Jesus?

Craig's Cosmological Argument

Craig's first reason to believe God exists is that the universe had a beginning. How does Craig know that the universe is not infinitely old? In the debate with Flew, he offers two arguments – one philosophical and one scientific.

The philosophical argument proceeds as follows. The claim that an actually infinite number of real things exists leads to self-contradictions. Thus, since past events are real, there cannot be an actually infinite number of past events.

And, together with the implicit premise that the universe cannot exist without events occurring, this implies that the universe began to exist a finite time ago.[6] I have my doubts about the first premise of this argument, and I have argued elsewhere that Craig's attempt to show that no collection of real objects can be actually infinite is at best incomplete.[7] To save space, I won't repeat my argument here. Instead, I will briefly discuss his scientific argument for a beginning and then examine his inference from a beginning of the universe to the existence of God.

Craig's scientific argument depends for its success on a rather speculative cosmological theory. Granted, science has proven an expanding known universe, but surely it has not yet established that the universe came into existence out of nothing. There remain other live options. For example, what we call the universe might very well be one small part of a larger system (the real universe) that is not expanding and that is infinitely old. After all, a few hundred years ago we thought our solar system included the stars and thus comprised the entire universe. Then we found out that there are many suns – or, as we now say, that our sun is just one of many stars. And less than a century ago we thought that the Milky Way was the whole universe. Then we found out that it is just one galaxy among many others. I, for one, would not be surprised if it turned out that the expanding system of galaxies that constitutes the known universe is just a relatively recent product of a much larger and infinitely more ancient physical system, a system that may contain many other expanding subsystems besides ours.

Suppose, however, there is no such larger system. Suppose that the universe really did begin to exist and that whatever begins to exist has a cause. Then the universe has a cause distinct from it. But what is the nature of this cause. Is it a Copleston-God? In other words, is it a supreme *personal* creator? Craig argues for the personal nature of the cause as follows:

1   The cause of the universe (which includes space and time) must itself be timeless.
2   A timeless cause cannot give rise to a temporal effect (like the universe) unless it is a person. Thus:
3   The cause of the universe is a person.

I think that both of the premises in this argument are questionable. The first is questionable because it assumes that nothing that is not a part of the physical space-time of our universe could be temporal. But instead of pursuing this objection, I would like to focus on the second premise. Craig defends it as follows:

> If the cause were an impersonal set of necessary and sufficient conditions, then the cause could never exist without the effect. If the cause were timelessly present, then the effect would be timelessly present as well. The only way for the cause to be timeless and for the effect to begin to exist in time is for the cause to be a personal agent who freely chooses to create an effect in time without any prior determining conditions.[8]

In short, Craig believes that a timeless cause of a temporal effect would have to be an agent-cause, because an agent-cause is not sufficient for its effect. A timeless *sufficient* cause could *never* (Craig's word) exist without its effect and so could only have timeless effects. One problem with this argument is that it assumes that agent-causation is the only type of non-sufficient causation. But why believe this? If quantum mechanics allows for natural temporal causes that are neither sufficient nor agents, then why is Craig so sure that supernatural timeless causes must be either sufficient causes or agents? Indeed, a timeless and hence changeless *person* is a harder concept to swallow than a timeless, non-personal, non-sufficient cause. So Craig's cosmological argument is at best incomplete. Even if it proves a first cause of the universe, it falls short of showing that this cause is a person and so fails to establish the existence of a Copleston-God.

Craig's Teleological Argument

Craig's teleological argument faces a similar problem. Even if it establishes an intelligent designer, it doesn't establish a creator of the universe and so it too falls short of establishing a Copleston-God. Perhaps, however, these gaps in Craig's cosmological and teleological arguments are not disastrous to his overall case. After all, even if neither argument by itself gets all the way to a Copleston-God, Craig could, with some plausibility, claim that the combination of the two arguments does reach that destination. For if his cosmological argument establishes a supernatural non-sufficient cause of the universe and his teleological argument establishes an intelligent designer capable of fine-tuning the universe for life, then surely the most likely theory is that the entities established by each argument are numerically identical, that the non-sufficient cause of the universe is also an intelligent being, and thus is, in all likelihood, an agent-cause of the universe.

Unfortunately, just as Craig's cosmological argument falls short of establishing a personal cause of the universe, Craig's teleological argument falls short of establishing intelligent design. In response to Flew's objection that complexity alone does not establish intelligent design, Craig claims that it is the great improbability of such complexity that rules out chance and so proves intelligent design.[9] Yet surely Craig can't mean that the support provided for intelligent design by complex order derives solely from the great improbability of that complexity, so that one would have proof of intelligent design if one had great improbability, whether or not one had complex order. For mere improbability is obviously not proof of intelligent design. Thus, Craig must mean that the complex order in our universe is much more probable with intelligent design than without it and, for that reason, raises the probability of intelligent design. This would be analogous to a case in which I win the lottery, Smith was capable of fixing the lottery, and I am Smith's only close friend. My winning in these circumstances is more probable given a fixed lottery (the design hypothesis) than given a fair one (the chance hypothesis), and so my winning raises the probability that the lottery was fixed. Compare this case to one in which an enemy of Smith wins, which is more probable (though still very improbable) if the lottery was fair than if it was fixed and so actually lowers the probability of design. Or compare it to a case in which no one knows who Smith likes or dislikes. In this case, my winning the lottery is no more or less likely on the chance hypothesis than on the design hypothesis and so is neither evidence for nor against design. The key point here is that, no matter how improbable an event is apart from intelligent design (no matter how big the lottery is), that event is not evidence for intelligent design unless it is more probable given intelligent design, and it is not *strong* evidence for intelligent design – evidence that might make design probable (depending on its prior probability) – unless it is *much* more probable given intelligent design.

Despite these obvious points, Craig never addresses the issue of how probable complex order is, given intelligent design. His entire case is built on the great improbability of complex order given naturalism or chance (together with a rejection of the view that complex order is necessary). But then his argument is, once again, incomplete. One might object that completing the argument is easy, for the evidence here is not just complex order, but a specific sort of complex order – the universe is fine-tuned for intelligent life. And it might seem obvious that this sort of order is vastly more probable on the hypothesis of intelligent design than on the hypothesis of chance. But is this really obvious? What is likely on intelligent design depends on what goals an intelligent designer is likely to have. Is it really obvious that a being capable of fine-tuning the universe would want humans to come into existence? Why not more magnificent beings? For that matter, why assume an intelligent designer would want any intelligent life at all? Human beings desire to interact with other intelligent beings, not because of their intelligence, but because of their social nature and curiosity. Why is Craig so sure that a non-human intelligent being – indeed a non-living intelligent being – would have a desire to interact with, or observe, other (much less) intelligent beings? Craig hasn't told us how he knows what the goals of such a being would be. And if we have no idea what the goals of such a being would be, then we don't know that human life is more likely on intelligent design than on chance.

Of course, Craig could add the goal of human life to his hypothesis of intelligent design. But an ad hoc manoeuvre like this won't help at all, for while it would increase the probability of complex order given his hypothesis, it would also decrease the prior probability of his hypothesis (that is, the probability of his hypothesis prior to considering complex order). Furthermore, it's far from clear that adding moral goodness to the hypothesis helps, since the existence of self-centred and violent creatures like humans might be even more improbable on morally good intelligent design than on the hypothesis of chance! So Craig has some explaining to do. His teleological argument, like his cosmological argument, is at best incomplete. Pointing out the great improbability of the complexity in our universe given naturalism does not by itself suffice to establish the existence of an intelligent designer.

Craig's Moral Argument

Craig's moral argument is supposed to show not just that a Copleston-God exists, but also that this God is the source of moral value and all goodness. Clearly this argument is crucial if Craig's cumulative case is to establish a theistic God rather than just a Copleston-God. In his opening speech, Craig sketches his moral argument. He claims that there are objective moral values and that such values cannot exist unless God exists. Unfortunately, philosophers mean many different things by 'objective' when they use that adjective to modify 'values', and it is not completely clear to me which of these meanings Craig has in mind. We can, however, circumvent this problem of interpretation by dividing Craig's general moral argument into two more specific arguments, each of which is based on one of Craig's two examples of 'objective' moral values: the 'specialness' of human beings and an 'absolute' right and wrong.

The argument from the 'specialness' of human beings runs as follows:

1   If God does not exist, then human beings are not special.
2   Human beings are special.
    Thus
3   God exists.

The argument from 'absolute' right and wrong runs:

1   If God does not exist, then there is no absolute right and wrong.
2   There is an absolute right and wrong.
    Thus
3   God exists.

In place of the question of what is meant by 'objective', we now have the question of what is meant by 'special' and 'absolute'. But the latter question is, at least for me, easier to answer than the former.

In the question and answer session, Flew responds to the first of these two specific arguments. He claims that human beings are special whether or not God exists: our rationality, for example, makes us special.[10] Craig replies:

> And as for rationality, that, of course, is a relative thing. Suppose there were extraterrestrials who came to earth who were as superior to us in intelligence as we are to animals such as cows and pigs, and they began to farm the earth and use us for labouring animals and began to eat human beings for food. What would we say to them to convince them that human beings are special, that we are of intrinsic value? Why should they treat us any differently than we treat horses and cows and pigs? On the atheistic view, I can't think of any reason. It seems to me that [on the atheistic view] to think humans are special is just specie-ism.[11]

This response is closely related to a passage written by J.P. Moreland that Craig quotes in his second rebuttal:

On an evolutionary secular scenario, ... human beings are nothing special ....
There is nothing intrinsically valuable about human beings in terms of having moral
non-natural properties .... The view that being human is special is guilty of specie-
ism – an unjustifiable bias toward one's own species.[12]

As Craig recognizes, Flew's appeal to rationality won't show that humans are special in the sense intended by Craig. First, not all humans are equally rational. So if rationality is what makes us special, then not all humans are equally special. Second, some human beings, because of brain damage or for other reasons, are less rational than some animals. So if rationality is what makes us special and no animal is special, then not all humans are special. And third (Craig's argument), some animals (like chimpanzees) are rational to some extent, though less rational than normal humans. So if this difference in rationality justifies us in, for example, capturing chimpanzees and performing scientific experiments on them, then an alien race that was more rational than us by the same amount would be justified in abducting us for use in scientific experiments. But, clearly, it would be wrong for such alien beings to treat us that way. Therefore, rationality can't be what makes us special.

Craig's reply to Flew's appeal to rationality, as well as the earlier quote from Moreland, makes it quite clear what Craig means when he says that human beings are special. He means that every human being has a special sort of inherent value that no animal has, and every human being has an equal amount of this value. Such equality is possible despite the great differences among humans, because the value in question does not supervene on any natural properties. It is a non-natural property that all (and only) humans possess. This is why our bias towards humans (for example, our willingness to do serious harm to animals for the sake of promoting relatively trivial human interests) is, according to Craig, a *justified* bias rather than specie-ism, by which Craig, following Moreland, means an *unjustifiable* bias towards members of one's own species.

My own view is that the second premise of Craig's first specific moral argument is false. Human beings are not special in Craig's sense. Our bias towards human beings is unjustified – it is not just bias, but *prejudice*. Animals have full moral standing in the sense that any moral duties we have that can sensibly apply to animals apply to them just as strongly as they apply to other humans. For example, since, unlike plants, some animals are conscious, it follows that some animals can be literally harmed – that is, harmed from their own internal point of view. Thus, our moral duty not to harm others applies just as strongly to them as it does to human beings. Human beings *are* special, but not in Craig's sense. Our natural properties make us special in the sense of being 'moral patients'. Any moral agent, human or not, has moral duties to humans because, unlike plants and rocks, humans (including humans that lack rationality) can be made better or worse off from their own internal point of view. But conscious animals are also special in this sense. Like very young children, they are not moral agents; lacking moral concepts, they have no moral duties themselves. But they are moral patients; moral agents have duties to them. And notice that conscious beings are special in this sense whether they are God's creatures or just the accidental by-products of a blind nature. Of course, one might ask about the status or source of these moral obligations to humans and animals. But that is a question about Craig's second specific moral argument, to which I will now turn.

In his first rebuttal, Craig explains what he means by 'absolute': 'in the absence of God, everything becomes socioculturally relative'.[13] So for Craig, the choice is between God and sociocultural relativism. Why a transcendent foundation for moral rightness and wrongness (or for the specialness of humans or for any other objective moral value) must be a Copleston-God rather than some other sort of supernatural being is never explained; so once again Craig's claim that each of his five reasons for believing in God is independent is open to question.

But even if we take this argument to be an argument not for God's existence, but just for supernaturalism, it still fails. I agree with Craig that some moral judgements (such as 'rape is wrong') are not relative to society or culture. What I don't understand is why Craig believes this position is coherent only if supernaturalism is true. He says very little about this in the debate. In fact, instead of responding to the most serious thinkers (both theistic and atheistic) who disagree with his position, he wastes his time quoting atheist thinkers who agree with him. Craig may win debating points this way, but he loses logical points. An appeal to an authority, even a qualified authority, is fallacious if there are many equally well-qualified authorities who deny the claim in question. Craig is well aware of the fact that many excellent philosophers (including the greatest Christian natural theologian of the twentieth century, Richard Swinburne) reject his claim that an absolute right and wrong requires God or any other sort of supernatural being. So finding atheists who agree with him on this point is evidentially worthless. In fact, it may even mislead the audience by making it appear as if the only way an atheist can challenge Craig's argument is by claiming that the wrongfulness of acts like rape is relative to society or culture. To make matters even worse, Craig goes so far as to say that the atheist must deny that rape is 'really wrong'.[14] But this wouldn't be true even if atheists were committed to sociocultural relativism. Craig doesn't seem to realize that some versions of relativism allow for the possibility that a society or culture can have mistaken views about morality, and thus allow for a distinction between something being believed to be wrong and its being really wrong.

Craig hints at something like an argument in his first rebuttal: 'There is no absolute right and wrong unless you have a transcendent vantage point to transcend sociocultural relativism.'[15] Apparently, Craig believes that God is needed to provide a transcendent vantage point, and a transcendent vantage point is needed to avoid sociocultural relativism. Swinburne would reject this argument because he believes that fundamental moral principles are necessary truths (analytic truths to be exact) and so are true whether or not God or any other supernatural being exists.[16] So in order for Craig's second specific moral argument to be convincing, he would need to show that neither the concepts of right and wrong themselves, nor those concepts combined with certain cross-cultural facts about human beings, place any substantive constraints on what moral judgements can be true or false – constraints that would apply to any society or culture. Also, he would need to deal with all those theories according to which moral standards can be derived from cross-cultural standards of rationality or from those standards combined with cross-cultural facts about human beings.[17] In short, the first premise of Craig's argument needs to be defended. It is far from obvious that a supernatural vantage point is needed to avoid sociocultural relativism. Even if there are no supernatural beings, morality, at least at its core, may still transcend the beliefs and values and other variable characteristics of any particular culture or society to which we belong.

Craig's Argument from Miracles

Craig's argument from miracles has two parts. The first part concludes that Jesus rose from the dead on the basis of certain alleged historical facts. The second part concludes that God exists on the basis of the alleged fact that Jesus rose from the dead. Although Craig does not spell out this second part, it is implicit in his claim that his five reasons for believing in God are independent of one another. Were it not for that claim, I would have been tempted to interpret Craig's argument from miracles not as an independent argument for God's existence, but rather as an argument for the conclusion that, if God exists, then the Christian God exists. On this interpretation, it would be the task of Craig's first three arguments to establish that a theistic God exists. This conclusion would then be used to show that the prior probability of the Resurrection is not negligibly low, thus making a historical case for the Resurrection seem less hopeless. Of course, even if Craig could successfully use this strategy to establish a Resurrection, there would still be more work to do, because there's a gap between the claim that a theistic God raised Jesus from the dead and the claim that Jesus is God incarnate.

But instead of wondering what Craig might be able to do with a Resurrection, let's first see whether or not he has one at his disposal. His argument for the conclusion that Jesus rose from the dead has the following structure.

1 After being buried, Jesus' tomb was empty.
2 Some people believed they saw Jesus (in the flesh) shortly after his death.
3 Jesus' disciples sincerely believed that Jesus rose from the dead.
4 The best available explanation of 1–3 is that Jesus rose from the dead.
   Thus
5 Jesus rose from the dead.

Now I must admit I have my doubts about premises 1–3, but I'm no historian, so let's assume for the sake of argument that Craig is right about them – let's assume they are very probably true. If this assumption is correct, then the success of the argument will depend on the truth of premise 4 and on the inference from 1–4 to 5. Since I'm short on space, I will limit my discussion to the latter.

Conclusion 5 is supposed to follow inductively from premises 1–4. The pattern of reasoning here is sometimes called 'inference to the best (available) explanation'. It is important to recognize, however, that not all such inferences are good inferences. There are many reasons why an hypothesis can be the best available explanation of a set of facts and yet still be improbable. For example, the hypothesis might start out with a very low probability. Or there might be several other available explanations of the facts that are nearly as good, or many that are not drastically worse. Or the most likely hypothesis might be that the true explanation is unavailable. Or there might not be enough facts to make any available explanation probable, including the best one. And so on.

The first point I want to make about Craig's inference is that what he likes to call his 'three great facts' are, in one respect, not so great, because they are not probabilistically or explanatorily independent of each other. Suppose, for example, the first fact obtains. The tomb was empty. This could easily cause sightings of Jesus, whether or not he rose from the dead. (I wonder how many more Elvis sightings there would be if his body was missing.) Furthermore, an empty tomb combined with sightings of Jesus could easily cause the disciples to believe quite sincerely that Jesus rose from the dead and so to become bold preachers of the Gospel willing to die for their beliefs – again, whether or not Jesus did in fact rise from the dead. Thus, the second and third facts don't add all that much to the first. Of course, one could object that the empty tomb can't by itself explain the details of the sightings in question (for example, the examining of wounds and so on). But Craig's argument isn't based on details – and for good reason. He emphasizes that his facts are accepted by a majority of scholars. Start adding details and this consensus would vanish quickly. No historical case can show that the Gospel writers never embellished their accounts with non-historical details.

Thus, since a missing body can explain both the sightings and the sincere belief, whatever the reason for its being missing, it follows that Craig has little more than a missing body upon which to base his case for the Resurrection. And surely that's far from enough. Just think of how many possible explanations there are for that! For example, perhaps the owner of the tomb changed his mind and decided not to bury Jesus there. Or perhaps the body was stolen by someone who hoped that touching even the dead body of Jesus could heal the sick. Or perhaps Jesus' enemies took his body, so that he would not have a dignified resting place. Do I believe that any of these possible explanations (or 47 others I could mention just off the top of my head) are true? No, of course not. Each is very improbable, because we just don't have enough evidence to make any of them probable – but this is also the case for the Resurrection explanation. This may be why Flew refuses to accept Craig's challenge to offer his own naturalistic theory of why the tomb was empty. Assuming the tomb was empty, how could he possibly know why? This is obviously a case in which there are too many possible explanations and too few facts to explain. None of the available explanations, not even the 'best' one (whichever one that is), is even close to being probable. Indeed, this is so even on the assumption that a God capable of raising Jesus from the dead exists.

Craig's Appeal to Religious Experience

Craig's final reason for believing in God is the immediate experience of God. According to Craig, people who have such experiences don't need arguments to know God exists. Craig emphasizes that this is not itself an argument. Thus, he is not claiming that the religious experiences of others can provide someone like me, who despite seeking God does not have such experiences, with evidence for God's existence. Instead, he claims that experiential evidence for God's existence is available to me because anyone who sincerely seeks God will immediately experience God.[18] This implies that I am at fault for not having Craig's fifth reason to believe. Although I have sought God, I have not *sincerely* sought God. Moreover, if my lack of sincerity constitutes or causes my irrevocably rejecting God, then, according to Craig, I am guilty of a sin of infinite gravity and proportion, which merits eternal punishment.[19] I will not respond to Craig's views about my spiritual state here.[20] Instead, I'd like to evaluate his position that experiences of God provide those who have them with direct evidence for God's existence.

In response to Flew's challenge to the veridicality of experiences of God, Craig asks rhetorically, '... in the absence of good arguments for atheism, why deny my experience?'.[21] This suggests that Craig accepts some version of the so-called 'principle of credulity'. According to this principle, perceptual experiences are epistemically innocent until proven guilty – in other words, in the absence of 'defeaters', what one seems to perceive is probably so. Although I have challenged this principle elsewhere,[22] here I will assume that it is true and focus instead on the issue of whether or not defeaters undermine Craig's appeal to religious experience.

It is important to realize that Craig is mistaken if he believes that the only possible sort of defeater for a sincere claim to perceive God is a good argument against the existence of God. Such an argument would be an 'overriding' defeater: an experience provides strong evidence for the truth of a perceptual claim, but there is equally strong or stronger evidence against the claim. A second type of defeater is 'undercutting'. For example, suppose I know that I suffer from what Alvin Plantinga has dubbed the 'dreaded dendrological disorder', which frequently causes its victims to seem to see trees when none is present, although it does not prevent them from seeing trees when they are there.[23] Because, when I seem to see a tree I don't know whether my visual experience is caused by a real tree or by the disorder, my knowledge that I suffer from the disorder is a defeater for the claim that a tree is present. But it is not an overriding defeater. It provides no evidence at all against the claim that a tree is present. Rather, it blocks the justification for this claim that would otherwise be conferred upon it by my perceptual experience – in fact, it does so even if I am, in this case, really seeing a tree.

I believe that Craig's appeal to religious experience faces an overriding defeater because a strong case can be made against God's existence. However, I also believe that a strong case can be made for God's existence, so this overriding defeater is offset by what I call a 'corroborating enhancer'. But this is a very long story I cannot tell here.[24] Instead, I would like to point out an undercutting defeater that has not, to my knowledge, been mentioned in the literature. Craig's claims are especially vulnerable to this defeater because he is an exclusivist Christian who appeals to experiences apparently of God that are specifically Christian in nature.[25] They are not just experiences of God – they are experiences of the Christian God. They occur in a specific religious context (for example, while reading the New Testament), and they cause their subjects to have specifically Christian beliefs.

To see why this creates a problem for Craig, let's modify the earlier example of the dendrological disorder. Instead of supposing that I *know* I suffer from the disorder, let's suppose that I do not suffer from it, but have good reason to believe I do. (Perhaps a blood test for the disorder that is very reliable comes back positive although, unbeknownst to me, it is a false positive.) Notice that the rest of the example remains the same. In these circumstances, I may be having a veridical visual experience of a tree and suffer from no cognitive disorder, and yet my believing that the tree exists is still not justified. This is because, relative to what I know, the probability of my having this experience given that a tree is really there isn't that much greater than the probability of my having it given that no tree is present. And this undercuts the justification that my sense experience would otherwise confer on my belief that a tree is present.

Now consider a different cognitive disorder or (more broadly) 'condition', which I will call 'senseless divinititus'. This condition makes its victims seem to experience revelatory acts of God even when no such acts are being performed. Craig cannot deny that many human beings suffer from this condition, for many non-Christians have experiences apparently of divine revelations, but these experiences are taken by their subjects to support religious beliefs that Craig, given his religious exclusivism, must reject as false. Thus, Craig must regard these non-Christian experiences as delusory – the product, perhaps, of wishful thinking or cultural conditioning. But the fact that these experiences are so common and so similar phenomenologically to Christian experiences, not to mention the fact that Christians themselves have experiences that support conflicting interpretations of Christian doctrine, gives Craig and other Christians good reason to believe that they, too, suffer from senseless divinititus. Given his belief that Muslims have delusory Muslim experiences, Jews have delusory Jewish experiences, and so on, Craig must admit that Christians would be fairly likely to have Christian experiences even on the assumption that Christianity is false. For example, he must admit that, given the culture in which he was raised and so on, he's fairly likely to sense God speaking to him when he reads the Gospels whether or not that really is the case.

This means that Christian experiences do not directly justify Christian beliefs. Just as the person who has good reason to believe he has the dreaded dendrological disorder should doubt his visual experiences of trees even if his visual faculties are in perfect working order, the Christian who has good reason to believe he has senseless divinititus should doubt his Christian experiences even if his *sensus divinitatus* is in perfect working order. A Christian theologian might describe this situation by claiming that one of the cognitive consequences of the Fall – an epidemic of senseless divinititus – makes immediately justified Christian belief impossible. Thus, even if the principle of credulity were true and there were no good arguments against God's existence, Craig's appeal to immediate experience would still fail. We may have a Christian *sensus divinitatus*, but its power to justify Christian belief is undermined by our susceptibility to senseless divinititus. Christians are likely to have Christian experiences, even on the assumption that Christianity is false.

Conclusion

William Lane Craig is an excellent philosopher. His work on the cosmological argument is a very important contribution to the philosophy of religion. But his project of using philosophical and historical argumentation to establish Christian theism, or even theism, or for that matter even the existence of a Copleston-God, is still a work in progress. The goal of completing this project, if that is possible, or even of making considerable progress, is of the greatest importance. Thus, I hope Craig continues to devote his time and considerable talent to its pursuit.[26]

Notes

1   See p. 19.
2   See p. 29.
3   Ibid.
4   See p. 30.
5   Ibid.
6   See p. 19.
7   Paul R. Draper, 'A Critique of the Kalam Cosmological Argument', in Louis P. Pojman (ed.), *Philosophy of Religion: An Anthology*, 4th edn (Belmont, CA: Wadsworth Publishing Company, 2003), pp. 42–47.
8   See p. 20.
9   See p. 30.
10 See p. 44.
11 See pp. 44–5.
12 See p. 35; citing J.P. Moreland and Kai Nielsen, *Does God Exist?* (Nashville, TN: Thomas Nelson, 1990), p. 112.
13 See p. 30.
14 See p. 22.
15 See p. 30.
16 Richard Swinburne, 'Duty and the Will of God', in Paul Helm (ed.), *Divine Commands and Morality*, (Oxford: Oxford University Press, 1981), pp. 120–34; also, idem, *The Existence of God* (Oxford: Clarendon Press, 1979), ch. 9.
17 For an interesting non-Kantian theory of this sort, see David Gauthier, *Morals by Agreement* (Oxford: Oxford University Press, 1987).
18 See pp. 23–4.
19 See p. 28.

20 I respond indirectly to those views in Paul R. Draper, 'Seeking But Not Believing: Confessions of a Practicing Agnostic', Daniel Howard-Snyder and Paul K. Moser (eds), *Divine Hiddeness: New Essays* (Cambridge: Cambridge University Press, 2002), pp. 197–214.

21 See p. 35.

22 Paul Draper, 'God and Perceptual Evidence', *International Journal for Philosophy of Religion*, 32 (1992) pp. 149–65.

23 I have modified Plantinga's original example. See Alvin Plantinga, 'Reason and Belief in God', in Alvin Plantinga and Nicholas Wolterstorff (eds), *Faith and Rationality: Reason and Belief in God* (Notre Dame, IN: University of Notre Dame Press, 1983), p. 83.

24 For more on the notion of a 'corroborating enhancer', see Draper, 'God and Perceptual Evidence', pp. 155–56. For more on what I take the evidence both for and against God's existence to be, see Section I of 'Seeking But Not Believing'.

25 See p. 39.

26 I am grateful to Kai Draper and Linda Draper for helpful comments.

Chapter 11

A Reply to Objections

William Lane Craig

Introduction

I am sure that I speak for both Professor Flew, as well as myself, in saying that it is an honour that so many of our eminent colleagues should have deemed it worth their while to subject our debate to such searching criticism. They have helped to advance the discussion far beyond the parameters permitted by a live debate, and I am grateful for the opportunity to expand a little further on what was said that evening in Madison.

In the original Copleston–Russell debate, Russell got away with sitting back, folding his arms, and playing the sceptic, thereby giving the impression that Copleston alone had to bear the burden of proof. I was determined that Flew should not escape so easily. The subject under debate did not take the propositional form 'Resolved: God exists' but rather took the form of a question 'Does God Exist?'. If Flew was prepared to answer negatively, as opposed to confessing, 'I don't know', he had to justify his answer.

In order to underline the fact that we did not face differential burdens of proof in the debate, I distinguished two questions that needed to be answered:

1 Are there good reasons to think that God exists?
2 Are there good reasons to think that God does not exist?

Failure on Flew's part to provide good reasons in response to question 2 leaves us at best with agnosticism, even if my arguments for theism completely fail.[1] How well, then, did Flew bear his burden of proof?

Reasons to Think that God does not Exist

Flew initially tries to play the mere sceptic's role in the debate, but it is evident that he does in fact offer three arguments for God's non-existence, namely:

1 the alleged incompatibility of omnipotence and evil;
2 the alleged incompatibility of God's love and justice with hell; and
3 the alleged impossibility of a bodiless person.

Also evident, I think, is how surprisingly weak those arguments are, for the reasons I explain in the debate. The question now becomes, have any of our respondents succeeded in advancing significantly better reasons for atheism? They have not. Even Michael Martin, as robust an atheist on the contemporary scene as one might find, declines to engage at this point. William Rowe, decrying Flew's purely defensive posture, alludes to the problem of apparently pointless suffering and to the alleged difficulty of certain great-making properties' having intrinsic maxima, but, since he fails to develop these assertions into arguments, we may leave it to the reader to consult the abundant literature in defence of the theistic position on these issues.[2] Rowe rightly chastises me for my saying that I had 'argued', rather than 'asserted' or 'contended', that there are no good reasons for atheism; such infelicities attend extemporaneous speaking. But the fact remains that, by refusing to accept what Martin calls 'Craig's gambit' – providing some warrant for the claim that God does not exist – Flew, as Rowe complains, does 'virtually concede the debate',[3] and our atheist respondents have done nothing to shore up his faltering end of the argument.

Reasons to Believe that God Exists

Have I, then, done any better in bearing my share of the burden of proof? Anticipating that Flew might try to raise the bar unreasonably high by demanding that I prove the existence of a being possessing all of God's great-making properties, I deliberately adopted the more modest conception of God which governed the original Russell–Copleston debate: 'a supreme personal being distinct from the world and the creator of the world'.[4] I also noted that my arguments are independent of one another – that is, the soundness of any one argument does not depend on the soundness of any other, and together give us a strikingly full concept of God. I have to smile when non-theists respond to such theistic arguments by complaining that they do not prove enough. It would be a strange form of atheism, indeed, which allows that there exists an immaterial, timeless, changeless, spaceless, beginningless, uncaused, unbelievably powerful, incomprehensibly intelligent, morally and paradigmatically perfect creator and designer of the universe, who has revealed Himself in the person of Jesus Christ and who can be immediately experienced today! If non-theists really thought that such a being existed, they would be wide-eyed and open-mouthed with astonishment. Rather than raise cavils about the failure to prove this being to be, say, omnipotent or omniscient, we ought rather to seek to find out whether this being has specially revealed Himself further so that we might discover answers to our remaining questions.

The Cosmological Argument

I open with a version of the cosmological argument based on the impossibility of an infinite temporal regress of events which I have styled the *kalam* cosmological argument. This is not the most popular version of the cosmological argument, and some of our respondents endorse formulations of the more widely accepted version from contingency developed by Leibniz:[5]

What is perhaps most interesting about these various versions of the cosmological argument is the necessity of the explanatory ultimate attained in the argument's conclusion. The God demonstrated by the Leibnizian formulation is broadly logically necessary in His existence – that is, He exists in every possible world. By contrast, in Yandell's formulation of the argument, like Swinburne's,[6] God is not broadly logically necessary in His existence: there are possible worlds in which He does not exist. For Yandell, God is such that it is logically impossible that His existence be explained, but it is not broadly logically necessary that God exists. Finally, in the *kalam* argument, God is shown to be necessary only in the weak sense that He is eternal and uncaused, but the question is left open whether He exists in all possible worlds and whether it is broadly logically possible that His existence be explained.

Now one riposte to the Leibnizian formulation would be to assert that the universe itself is a broadly logically necessary entity which exists by a necessity of its own nature. Similarly, one might respond to Yandell that it is logically impossible that the universe or physical stuff should have an explanation. One of the ways in which one could respond to this challenge is by using the *kalam* cosmological argument. For, by showing that the universe began to exist, the argument reveals that its existence is not necessary and uncaused. The universe's existence could be necessary only by being necessarily caused by a higher being, which explains its existence, contrary to the hypothesis; and it could be uncaused only if it is not necessary in its existence, since it does not exist eternally but sprang into being a finite time ago, thereby revealing that its existing is contingent, contrary to the hypothesis. Thus, by demonstrating that the universe began to exist, the *kalam* argument powerfully supplements contingency arguments for God's existence.

Whatever begins to exist has a cause This first premise of the argument certainly seems to be more plausibly true than its contradictory. It is supported by the metaphysical intuition that things do not pop into being out of nothing and by our unfailing experience of the physical world. Martin rejects my appeal to metaphysical intuition because intuitions are 'unreliable'. But he says nothing against this particular intuition, and since metaphysical intuitions are indispensable, we have no recourse but to accept those which press themselves upon us and for which we have no defeaters. Moreover, this intuition is, *pace* Martin, constantly confirmed empirically.[7]

In fact, a more modest premise will serve us just as well: *if the universe began to exist, then the universe has a cause of its existence*. It seems inconceivable that the space-time universe could have come into being without a cause, for in that case there was not even the potentiality of the universe's existence prior to the beginning (since there was no 'prior'). But how could the universe become actual if there was not even the potentiality of its existence? It seems more plausible to hold that its potentiality lay in the power of its cause to create it.

Martin argues that the beginning of the universe cannot have a cause, since causes temporally precede their effects and no time existed prior to the universe's beginning. There are various ways of countering this objection;[8] my preferred position is to say that God's action of causing the universe to begin is simultaneous with the universe's beginning to exist. God is therefore temporal since the moment of creation even if, *sans* creation, God exists atemporally.[9]

Martin seems to suggest that if God's existence could be a brute fact, then the universe's existence could be a brute fact. But this response to the cosmological argument is plausible only in the case that the universe is eternal. There is an obvious and significant disanalogy in something's existing eternally without a cause and something's coming into being without a cause. Only in the second case do we get something from nothing. The possibility of an eternal, uncaused being provides absolutely no warrant for thinking that beings can come into existence uncaused from nothing.

The universe began to exist   This second, more controversial premise is supported both by a deductive, philosophical argument and an inductive, scientific argument.

The deductive argument is based on the impossibility of the existence of an actually infinite number of things. My claim here is that, although infinite set theory and transfinite arithmetic each constitute a logically consistent universe of discourse, given their axioms and conventions, the instantiation of an actual infinite in the real world leads to intolerable absurdities. For example, the subtraction of infinite quantities leads to contradictory results.

David Yandell raises three objections to this argument.

1   *It implies that we have no coherent idea of infinity.* It is far from evident that we do have, in one sense, a coherent notion of the actual infinite. We may, with Cantor, define a collection as actually infinite if, and only if, a proper subset of the collection has the same cardinal number of members as the entire collection. But as is well-known, naive infinite set theory is plagued with paradoxes,[10] and the standard way of dealing with these is through axiomatization, which eschews providing any definition of an infinite set. I am quite happy to grant the coherence and consistency of infinite set theory and transfinite arithmetic, while denying that the actual infinite can exist in reality. In order to maintain consistency, transfinite arithmetic simply prohibits performing inverse operations, such as subtraction, with transfinite numbers. But while we may slap the hand of the mathematician who tries to subtract transfinite cardinal numbers, we cannot prevent, for example, an arbitrary number of guests from checking out of Hilbert's infamous, actually infinite hotel.[11] In any case, should the intuitionists turn out to be right, I shall not weep for infinite set theory. But my argument does not require so strong a thesis as that mathematical theories of the infinite are incoherent. It is the real existence of the actual infinite which I reject.
2   *God's existence entails the existence of an actual infinite.* I deny that the divine attributes entail the existence of an actual infinite. In general, God's infinity is a qualitative, not a quantitative, notion. It has nothing to do with an infinite number of definite and discrete finite particulars. Attributes such as omnipotence, moral perfection, timelessness, aseity, omnipresence and so on just are not quantitative notions.[12] Even omniscience need not entail

that God has an actually infinite number of true beliefs if, with William Alston and in line with Christian tradition, we take God's knowledge to be non-propositional in nature, though represented by us finite cognizers as knowledge of individual propositions.[13]

3 *The subtraction of infinite quantities is not contradictory.* It is true that every time one subtracts all the even numbers from the set of natural numbers, one gets all the odd numbers, which are infinite in quantity. But that is not where the contradiction is alleged to lie. Rather the contradiction lies in the fact that one can subtract equal quantities from equal quantities and arrive at different answers. For example, if we subtract all the even numbers from all the natural numbers, we get an infinity of numbers, and if we subtract all the numbers greater than three from all the natural numbers, we get only four numbers. Yet, in both cases, we subtracted an *identical number* of numbers from an *identical number* of numbers and yet did not arrive at an identical result. In fact, one can subtract equal quantities from equal quantities and get any quantity between zero and infinity left over. For this reason, subtraction and division are simply prohibited with transfinite numbers – an arbitrary stipulation which has no probative ontological force.

This is but one of the many absurdities which would attend the real existence of the actual infinite and which lead me to embrace the Aristotelian tradition that only the potential infinite exists in reality.[14] Keith Yandell in his Introduction asserts that Aristotle's distinction is vacuous, since there is no potential for an actually infinite series, if such a series is impossible. But Aristotle himself made quite clear that, in speaking of the potential infinite, he was not making the customary distinction between potency and actuality which figures so largely in his metaphysics;[15] rather a potential infinite is a collection which is, at any time, finite but which, over time, increases toward infinity as a limit. Such a limited concept of infinity finds no place in set theory, but plays a central role in the calculus. In his response Yandell seems to recognize this, but then wrongly infers that the potential infinite is therefore a 'red herring'. Not at all; all that follows is that the name is misleading.

Yandell also seems to think that the existence of abstract objects provides a decisive counterexample to the claim that an actual infinite cannot exist. Geivett would avert this objection by limiting the scope of the claim to the spatio-temporal realm.[16] But I see no reason to accept Yandell's counterexample in the first place. First, the counterexample presupposes that the intuitionists are wrong in allowing only potential infinites to exist; but we have seen Yandell's argument against the potential infinite to be a *non sequitur*. Second, and more important, the counterexample begs the question by assuming Platonism or realism to be true. Realism is a necessary condition of abstracta's constituting a bona fide counterexample to our claim. But why make this assumption? In order to defeat Yandell's putative counterexample, all the defender of the *kalam* argument has to do is deny that Platonism has been shown to be true. In other words, the burden of proof rests on Yandell to prove that realism is true before his counterexample can even be launched. A conceptualist understanding of abstract objects combined with the simplicity of God's cognition is at least a tenable alternative to Platonism. Indeed, historically, this has been the mainstream theistic tradition, from Boethius through Ockham. In fact, theists had better hope that there *is* such an alternative to Platonism, since the latter entails a metaphysical pluralism which leaves God as but one infinitesimal being among an unimaginable plenitude of beings existing independently of Him, in contradiction to divine aseity and the doctrine of *creatio ex nihilo*.

The inductive evidence for the beginning of the universe is drawn from contemporary cosmology. Here I need to correct a mistake on Keith Yandell's part. He rightly claims that physics cannot explain how there can come to be any physical stuff at all. But he errs in inferring that one cannot therefore 'claim to have found evidence in Big Bang physics for "the beginning of the universe"'.[17] The beginning predicted by the standard model involves an initial cosmological singularity which constitutes an edge or boundary to physical space and time themselves. Physicists John Barrow and Frank Tipler emphasize, 'At this singularity, space and time came into existence; literally nothing existed before the singularity, so, if the Universe originated at such a singularity, we would truly have a creation *ex nihilo*.'[18] The standard model does not – indeed, cannot – explain *why* the Big Bang occurred, but it can predict *that* it occurred. So the question reduces to whether we have good evidence for this prediction of the standard model. The Hawking–Penrose singularity theorems governing objects in gravitational self-collapse render such an initial cosmological singularity inevitable so long as the equations of classical General Relativity apply. Some theorists have hoped to avert the initial singularity by the introduction of a quantum theory of gravitation. But even on quantum gravitational cosmological models, such as the Hartle–Hawking model, while the singular beginning point is smoothed away, the prediction of a finite past and an absolute beginning of the universe remains unaltered, so that, in Hawking's words, the universe 'would quite literally be created out of nothing'.[19] Thus, Barrow comments, 'This type of quantum universe has not always existed; it comes into being, just as the classical cosmologies could, but it does not start at a Big Bang where physical quantities are infinite ....'[20]

Moreover, the thermodynamic properties of the universe point to the absolute beginning predicted by the Big Bang theory, for if the universe were infinitely old it becomes inexplicable why the universe does not exist in an equilibrium state or 'heat death' (compare Yandell's own story about Azads and Bezubs).[21] Indeed, Roger Penrose has argued that it is a mistake to try to avert the initial cosmological singularity of classical cosmology, since it provides the best hope of explaining the otherwise inexplicable low-entropy state of the early universe and the Second Law of Thermo-dynamics.[22]

Now, of course, as Paul Draper reminds us, there remain other live options than the standard model. But that does nothing to show that the standard model is not the best explanation of the evidence or that the evidence fails to render the second premise of the *kalam* argument more plausible than its contradictory. The devil is in the details, and, once we get down to specifics, we find that there is no mathematically consistent model which has been as successful in its predictions or as corroborated by the evidence as the standard Big Bang model.[23] Models which seek to avert the prediction of the standard model of an absolute beginning of the universe have repeatedly been shown either to be untenable or else to imply the very beginning of the universe which their proponents sought to avoid. So, we must ask, what is Draper talking about when he says that 'the universe might very well be one small part of a larger system (the real universe) that is not expanding and that is infinitely old'?[24] What model does he mean to endorse? Does he think that vacuum fluctuation models, proposed in the 1970s, according to which our observable universe is one of myriads formed via fluctuations of the energy in the quantum vacuum of a wider universe, is better supported by the evidence than the standard model? How, then, will he deal with what quantum cosmologist Christopher Isham has called the 'fairly lethal' problem that, on such models, there is a non-zero probability at any point in the quantum vacuum of a fluctuation's occurring and spawning a universe, so that if the wider universe were infinitely old, there would, by now, have been universes formed at every point in the quantum vacuum, with the result that they would all by now have coalesced into one infinitely old universe – which contradicts observation?[25] Why is it that, according to Isham, these models were therefore 'jettisoned twenty years ago' and 'nothing much' has been done with them since? Or does Draper perhaps mean to endorse eternal inflationary models, such as Linde's chaotic inflationary model, according to which our observable universe is but one domain in an infinite series of inflating domains, each begotten by and begetting further domains in a wider universe? How, then, will he answer Borde and Vilenkin, who in 1994 demonstrated that any future-eternal inflationary model must possess an initial cosmological singularity, thereby forcing one to address the metaphysical question of what, if anything, came before?[26] How is it that Linde himself, confronted with these results, now concedes that there must have been Big Bang singularity at some point in the past?[27] In the absence of some theory of how the universe could be eternal on the evidence we have, Draper's speculations are empty.

Therefore, the universe has a cause From the two premises, the conclusion deductively follows. I then flesh out, via a conceptual analysis, some of the properties of the first cause. Draper challenges my argument for the personhood of the first cause, appealing to quantum indeterminacy as grounds for postulating 'a timeless, non-personal, non-sufficient cause'.[28] The objection presupposes, without justification, that quantum indeterminacy is ontic rather than epistemic, which I, along with a considerable number of philosophers of science, find highly dubious.[29] But let that pass. Draper's claim cannot be that the origin of the universe is literally due to quantum effects, for we have seen that the cause of the universe must transcend physical space and time and therefore cannot be any entity describable by physics. But, then, what is Draper talking about? The only entities we know of which are immaterial and can be conceived to exist timelessly and spacelessly are minds and abstract objects. But the latter do not stand in causal relations. Therefore, the cause of the universe is of the order of mind. Draper may find this hard to swallow, but he shows no incoherence in the notion of a timeless person, and a number of studies have, to my mind at least, convincingly demonstrated its coherence.[30]

I appeal to agent causation to explain the origin of the universe. I agree with Rowe that we do not want to say that, in agent causation, the agent causes his causing of some effect. Partisans of agent causation typically say that the agent's causing some effect is not an event requiring a cause, either because it is not itself an event, but just a way of describing an agent's causing an event; or, if it is an event, then it is not further caused.[31] I do not think that either alternative requires revision of my first premise, which concerns not events, but substances which come into being.

Both David Yandell and Michael Martin raise objections concerning the coherence of the creation of a temporal universe by a timeless free agent. Since this issue did not arise in the debate proper, our respondents may have missed the statement of my position in the question and answer session that God is timeless *sans* creation and temporal since the moment of creation.[32] Indeed, I should say that the act of creating the universe, as opposed to the timeless intention to create a universe with a beginning, is what temporalizes God. Such a model removes the teeth from Yandell's and Martin's objections to unqualified divine timelessness. It does, of course, raise a host of further perplexities, which I have sought to address in my most recent work.[33]

Martin also complains that the argument does not exclude the possibility that a plurality of gods created the universe. But, in the absence of any evidence in its favour, Ockham's razor shaves away this hypothesis, since we should not multiply causes beyond necessity. As for the moral qualities of the personal creator, I agree that, for all the cosmological argument tells us, He might be an absolute stinker; that question lies beyond the scope of the argument.

Finally, let me say a word about David Yandell's query concerning the necessity of God's being. I hold that God's existence is broadly logically necessary, although, as mentioned, the *kalam* cosmological argument does not itself attain such heights. Yandell disputes the idea that God's existence is logically necessary because 'God exists contingently' and 'God does not exist' are not contradictions. I was surprised to find both David and Keith operating with a concept of necessity so out of step with contemporary philosophizing on the nature of necessity.[34] In asserting the necessity of statements such as 'God exists' or 'An actual infinite does not exist', one is not talking about strict logical necessity or claiming that their negations are, or imply, contradictions; rather, one is speaking in terms of broad logical possibility/necessity – terms in which possible worlds semantics are framed. Broad logical modality is usually identified with metaphysical modality, so that if something is broadly logically possible then it is capable of being actualized or realized. A metaphysical impossibility may not involve a logical contradiction. Nor can one conclude from the absence of strict logical inconsistency that some notion is metaphysically possible. This is important not only for God's existence, but also for my claim that an actual infinite cannot exist, for that claim is to be understood in terms of actualizability or metaphysical possibility, not strict logical possibility.[35] At least that is how I understand, and am using, the modal locutions involved in my arguments.

The Teleological Argument

Since Flew did not address my teleological argument in the debate proper, one of the advantages of the present exchange is that it gives us the opportunity to explore further this important argument.

The fine-tuning of the initial conditions of the universe is due to either law, chance or design When one speaks of 'fine-tuning', the notion of intelligent choice must not be imported into the expression's meaning, lest one beg the question. Rather, one means that there is a remarkably narrow, interconnected range of values which various fundamental constants and quantities must take if the universe is to permit the existence of intelligent, carbon-based life. That the universe is, in this sense, fine-tuned seems to me undeniable, and none of our respondents disputes this fact. Neither do any suggest another alternative to law, chance or design as the best explanation of this fine-tuning.

It is not due to either law or chance As becomes evident in my development of this premise in my first rebuttal, I am relying on William Dembski's analysis of design inferences in terms of specified complexity in order to eliminate law and chance and thereby infer design as the best explanation of the cosmic fine-tuning – an approach which subverts many of the objections to the teleological argument raised by Parsons and Draper.[36] An application of Dembski's Generic Chance Elimination Argument to cosmic fine-tuning yields the following procedure:

1 One discovers that certain physical constants and quantities given in the Big Bang possess certain values.
2 Examining the circumstances of the Big Bang, one finds that there is no theory which would render physically necessary the values of all the constants and quantities, so they must be attributed to sheer accident.
3 One discovers that the values of the constants and quantities are incomprehensibly fine-tuned for the existence of intelligent, carbon-based life.
4 The probability of each value and of all the values together occurring by chance is vanishingly small.
5 There is only one universe; it is illicit in the absence of evidence to multiply one's probabilistic resources (that is, postulate a world ensemble of universes) simply to avert the design inference.
6 Given that the universe has occurred only once, the probability of the constants and quantities all having the values they do remains vanishingly small.
7 This probability is well within the bounds needed to eliminate chance.
8 One has physical information concerning the necessary conditions for the existence of intelligent, carbon-based life.

9   This information about the finely-tuned conditions necessary for a life-permitting universe is independent of the pattern discovered in step (3).
10 One is therefore warranted in inferring that the physical constants and quantities given in the Big Bang are the result of design.

Step 2 of the argument aims to eliminate the hypothesis of law (physical necessity), and steps 3–9 are intended to eliminate the hypothesis of chance. Although Parsons holds out hope for a Theory of Everything (TOE) that would show a life-permitting universe like ours to be physically necessary, his own references in his endnote 20 betray him. If this alternative is to be more than an 'atheism of the gaps', appealing to ignorance in hopes that some unknown naturalistic possibility might be found to explain the data, then there must be evidence for this alternative, but, as Davies states, there is 'absolutely no evidence' that the values of the constants and quantities are physically necessary. Like a bump in the carpet, fine-tuning stubbornly resists being smoothed away: suppressed at one point, it always pops up at another. For example, attempts to eliminate fine-tuning of the density parameter Ω_0 and the Hubble constant H_0 by appeal to so-called inflationary models of the early universe only suppressed fine-tuning at this point to have it pop up again at another – namely, the fine-tuning of the cosmological constant Λ. Similarly, in the most promising candidate for a TOE to date, super-string theory or M-Theory, the success of the theory depends crucially on the precise number of space-time dimensions, which remains unexplained by anything in the theory. There is no reason to think that a successful TOE would succeed in explaining everything or eliminating fine-tuning.

In the end, Parsons is willing just to bite the bullet and accept the finely-tuned initial conditions of the universe as inexplicable or brute facts. The plausibility of that alternative depends on whether they exhibit that specified complexity indicative of design.

On Dembski's analysis, the hallmarks of design are high improbability plus an independently given pattern, resulting in specified complexity. As my illustrations of the archaeologists and SETI investigators intend to show, we use this procedure of inferring design all the time. In the face of Dembski's analysis, Draper's generalizations about our ignorance of the designer's goals are simply irrelevant.

Parsons challenges the claim of step 4 that a life-permitting universe is improbable. While I regard the articulation of the relevant notion of probability a fascinating and valuable project, I do want to say at the outset that one does not need to have a philosophical analysis of probabilistic notions in order to recognize that something cries out for explanation and should not be taken merely as a brute fact. That said, let me lay out the way in which we should understand the claim that life-permitting universes are highly improbable. John Barrow provides the following illustration which makes quite clear the sense in which our life-permitting universe is improbable.[37] Take a sheet of paper and place upon it a red dot. That dot represents our universe. Now alter slightly one or more of the finely-tuned constants and physical quantities which have been the focus of our attention. (In order to avoid problems arising from the nature of the continuum, we simply stipulate some appropriately fine-grained standard of deviation, so that only a finite number of universes are designatable within a finite area.) As a result we have a description of another universe, which we may represent as a new dot in the proximity of the first. If that new set of constants and quantities describes a life-permitting universe, make it a red dot; if it describes a universe which is life-prohibiting, make it a blue dot. Now repeat the procedure arbitrarily many times until the sheet is filled with dots. What one winds up with is a sea of blue with only a few pinpoints of red. That is the sense in which it is overwhelmingly improbable that the universe should be life-permitting. There are simply vastly more life-prohibiting universes in our local area of possible universes than there are life-permitting universes.

It might be objected that we do not know if all these possible universes are equally probable. This objection might be understood as the claim that, since we really do not know how much certain constants and quantities could have varied from their actual values, the range of possible values for a certain constant or quantity may be very narrow. But this admitted uncertainty becomes less important when the number of variables to be fine-tuned is high. For example, the chances of all 50 known variables being fine-tuned, even if each variable has a 50 per cent chance of being its actual value, is less than 3 out of 10^{17}. Moreover, in the absence of any physical reason to think that the values are constrained, we are justified in assuming a principle of indifference to the effect that the probability of our universe's existing will be the same as the probability of any other universe's existing, which is represented on our sheet.[38]

But why should we consider only universes represented on the sheet? Perhaps universes are possible which have wholly different physical variables and natural laws and are life-permitting. Perhaps these would contain forms of life vastly different from life as we know it. The teleologist need not deny the possibility, for such worlds are irrelevant to the argument. All one needs to show is that our universe is highly improbable within the local group of possible universes. John Leslie gives the illustration of a fly resting on a large, blank area of the wall.[39] A shot is fired, and the bullet strikes the fly. Now even if the rest of the wall outside the blank area is covered with flies, such that a randomly fired bullet would probably hit one, nevertheless it remains highly improbable that a single, randomly fired bullet would strike the solitary fly within the large, blank area. In the same way, we need only concern ourselves with the universes represented on our sheet in order to determine the conditional probability of the universe's being fine-tuned for intelligent, carbon-based life.

Parsons also disputes step 5 of the argument, appealing to Linde's inflationary cosmology and Smolin's evolutionary cosmology to justify the postulation of a world ensemble, thereby multiplying one's probabilistic resources. (There is a certain appearance of inconsistency in Parson's argument here, for many of his own objections against probability assessments of fine-tuning relative to possible universes seem to return to haunt the claim that, relative to a world ensemble, it is highly probable that the fine-tuned cosmic conditions are somewhere actualized.) But there are very substantial reasons for scepticism concerning this manoeuvre on the naturalist's part.

In the first place, it needs to be recognized that the world ensemble hypothesis is no more scientific, and no less metaphysical, than the hypothesis of a cosmic designer. As the scientist–theologian John Polkinghorne says, 'People try to trick out a "many universe" account in sort of pseudo-scientific terms, but that is pseudo-science. It is a metaphysical guess that there might be many universes with different laws and circumstances.'[40] But as a metaphysical hypothesis, the world ensemble hypothesis is arguably inferior to the design hypothesis because the design hypothesis is simpler. According to Ockham's razor, we should not multiply causes beyond what is necessary to explain the effect. But it is simpler to postulate one cosmic designer to explain our universe than to postulate the infinitely bloated and contrived ontology of the many worlds hypothesis. Only if the world ensemble theorist could show that there exists a single, comparably simple mechanism for generating a world ensemble of randomly varied universes would he be able to elude this difficulty. But, as we shall see, no one has been able to identify such a mechanism.

Second, there is no known way for generating a world ensemble. No one has been able to explain how or why such a collection of universes should exist. Parsons alludes to Lee Smolin's speculation that if we suppose that black holes spawn other universes beyond our own, then universes which produce large numbers of black holes would have a selective advantage in producing offspring, so that a sort of cosmic evolution would take place. If each new universe is not an exact reproduction of its parent universe but varies in its fundamental constants and quantities, then universes which are proficient in producing black holes would have a selective advantage over those which are less proficient. Thus, in the course of cosmic evolution, universes whose fundamental parameters are fine-tuned to the production of black holes would proliferate. Since black holes are the residue of collapsed stars, cosmic evolution has the unintended effect of producing more and more stars and hence, more and more planets where life might form. Eventually observers would appear who marvel at the fine-tuning of the universe for their existence. The fatal flaw in Smolin's scenario, wholly apart from its ad hoc and even disconfirmed conjectures, was his assumption that universes fine-tuned for black hole production would also be fine-tuned for the production of stable stars.[41] In fact, the opposite is true: the most proficient producers of black holes would be universes which generate them prior to star formation, so that life-permitting universes would actually be weeded out by Smolin's cosmic evolutionary scenario.

Other suggested mechanisms for generating a world ensemble turn out to require fine-tuning themselves. For example, although some cosmologists appeal to inflationary theories of the universe to generate a world ensemble, we have mentioned that inflation itself requires fine-tuning. The total cosmological constant Λ_{tot} is usually taken to be zero, but this requires that the energy density of the true vacuum be tuned to zero *by hand*; there is no understanding of why this value should be so low. Worse, inflation requires that Λ_{tot} was once quite large, though zero today; this assumption is without any physical justification. Moreover, in order to proceed appropriately, inflation requires that the two components of Λ_{tot} cancel each other out with an enormously precise, though inexplicable, accuracy. A change in the strengths of either the gravitational constant or the weak force by as little as one part in 10^{100} would destroy this cancellation on which our lives depend. In these and other respects, inflationary scenarios actually require, rather than eliminate, fine-tuning.

Third, there is no evidence for the existence of a world ensemble *apart from the fine-tuning itself*. But the fine-tuning is equally evidence for a cosmic designer. Indeed, the hypothesis of a cosmic designer is, again, the better explanation because we have independent evidence of the existence of such a designer in the form of the other arguments for the existence of God.

Fourth, the world ensemble hypothesis faces a severe challenge from biological evolutionary theory.[42] First, a bit of background: the nineteenth-century physicist Ludwig Boltzmann proposed a sort of world ensemble hypothesis in order to explain why we do not find the universe in a state of 'heat death' or thermodynamic equilibrium.[43] Boltzmann hypothesized that the universe as a whole *does*, in fact, exist in an equilibrium state, but that, over time, fluctuations in the energy level occur here and there throughout the universe, so that by chance alone there will be isolated regions where disequilibrium exists. Boltzmann referred to these isolated regions as 'worlds'. We should not be surprised to see our world in a highly improbable disequilibrium state, he maintained, since in the ensemble of all worlds there must exist, by chance alone, certain worlds in disequilibrium, and ours just happens to be one of these. The problem with Boltzmann's daring world ensemble hypothesis is that, if our world were merely a fluctuation in a sea of diffuse energy, then it is overwhelmingly more probable that we should be observing a much tinier region of disequilibrium than we do. In order for us to exist, a smaller fluctuation – even one that produced our world instantaneously by an enormous áccident – is inestimably more probable than a progressive decline in entropy to fashion the world we see. In fact, Boltzmann's hypothesis, if adopted, would force us to regard the past as illusory – everything having the mere appearance of age, and the stars and planets as illusory, mere 'pictures' as it were – since that sort of world is vastly more probable, given a state of overall equilibrium, than a world with genuine, temporally and spatially distant events. As a result, Boltzmann's world ensemble hypothesis has been universally rejected by the scientific community, and the present disequilibrium is usually taken to be just a result of the initial low-entropy condition mysteriously obtaining at the beginning of the universe.

Now a precisely parallel problem attends the world ensemble hypothesis as an explanation of fine-tuning. According to the prevailing theory of biological evolution, intelligent life like ourselves, if it evolves at all, will do so as late in the lifetime of the sun as possible. The less the timespan available for the mechanisms of genetic mutation and natural selection to function, the lower the probability of intelligent life's evolving. Given the complexity of the human organism, it is overwhelmingly more probable that human beings will evolve late in the lifetime of the sun rather than early. In fact, Barrow and Tipler list ten steps in the evolution of *Homo sapiens*, each of which is so improbable that, before it would occur, the sun would have ceased to be a main-sequence star and incinerated the earth![44] Hence, if our universe is but one member of a world ensemble, then it is overwhelmingly more probable that we should be observing a very old sun rather than a relatively young one. If we are products of biological evolution, we should find ourselves in a world in which we evolve much later in the lifetime of our star. (This is the analogue to its being overwhelmingly more probable that we should exist in a smaller region of disequilibrium on the Boltzmann hypothesis.) In fact, adopting the world ensemble hypothesis to explain away fine-tuning also results in a strange sort of illusionism: it is far more probable that all our astronomical, geological and biological estimates of age are wrong, that we really do exist very late in the lifetime of the sun and that the sun and the earth's appearance of youth is a massive illusion. (This is the analogue of its being far more probable that all the evidence of the old age of our universe is illusory on the Boltzmann hypothesis.) Thus, the world ensemble hypothesis is no more successful in explaining cosmic fine-tuning than it was in explaining cosmic disequilibrium.

Therefore, it is due to design Parsons tries to attack the adequacy of the conclusion, with a view towards making the alternatives more palatable. But, as already explained, it is no indictment of the teleological argument that the moral qualities of the cosmic designer are left out of account. Any non-transcendent, physical beings such as super-intelligent aliens will depend on cosmic fine-tuning for their very existence. And *modus operandi* objections are relevant only to scientific explanations, not to personal explanations involving agents and their basic actions.

The teleological argument thus gives us a personal, intelligent designer of the cosmos. And as Geivett reminds us, the resistance of the origin of life and the evolution of biological complexity to naturalistic explanations only adds weight to the argument from fine-tuning.

The Moral Argument

My statement of the moral argument seemed to provoke the most heated reactions from our respondents, some claiming that it is based on mere authority or assertion. When one reads, however, my cumulative remarks on this count in my opening speech, third speech, closing statement and question and answer session, this allegation is belied.

If God does not exist, objective moral values do not exist Stated simply for a popular audience, premise 1 should actually be understood to express a counterfactual proposition having an impossible antecedent. I take it that, contrary to Stalnaker–Lewis semantics, but in line with customary usage, there are such counterfactuals which are non-trivially true, and this is one of them.[45]

Rowe dismisses this premise as 'absurd', and Keith Yandell concurs with

Swinburne that moral truths, being necessarily true, cannot depend on God for the explanation of their truth. But when we recall that, for both Swinburne and Yandell, the proposition *God exists* is not true in every possible world, whereas *Objective moral values exist* is, then it is obvious why they cannot countenance moral values being grounded in God. But the mainstream Christian tradition has held that God's existence is broadly logically necessary, so that He can be the explanatory basis of necessary truths. Such truths, being explained not by God's will but by His nature, could not have been false but are nonetheless not explanatorily ultimate. The key presupposition of Swinburne and Yandell is that necessary truths cannot stand in relations of explanatory priority to one another. That assumption strikes me, not merely as not evidently true, but as plainly false.[46] For example, the proposition *A plurality of persons exists* is necessarily true (in a broadly logical sense) because *God exists* is necessarily true and God is essentially a Trinity. Or again, *States of consciousness exist* is necessarily true for the same reason. To give a non-theological example, *Addition is possible* is necessarily true because *Numbers exist* is necessarily true and numbers have certain essential properties. Or again, *No event precedes itself* is necessarily true because *Temporal becoming is an essential and objective feature of time* is necessarily true. I should reject as utterly implausible the suggestion that the relation of explanatory priority obtaining between the relevant propositions is symmetrical. Hence, necessary truths can stand in relations of asymmetrical explanatory priority.

One could even agree with Yandell that 'there is no such thing as explaining that a necessary truth is true *rather than false*'.[47] But it does not follow that there is no such thing as explaining that (or why) a necessary truth is true. Intriguingly, Yandell does allow in his Introduction that a metaphysical *analysis*, rather than *explanation*, can be given, according to which necessary moral principles are true in virtue of the existence of some necessary being. What I call an 'explanation' Yandell calls an 'analysis' because he has built into his definition of 'explanation' that it must eliminate possible falsehood. But whether we call such an account of the basis of morality an explanation or an analysis, it clearly grounds necessary moral truths asymmetrically in some necessary being.

Yandell even gives us the two candidates for the ground of necessary moral truths: God or abstract objects. I agree that these are the alternatives, and it is unclear to me whether Draper, Martin and Rowe, in rejecting theistic ethics, would embrace Platonism. In a debate situation, one waits for one's opponent to bring up the alternatives; now that it has been raised, let me say a word about why I find theism a more plausible ground for moral values and duties than Platonism.

First, it is difficult even to comprehend the Platonist view. What does it mean to say, for example, that the moral value *Justice* just exists? It is hard to know what to make of this. It is clear what is meant when it is said that a person is just; but it is bewildering when it is said that, in the absence of any people, *Justice* itself exists. Moral values seem to exist as properties of persons, not as mere abstractions – or at any rate, it is hard to know what it is for a moral value to exist as a mere abstraction. Lacking any adequate foundation in reality for moral values, Platonism seems to just leave them floating unintelligibly in an ideal space.

Second, the nature of moral duty or obligation remains unaccounted for on Platonism. Let us suppose, for the sake of argument that moral values do exist independently of God. Suppose that values like *Mercy, Justice, Love, Forbearance*, and the like just exist. How does that result in any moral obligations for me? Why would I have a moral duty, say, to be merciful? Who or what lays such an obligation on me? As Richard Taylor points out, 'A duty is something that is owed .... But something can be owed only to some person or persons. There can be no such thing as duty in isolation ...'.[48] God serves as a ground of moral obligation because His commands constitute for us our moral duties; we are obligated to do as He commands. Taylor writes:

> Our moral obligations can ... be understood as those that are imposed by God ....
> But what if this higher-than-human lawgiver is no longer taken into account? Does
> the concept of a moral obligation ... still make sense? ... the concept of moral
> obligation [is] unintelligible apart from the idea of God. The words remain but their
> meaning is gone.[49]

As a non-theist, Taylor therefore thinks that we literally have no moral obligations, that there is no right or wrong. The Platonist rightly finds this abhorrent, but, as Taylor clearly sees, on an atheistic view there simply is no ground for duty, even if moral values somehow exist.

Third, it is fantastically improbable that just that sort of creatures would emerge from the blind evolutionary process who correspond to the abstractly existing realm of moral values. This seems to be an utterly incredible coincidence when one thinks about it. It is almost as though the moral realm *knew* that we were coming. It is far more plausible to regard both the natural realm and the moral realm as under the hegemony of a divine creator and law-giver than to think that these two entirely independent orders of reality just happened to mesh.

Thus I think that Platonism is not as plausible a view as theism but serves as a convenient halfway house for atheist philosophers who do not have the stomach for the moral nihilism which their atheism seems to imply. As an alternative to Platonism, I should commend the Augustinian tradition of the Divine Ideas, which, in contrast to Platonism, preserves divine aseity with respect to abstract objects by making them dependent upon divine intellection for their being.[50] My postulating relations of asymmetrical explanatory priority between certain necessary moral truths and certain necessary truths about the divine nature and will is simply a part of this Augustinian programme. Indeed, the tradition of divine command morality, except in its voluntaristic forms, is committed to God's explanatory priority to necessary moral truths.[51] So I find myself in very good company in asserting premise 1.

Our respondents' vigorous affirmations that certain moral truths are necessary therefore only reinforces the second premise of the moral argument and does nothing to defeat the first. We are still left wondering why, on the atheistic view of man, human beings would have intrinsic moral value and stand in relations of moral obligation to one another. I speak, of course, of objective moral values and duties – that is, values and duties which are valid and binding independently of their apprehension by human beings. The existence of such objective values and duties hardly passes well with the naturalistic world-view. For on a naturalistic world-view we are just animals, relatively advanced primates, and animals do not have moral duties towards one another nor is any species invested with special value or, indeed, any value.

Remarkably, Draper agrees that human beings are not special in this moral sense and that it is mere prejudice to think so. But he would rescue some vestige of the moral worth of human beings by maintaining that all conscious animals, including humans, are moral patients, in that they can be made to suffer consciously and wrongfully. The word 'wrongfully' is key here, for, in its absence, the pain inflicted upon and experienced by animals has no moral dimension. They would be patients, but not moral patients. But then I cannot see any reason why on naturalism animals should be thought to be moral patients. Why, on the naturalistic evolutionary scenario, is it morally wrong to inflict suffering on other sentient life? Why is suffering evil rather than an expected and neutral feature of the evolutionary struggle? On the Judeo-Christian view, human beings are commanded by God, and therefore morally obliged, to act as stewards of the biosphere. On this basis we can articulate a coherent environmental ethic which will extend even beyond duties to behave in certain ways towards sentient life to duties to act in certain ways with respect to the environment itself. But given a naturalistic world-view, I just do not see why suffering would be evil or the infliction of suffering wrong.

In order to justify his view, Draper ultimately must fall back on the view that moral principles are necessarily true and therefore inexplicable. But we have seen reason to question the assumption that necessary truths cannot stand in asymmetrical relations of explanatory priority. And to all appearances, some moral principles, at least – for example, *It is wrong to torture a child for fun* – are metaphysically necessary, synthetic truths, not merely analytic statements.[52] Both Draper and Martin would saddle me with the task of refuting all atheistic objectivist theories of ethics, which, of course, cannot be done in the space of a debate or this brief essay. But the mere mentioning of such theories does not serve to defeat premise 1, for I have given a reason for considering it to be true. Now it is up to our respondents to show how some atheistic ethical theory can justifiably be objectivist. Neither Martin nor Draper tells us which of the many non-theistic meta-ethical theories they endorse, but my experience with such theories is that they inevitably just assume gratuitously that on a naturalistic view of man, some feature of human existence, say, pleasure, is an intrinsic good, and they proceed from there. But the advocates of such theories are typically at a loss to justify their starting point. If their approach to meta-ethical theory is to be what Frank Jackson has called 'serious metaphysics' rather than just 'a shopping list' approach,[53] whereby one simply helps oneself to the supervenient moral properties needed to do the job, then some sort of explanation is required for why moral properties supervene on certain natural states. It is insufficient for the naturalist to point out that we do, in fact, apprehend the goodness of some feature of human existence, for that only goes to establish premise 2 of the moral argument. The issue is whether human beings would still have the value they in fact do were the naturalistic world-view true. I have yet to see any justification for the affirmation that, in a naturalistic universe, moral values would be anything more than the by-products of sociobiological evolution or expressions of personal taste.

Objective moral values do exist I take it that in moral experience we do apprehend a realm of objective moral values, just as in sensory experience we apprehend a realm of objectively existing physical objects. Just as it is impossible for us to step outside our sensory input to test its veridicality, so there is no way to test independently the veridicality of our moral perceptions. In the absence of some defeater, we rationally trust our perceptions, whether sensory or moral.

It is noteworthy that none of our respondents denies the truth of premise 2. Indeed, many insist on its necessary truth. Thus, some of them emphatically affirm, for example, that rape is wrong, even though the physical activity that counts as rape among human beings goes on all the time in the animal kingdom – just as acts that count as murder and theft when done by one human to another occur constantly between members of other animal species – without any moral significance whatsoever. This is surely strange and cries out for explanation. But unless our respondents are willing to embrace Platonism (itself a dubious move for a naturalist), they are just left with inexplicable moral principles governing the behaviour of *Homo sapiens* which are mysteriously true.

Therefore, God exists If at least some moral principles are, as I believe, necessarily true, then it follows that God, as their ground, exists necessarily. Thus, the moral argument advances our conception of God over the conclusions of the *kalam* cosmological argument and teleological argument in establishing not only the goodness of God, but the metaphysical necessity of His being.

Martin presses into service the old Euthyphro argument in order to prove the untenability of theistic ethics. But my non-voluntaristic version of divine command ethics avoids the dilemma he poses, for our moral duties are constituted by the commands of an essentially just and loving God. For any action A and moral agent S, we can explicate the notions of moral requirement, permission and forbiddenness of A for S as follows:

A is required of S if, and only if, a just and loving God commands S to do A.

A is permitted for S if, and only if, a just and loving God does not command S not to do A.

A is forbidden to S if, and only if, a just and loving God commands S not to do A.

Since our moral duties are grounded in the divine commands, they are not independent of God nor, plausibly, is God bound by moral duties, since He does not issue commands to Himself.

If God does not fulfil moral duties, then what content can be given to the claim that He is good? Here Kant's distinction between *following a rule* and *acting in accordance with a rule* proves helpful. God may act naturally in ways which, for us, would be rule-following and so constitutive of goodness in the sense of fulfilling our moral duties, so that God can be said similarly to be good in an analogical way. This fact also supplies the key to the arbitrariness objection, for our duties are determined by the commands, not merely of a supreme potentate, but of a just and loving God. God is essentially compassionate, fair, kind, impartial and so forth, and His commandments are reflections of His own character. Thus, they are not arbitrary, and we need not trouble ourselves about counterpossibles such as 'If God were to command child abuse ...'. God may be said to be good in the sense that He possesses all the moral virtues He possibly can and He does so essentially and to the maximal degree. Thus, God's axiological perfection should not be understood in terms of duty-fulfilment, but in terms of virtue. This conception helps us understand the sense in which God is to be praised – not in the sense of commendation for fully executing His duties or even for His acts of supererogation, but rather in the sense of adoration for His axiological perfection.

The question might be pressed as to why God's nature should be taken to be definitive of goodness. But, unless we are nihilists, we have to recognize some ultimate standard of value, and God seems to be the least arbitrary stopping point. Moreover, God's nature is singularly appropriate to serve as such a standard because, by definition, He is a being *worthy of worship*. And only a being which is the locus and source of all value is worthy of worship. Thus, God's nature and will serve to explain the existence of objective moral values and duties.

The Argument from Miracles

The argument based on the historical Resurrection of Jesus is, as Draper observes, an argument from miracles. While I do think that it is best used, as several respondents suggest, to discriminate between theisms,[54] nonetheless I include it in the debate as part of a cumulative case for theism. It represents an inference to the best explanation. Given the historical facts of the empty tomb, the post-mortem appearances of Jesus, and the origin of the disciples' belief in his Resurrection, the best explanation of these facts, when judged by such criteria as explanatory power, explanatory scope, plausibility, accord with accepted beliefs, absence of ad hoc hypotheses and so on, is the hypothesis 'God raised Jesus from the dead'.

While Keith Yandell is correct to emphasize that 'a very detailed and sustained examination' of the evidence and issues is necessary to sustain a cogent argument, it is still worth emphasizing that the majority of New Testament scholars who have written on the fate of Jesus of Nazareth agree with the three facts which form the inductive database for my argument. It is most definitely not a matter of merely quoting one scholar over against another. Most scholars shrink back from drawing the inference that God raised Jesus from the dead, but most would not dispute the database.

Parsons, however, does. In denying the fact of the empty tomb, Parsons rightly discerns the critical importance of the burial narrative, the mention of which I omitted in the debate due to time constraints. In dealing with the Resurrection, I often speak of four established facts, including the fact that Jesus was buried late Friday afternoon by Joseph of Arimathea, which the late John A.T. Robinson has characterized as 'one of the earliest and best-attested facts about Jesus'.[55] I refer the reader to my published work for the multiple, independent lines of evidence which have led most critics to accept this stated core fact of the burial account.[56]

Unfortunately, Parsons' citations of sources such as *Free Inquiry* magazine, the popular author J.S. Spong, the infamous G.A. Wells (a German teacher who has denied that Jesus ever existed) and so on, suggest that he has yet to carry out that detailed and sustained examination of the evidence called for by Yandell. Parsons misinterprets most critics' scepticism about Joseph of Arimathea's being a secret disciple as a reason for denying the historical role of Joseph in burying Jesus. In fact, the criterion of embarrassment strongly supports Joseph's role, for as Parsons notes, a later, Christian, legendary account would surely have made the disciples themselves or the women at the cross the persons responsible for Jesus' honourable burial. There was deep hostility in the early Church towards the Jewish leadership who had instigated Jesus' crucifixion, and thus the Christian invention of a Jewish Sanhedrist who does what is right for Jesus, while all his disciples desert him, would be, in Raymond Brown's words, 'almost inexplicable'.[57] Acts 13:29 is to be understood in the same light: it represents not an independent burial tradition, but Luke's tendency to hold the Jewish leaders responsible for Jesus' fate, as is evident from Luke's earlier statements that the *Jews* crucified Jesus (Acts 2:23; 36:4–10). In any case, Joseph was, after all, a Sanhedrist, so that no alternative form of burial is envisaged when Acts 13:29 says of the Jews that they 'laid him in a tomb'[58]. Thus, even Parsons' own source, Fuller, who is, as Parsons notes, very sceptical, accepts the historicity of Jesus' entombment. The historical fact of Jesus' burial by Joseph is very important because it implies that the location of Jesus' tomb was known in Jerusalem to friend and foe alike. A movement founded on belief in his Resurrection could not have arisen in Jerusalem in the face of an occupied tomb.

So what about the fact of the empty tomb? Parsons' deprecatory remarks concerning Mary Magdalene are merely embarrassing coming from a modern scholar rather than from a Celsus of the second century. The fact of the empty or occupied tomb was a publicly inspectable fact not dependent on the private witness of any one person. The summary quotation of Michael Martin stands unsupported, and his reservations have been addressed elsewhere.[59] Ironically, the lack of veneration of Jesus' tomb actually supports the historicity of the empty tomb, for the tombs of holy men were preserved as resting places for their bones in hope of the eschatological Resurrection; but in Jesus' case, the bones were no longer present, since the Resurrection had already occurred. Doubtless the site of the tomb was remembered, but it was not venerated as it would have been had the bones of Jesus rested there. Finally, Spong's point about the inadequacy of an empty tomb to generate belief in Jesus' Resurrection is quite correct and generally acknowledged; but Spong seems to have misunderstood New Testament scholars if he thinks that this implies the lateness of the tradition, for no one alleges that the Easter faith arose from the discovery of the empty tomb alone. On the contrary, his point supports my claim that the origin of the disciples' belief cannot be explained even by the discovery of the empty tomb. In short, Parsons needs to do much more of the careful work called for by Yandell if he seeks to undermine the credibility of the discovery of the empty tomb.

What, then, of the Resurrection appearances? At this point in his essay Parsons begins to refer to persons who accept the historicity of the post-mortem appearances as 'apologists', apparently unaware that the appearances are virtually universally acknowledged among New Testament scholars today as historical – which is why we find even Lüdemann, quoted in my opening speech, saying that it is 'historically certain' that the disciples had such experiences. Parsons does not seem to appreciate that in accepting Lüdemann's treatment as 'wholly convincing' he has committed himself to the historicity of the appearances.

With respect to the pre-Pauline tradition cited in I Corinthians 15:3–7, Parsons raises a number of points, the evidentiary significance of which he fails to explain.

1   *The early date of the tradition.* The earlier the tradition the less likely it is to be legendary. The Darwin story footnoted by Parsons is not relevant because it stemmed from a single person in an alleged, private conversation with Darwin and has nothing to do with the Jewish transmission of oral tradition.

2   *The witnesses.* Both groups and individuals, on multiple occasions, are said to have experienced the appearances. Three years after Jesus' death on a fact-finding trip to Jerusalem, Paul spent two weeks with the two named witnesses, Peter and James, both of whom eventually went to their deaths holding to the truth of Jesus' Resurrection. Paul also knew some of the 500 brethren, since he was aware that some had passed away in the interim.[60] Moreover, we have multiple, independent attestation of at least two of these appearances, which is one of the primary criteria of historicity: the appearance to Peter is attested in Paul and Luke, while the appearance to the Twelve is attested in Paul, John and Luke.

3   *The nature of the appearances.* From Paul's tradition we can draw no inference as to the nature of the appearances. But the remainder of the chapter makes it clear that Paul believed in a literal Resurrection body.[61]

4   *The empty tomb.* Paul's tradition implies the empty tomb in affirming that Christ 'was buried, and he was raised' and in dating the Resurrection 'on the third day', the day on which the women discovered the tomb empty. As I Corinthians 15:35–57 shows, Paul himself believed that the remains of the dead would be raised and transformed into supernatural bodies, thereby implying his belief in the empty tomb.

5   *Paul's personal experience.* Paul, who was an ecstatic, and the entire New
Testament draw a distinction between the Resurrection appearances and
visions of Christ. The only tenable basis for understanding this differentia-
tion is that the Resurrection appearances, unlike ecstatic visions, involved a
real, extra-mental component. None of Parson's points thus succeeds in
undermining the historical importance of Paul's information.

  With respect to the Resurrection appearance stories in the Gospels, Parsons'
only indictment of these is their alleged inconsistency. This objection is not
serious for the following reasons. First, Fact 2 does not depend on all – or, for
that matter, even any – of these stories' being accurate transcripts of what
happened during these experiences. Second, inconsistencies in the secondary or
circumstantial features of accounts do not prompt historians to discard those
accounts as historically worthless. For example, the only accounts we have of
Hannibal's crossing the Alps with elephants to mount an attack upon Rome in
the Second Punic War are two inconsistent reports by Martial and Livy; yet no
historian doubts that Hannibal did, in fact, mount such a campaign. Third, the
Resurrection appearances can be arranged in a coherent chronological and
geographical order: to the women at the tomb, to Peter in Jerusalem, to two
disciples on the road to Emmaus, to the Twelve gathered in the upper room, a
week later to the Twelve, including Thomas, as the disciples remained in
Jerusalem for the duration of the feasts of Passover/Unleavened Bread before
returning to Galilee, to seven disciples fishing at the Sea of Tiberius in Galilee
as they awaited their rendezvous with Jesus on the mountain, to the Twelve
and others who gathered with them (the 500 brethren perhaps?) on the
mountain in Galilee, to James sometime in Galilee, and finally to all the
apostles upon their return to Jerusalem for the feast of Pentecost. Thus, the
accounts, while complementary, are not inconsistent. The Evangelists pick and
choose which appearances to narrate according to their editorial purposes.
Luke, for example, wants to show how the Christian faith comes to be centred
in Jerusalem, so he omits any Galilean appearance stories, even though he
mentions that the appearances (which he neglects to narrate) went on over a
period of 40 days prior to Pentecost. In summary, we have abundant,
independent, early sources for the fact of Jesus' post-mortem appearances,
which is why virtually no New Testament historian denies than the disciples
had such experiences.

  Finally, we turn to that third fact, the origin of the disciples' belief that God
had raised Jesus from the dead. Parsons does not deny that the Christian
movement sprang into being because the earliest disciples sincerely believed
that God had raised Jesus from the dead. But he tries to soften the impact of
that fact by denying that it was contrary to the disciples' every predisposition.
Given their belief that the New Age had begun, they were not predisposed
against belief in Jesus' Resurrection. But Parsons puts the cart before the horse.
His citation from Kee *et al.* is precisely to the point: Christians believed that the
New Age had dawned *because* they believed that God had raised Jesus from the
dead. The question remains why the disciples, confronted with Jesus'
crucifixion, would have come to believe something so outlandish and un-

Jewish as that the eschatological Resurrection had somehow occurred in advance in Jesus, when acceptable, alternative explanations (for example, translation) were available to explain any hallucinatory experiences they might have had and even the empty tomb itself. So long as an acceptable Jewish category is available to account for their experience, the claim that the disciples instead appropriated some other category at odds with Jewish thinking requires justification.

Draper thinks that the facts of the empty tomb, the post-mortem appearances and the origin of the disciples' belief in Jesus' Resurrection are 'not so great' because they could be explanatorily connected. For example, the discovery of the empty tomb might be conducive to hallucinations, and together these might lead the disciples to infer that Jesus was risen. I grant the possibility, and in my published work try to exhibit the explanatory deficiencies of such scenarios. But that does not affect my point here that we have in the empty tomb, post-mortem appearances and origin of the disciples' belief three independently established facts (for example, the evidence for the empty tomb is independent of the evidence for the appearances) which constitute data which must be plausibly explained *in toto* by any tenable hypothesis. So with these facts in place, we now come to the question of which of the live options for explaining these four facts concerning Jesus' fate constitutes the best explanation.

Rowe presents a very curious philosophical argument against allowing the Resurrection of Jesus even to be included in the pool of live options. As I understand him, the argument is that relative to our background information, not including the fact of God's existence, human immortality is enormously improbable. Let us concede the point – but where does the argument go from there? The next step is the claim that this 'easily counterbalances' or 'overwhelms' the evidence for the Resurrection of Jesus. But this looks for all the world like Hume's old, oft-refuted argument against miracles, and it is hard to believe that Rowe is advancing that as his disproof of the Resurrection.

Probability theorists from Condorcet to John Stuart Mill wrestled with the question, raised by Hume's original argument, concerning what evidence is required in order to establish the occurrence of highly improbable events.[62] It was soon realized that if one simply weighed the probability of the event against the reliability of the witness, then we should be led into denying the occurrence of events which, though highly improbable, we reasonably know to have occurred.[63] What also needs to be considered is the probability that if the reported event has *not* occurred, then the witness's testimony is just as it is. As Mill wrote:

> To know whether a coincidence does or does not require more evidence to render it credible than an ordinary event, we must refer, in every instance, to first principles, and estimate afresh what is the probability that the given testimony would have been delivered in that instance, supposing the fact which it asserts not to be true.[64]

In the case of the Resurrection the question that must be assessed is whether the evidence for the empty tomb, the Resurrection appearances and the origin of the Christian Way would be just as it is if Jesus did not rise from the dead. This realization has been embodied in Bayes' Theorem, which requires that the Resurrection hypothesis R will have a high epistemic probability on our background information B and the specific evidence E – that is, $Pr(R/B\&E) > 0.5$ – just in case it has a greater balance of inherent plausibility and explanatory power than its denial – that is, $Pr(R/B) \times Pr(E/B\&R) > Pr(\neg R/B) \times Pr(E/B\&\neg R)$.[65]

Now Rowe's claim is that (R/B) is so wildly improbable that the values assigned to the other probabilities in question cannot overcome it. I, however, see no reason to think that $Pr(R/B) \ll 0.5$. What our background evidence renders highly improbable is that someone should rise naturally from the dead; but the Christian agrees wholeheartedly with that conclusion and rightly sees therein nothing that renders improbable the hypothesis that God raised Jesus miraculously from the dead. Does Rowe think that the Resurrection of Jesus is improbable because such an event is so rare? The problem, then, is that the frequency model of probability simply will not work in this context. For, as Earman has pointed out, trying to ground all the terms in Bayes' Theorem in objective frequencies would disqualify the probabilification of many of the theoretical hypotheses of the advanced sciences.[66] Earman concludes that, in the case of $Pr(R/B)$, the guidance for assigning probability 'cannot take the simple minded form' of using the value of the frequency of R-type events in past experience; that frequency may be flatly zero (as in proton decay), but it would be unwise to therefore set $Pr(R/B) = 0$.[67] In short, I do not think Rowe has given any good reason for thinking either that $Pr(R/B) \ll 0.5$ or that any improbability cannot be overcome by the improbability that the evidence would be just as it is in the absence of Jesus' Resurrection.

In any case, even if I have misunderstood him, Rowe's argument misfires because what the background evidence renders highly probable on Rowe's account is 'that there is no conscious life at all after the death and destruction of the human body'.[68] But that, at best, renders improbable the existence of an intermediate state between a person's death and Resurrection. This is really an argument against the immortality of the soul, not the Resurrection of the body. Hence, it does nothing to render improbable the claim that Jesus rose bodily from the dead.

Parsons, on the other hand, opts for the hallucination hypothesis, championed anew by Lüdemann, as the best explanation. In my *Jesus' Resurrection: Fact or Figment*, co-authored with Lüdemann, I argue that the hallucination hypothesis has weak explanatory power, has inadequate explanatory scope, is implausible in multiple respects, is *ad hoc* in several ways, contradicts a number of propositions accepted by the majority of New Testament scholars, and does not outstrip the Resurrection hypothesis in meeting the criteria for the best explanation.[69] The reader may decide for himself whether Lüdemann or any of our respondents in that book is able to meet this challenge.

If I am correct about the inadequacy of the hallucination hypothesis, then Draper's hypothesis of hallucinations induced by the discovery of the empty tomb is also undercut. Moreover, it is doubtful that discovery of an empty tomb would have led to hallucinations in the first place, as Draper surmises. Ironically, here Parsons has the more accurate historical understanding; he agrees with Spong that: 'The disciples ... would have concluded that even the dead body of this Jesus had not been spared degradation. No Easter faith would have resulted from an empty tomb.'[70] Furthermore, it is unlikely that hallucinations, even conjoined with an empty tomb, would have led to the disciples to think that God had raised Jesus from the dead, an idea which, while familiar to us in the Christian era, ran contrary to first-century Jewish thinking. Draper needs to explain why, in line with Jewish beliefs, they did not proclaim Jesus' translation or assumption into heaven, rather than, contrary to Jewish beliefs, his Resurrection. And, of course, there remains the empty tomb itself to explain. Draper knows too much about inference to the best explanation to think that his merely mentioning other explanations in the pool of live options suffices to show them to be as good an explanation as the Resurrection hypothesis. Each one must be subjected to careful scrutiny using the criteria for a best explanation. It is dubious that many of these will survive. The idea that Jesus' enemies stole the corpse, for example, is enormously implausible in light of their silence once the disciples began to proclaim in Jerusalem that Jesus was risen. I have yet to see a naturalistic explanation of the facts of the matter that is as good as the Resurrection hypothesis.

Belief in God as Properly Basic

My final reason for theistic belief is that belief in (Christian) theism is properly basic both with respect to rationality and warrant for a person who has experienced the regenerating work of the Holy Spirit and so come into personal relationship with God. Philosophers of religion will recognize this as the religious epistemology articulated and defended so ably by Alvin Plantinga in his epochal trilogy on warrant.[71] My main differences with Plantinga are that I eschew any innate *sensus divinitatis* in favour of reliance solely on the inner witness of the Holy Spirit (*testimonium spiritu sancti internum*) and that I construe the latter, not as a belief-forming process analogous to a cognitive faculty, but as part of the circumstances in which a person whose cognitive faculties are functioning properly forms for himself the relevant beliefs, such as 'God loves me'.[72] The claim is that I am rational and warranted in holding such beliefs in the absence of any defeater of them. As a couple of our respondents remind us, such defeaters need not be rebutting defeaters, such as arguments for God's non-existence, but may be undercutting defeaters, removing any warrant I have for thinking my belief to be true. The goal of this argument for the proper basicality of belief in God is not, of course, to hold forth my experience as evidence to others of God's existence, but to invite others to embark on what Geivett calls 'a devotional experiment' with a view to finding the knowledge of God themselves: 'Taste and see that the Lord is good!'.[73]

The Christian can urge non-believers to undertake such a spiritual quest, confident in Jesus' promise that 'he who seeks finds'.[74] I take this to be one of the promises of God to be claimed by faith. The fact that apparently sincere seekers have not yet found God is not, as Rowe and Martin think, a powerful objection to Christian theism for two reasons. First, the human penchant for self-deception is enormous. Many people seek to come to God on their own terms rather than in humility and openness, in which case the knowledge of God will elude them. Second, disappointed seekers may yet find God! One must not give up the quest too soon or think that anyone is beyond saving.

The most significant objection to such a religious epistemology, as several respondents observe, arises from the diversity of the religious claims supported by religious experience. Since these claims are logically incompatible in many cases, the experiences cannot ground them all as properly basic with respect to warrant (assuming that truth is not pluralistic and person-relative, but is one and objective). Either at least some of the experiences are non-veridical or else veridical experiences of the divine have been conceptualized in false propositional claims. For example, while the Christian theist may claim to know the great truths of the Gospel through the inner witness of the Holy Spirit, the Mormon polytheist will claim to know the truth of the Book of Mormon through the 'burning in the bosom' he experiences as he reads it. Does not the presence of the confident claim of the Mormon to know the truth of LDS doctrine based on religious experience serve to undercut the claim of the Christian to know the Gospel truth via a similar religious experience?

This is far from obvious. It is clear, I think, that false claims to an experience of God do absolutely nothing to undermine the veridicality of a genuine experience of the Spirit's witness, any more than the insistence of a colourblind person that there is no difference in colour between a red object and a green object undermines my veridical perception of their difference in colour. Even if I were utterly at a loss to show him that his faculties are not functioning properly or that mine are, that inability in no way affects the veridicality of my experience. So what the detractor of religious experience owes us here is what Plantinga calls a *de jure* objection to theistic belief: an objection, in this case, to the rationality or warrantedness of theistic belief even given the veridicality of my religious experience.

Draper offers just such an argument. By way of illustration, he imagines that while I do not suffer from dendrological disorder, nonetheless I 'have good reason to believe I do'.[75] Then my confidence that a tree really exists when I see a tree is undermined, leaving me without adequate warrant for thinking that a tree exists. (Draper speaks of reduced probability in this connection, but this is a mistake, treating my beliefs not as properly basic, but as inferences from experience; the key issue here is the reduction in confidence I experience because I have reason to doubt the veridicality of my experience.[76]) Analogously, as a Christian, I have good reason to think that masses of humanity suffer from 'senseless divinititus' – that is, have non-veridical religious experiences. The prevalence and phenomenological similarity of these experiences to Christian experience give me good reason to think that I, too, have senseless divinititus. But then, even if my experiences of God are veridical, I ought to doubt them to such an extent that they are no longer properly basic for me with respect to rationality or warrant.

Now suppose we agree with Draper that 'Just as the person who has good reason to believe he has the dreaded dendrological disorder should doubt his visual experiences of trees even if his visual faculties are in perfect working order, the Christian who has good reason to believe he has senseless divinititus should doubt his Christian experiences even if his *sensus divinitatus* [sic] is in perfect working order.'[77] The key question, then, is whether the Christian does have good reason to believe that he has senseless divinititus – that is, suffers from non-veridical religious experiences. The proffered reason is that so many non-Christians must be regarded as having non-veridical religious experiences, which are similar to mine. But, so far as I can see, this gives me only good reason for thinking that *they* have the disease, not that *I* have it. In Draper's illustration of dendrological disorder, *I* had good reason to think that *I* had the disease – namely, the results of my blood test. In the absence of such evidence, the fact that many other persons have non-veridical perceptions of trees indistinguishable from my own does not give me reason to think that my perceptions are non-veridical. It is not enough to have evidence that they have the disease; in order for my beliefs to be undercut I must have good evidence that I have the disease.

Likewise, in the case of religious experience, the fact that many, or even most, claims made on the basis of religious experience are unwarranted does not in itself undercut the warrant my beliefs have on the grounds of my experience. With respect to competing religious claims, say, those of Mormonism, I may have good reasons (namely, the personal follies of Joseph Smith, the historical inaccuracies of the Book of Mormon, the outrageous Mormon pantheon of physical, humanoid deities, and so on) to think that Mormons have non-veridical religious experiences or have misconstrued genuine religious experiences. But that gives me no reason to doubt the veridicality of my experiences. To do so, I should have to have some reason to think that my experiences are non-veridical – for example, arguments or evidence that Christian theism is false. But then the objection is no longer an independent *de jure* objection distinct from *de facto* considerations.

But what about a case where I have no evidence that some non-Christian claimant to religious experience is mistaken other than the incompatibility of his truth-claims with Christian truth-claims? Does that give me reason to be agnostic about the veridicality of my experience? I think not. Consider, by analogy, beliefs formed on the ground of moral experience. Should I regard as unwarranted my belief that anti-Semitism is immoral just because Nazis regarded it as moral? Certainly not; their warped perceptions should not lead me to think that my perceptions are warped, even though there is no court of appeal beyond moral experience itself. Similarly with religious experience; in order for the proper basicality of my religious beliefs to be undercut I must have some good reason to think that my own experience, as opposed to that of others, is non-veridical or misconstrued.

Two further points should be made. We have been assuming, for the sake of argument, that all religious experiences are phenomenologically similar. But this is clearly false. Christian experience is very different from Advaita Vendanta Hindu or Buddhist experience, for example.[78] A feeling of oneness with the All or of absolute dependence is not at all similar to the testimony of the Holy Spirit described by Paul.[79] The Christian experiences a personal fellowship with God which is utterly foreign to most of the religions of mankind. As a simple sociological fact, the masses of humanity have no such experience. This has two important implications. First, the Christian need not deny the veridicality of all non-Christian religious experiences. He may happily concede that people in many different religious traditions do experience God as a ground of being or the most real being or the transcendent and ineffable and so forth. Second, since Christian experience is not able to be assimilated to generic religious experience, the fact that many persons have non-veridical religious experiences does not undermine the Christian's confidence in the veridicality of his experience.

Finally, I have contended elsewhere that the testimony of the Holy Spirit is self-authenticating.[80] It is what Plantinga calls an intrinsic defeater-defeater.[81] It confers so much warrant on the beliefs it grounds that it overwhelms defeaters brought against it. If this is correct, then the undercutting defeater constituted by the prospect of non-Christian religious experience may, at best, diminish my confidence in the veridicality of my experience, but it will not defeat it. Non-Christian religious experience, even if it furnished, in Draper's words, a 'good reason' to think my experience non-veridical, does not furnish an overriding reason to think my experience non-veridical. Now, of course, adherents to other religions can, and do, likewise claim to have self-authenticating experiences grounding non-Christian beliefs. But the Christian, as the recipient of a bona fide self-authenticating experience of God, knows that such claims are spurious. He will therefore do his best to convince the non-Christian of the truth of the Gospel by presenting him arguments and evidence, such as I have done in this debate, in the hopes that the false confidence of the non-Christian will crack under the weight of the evidence and that he will attend to the convicting witness of the Holy Spirit, drawing him to the true God and eternal life.

Notes

1   I had, of course, anticipated that Flew might appeal to some 'presumption of atheism' in order to justify differential burdens of proof; but, although several respondents comment on this alleged presumption, Flew never raised it in the debate. (For my take on the presumption of atheism, see J.P. Moreland and William Lane Craig, *Philosophical Foundations of a Christian Worldview* (Downer's Grove, Ill: InterVarsity Press, 2003, ch. 7.) With good reason: it depends upon a revisionist definition of 'atheism' which identifies it with a belief state rather than a metaphysical position and forces us to the absurd conclusion that infants count as atheists, since they lack belief in God. So the alleged presumption of atheism does not lighten the burden resting on the atheist's shoulders.

2   On the problem of gratuitous evil, see Daniel Howard-Snyder (ed.), *The Evidential Argument from Evil* (Bloomington, IN: Indiana University Press, 1996); and, more recently Alvin Plantinga, 'Degenerate Evidence and Rowe's New Evidential Argument from Evil', *Noûs*, 32 (1998), pp. 531–44; William L. Rowe, 'Reply to Plantinga', *Noûs*, 32 (1998), pp. 545–52.

On the divine attributes, see William Lune Craig (ed.), *Philosophy of Religion A Reader and Guide* (Edinburgh: Edinburgh University Press, 2001). See also no. 12 below.

3   See p. 71.

4   See p. 29.

5   Stephen Davis has offered a disarmingly simple version of this argument in his 'The Cosmological Argument and the Epistemic Status of Belief in God', *Philosophia Christi*, NS1 (1999), pp. 5–15. Davis argues that any thing that exists has an explanation of its existence, either in the necessity of its nature or in an external cause. If the universe has an explanation of its existence, it is plausible that that explanation is God. Since the universe is an existing thing, it therefore follows that God is the explanation of the existence of the universe and exists Himself by a necessity of His own nature. I find this argument quite persuasive.

6   Richard Swinburne, *The Existence of God*, rev. edn (Oxford: Clarendon Press, 1991), ch. 7.

7   On Hawking's quantum cosmology, mentioned by Martin, see my '"What Place, Then, for a Creator?" Hawking on God and Creation', *British Journal for the Philosophy of Science*, 41 (1990), pp. 229–34.

8   See my 'Professor Grünbaum on Creation', *Erkenntnis* 40 (1994), pp 325–41; 'Creation and Big Bang Cosmology', *Philosophia Naturalis*, 31 (1994), pp. 217–24; 'A Response to Grünbaum on Creation and Big Bang Cosmology', *Philosophia Naturalis*, 31 (1994), pp. 237–49.

9   For an extended discussion of God's relation to time, see my *God, Time and Eternity* (Dordrecht: Kluwer Academic Publishers, 2001).

10 For a brief discussion see my *The* Kalam *Cosmological Argument* (London: Macmillan & Co., 1979), pp. 89–92; also A.W. Moore, *The Infinite* (London: Routledge, 1990), pp. 123–30.

11 For an account of Hilbert's Hotel, see my *Reasonable Faith* (Wheaton, Ill.: Crossways, 1994), pp. 95–6.

12 On the divine attributes, see the introduction and selections in William Lane Craig (ed.), *Philosophy of Religion: A Reader and Guide* (Edinburgh: Edinburgh University Press, 2001), section III, particularly the piece 'Maximal Power' dealing with omnipotence.

13 See William Alston, 'Does God Have Beliefs?', *Religious Studies*, 22 (1986), pp. 287–306.

14 See further my *The* Kalam *Cosmological Argument*, pp. 69–87. For the logic of the argument see my 'Time and Infinity', in William Lane Craig and Quentin Smith (eds), *Theism, Atheism, and Big Bang Cosmology* (Oxford: Clarendon Press, 1993), pp. 98–99.

15 Aristotle *Physica*, 3.6.206a15–20.

16 Here, a second *kalam* cosmological argument is relevant: the argument based on the impossibility of the formation of an actual infinite by successive addition. Although Keith Yandell treats this argument dismissively, there are, in fact, enormous difficulties in the idea that the series of past events is infinite and yet has been instantiated by successive addition. See my *The* Kalam *Cosmological Argument*, pp. 102–10; also 'Time and Infinity', pp. 99–106.

17 See p. 102.

18 John Barrow and Frank Tipler, *The Anthropic Cosmological Principle* (Oxford: Clarendon Press, 1986), p. 442.

19   Stephen Hawking and Roger Penrose, *The Nature of Space and Time*, The Isaac Newton Institute Series of Lectures (Princeton, NJ: Princeton University Press, 1996), p. 85.

20   John D. Barrow, *Theories of Everything: The Quest for Ultimate Explanation* (Oxford: Clarendon Press, 1991), p. 68.

21   See my *The Kalam Cosmological Argument*, pp. 130–40.

22   Roger Penrose, 'Some Remarks on Gravity and Quantum Mechanics', in M.J. Duff and C.J. Isham (eds), *Quantum Structure of Space and Time* (Cambridge: Cambridge University Press, 1982), pp. 3–10.

23   See my 'The Ultimate Question of Origins: God and the Beginning of the Universe', *Astrophysics and Space Science*, 269–270 (1999), pp. 723–40, with the attendant commentary by G.F.R. Ellis; for an expanded version of the same see my 'Naturalism and Cosmology', in William L. Craig and J.P. Moreland (eds), *Naturalism: A Critical Appraisal*, Routledge Studies in Twentieth-Century Philosophy (London: Routledge, 2000), pp. 215–52.

24   See p. 143.

25   Christopher Isham, 'Space, Time, and Quantum Cosmology', paper presented at the conference 'God, Time, and Modern Physics', March 1990; Christopher Isham, 'Quantum Cosmology and the Origin of the Universe', lecture presented at the conference 'Cosmos and Creation', Cambridge University, 14 July 1994.

26   A. Borde and A. Vilenkin, 'Eternal Inflation and the Initial Singularity', *Physical Review Letters*, 72 (1994), pp. 3305–7.

27   Andrei Linde, Dmitri Linde and Arthur Mezhlumian, 'From the Big Bang Theory to the Theory of a Stationary Universe', *Physical Review*, D 49 (1994), pp. 1783–826.

28   See p. 144.

29   See, for example, James T. Cushing, *Philosophical Concepts in Physics* (Cambridge: Cambridge University Press, 1998); idem, *Quantum Mechanics: Historical Contingency and the Copenhagen Hegemony*, Science and its Conceptual Foundations (Chicago: University of Chicago Press, 1994).

30   See discussion and literature cited in my 'Divine Timelessness and Personhood', *International Journal for Philosophy of Religion*, 43 (1998), pp. 109–24.

31   For a good airing of the issue, see Timothy O'Connor, *Persons and Causes: The Metaphysics of Free Will* (Oxford: Oxford University Press, 2000), ch. 3.

32   I have defended this position since first enunciating it in my 'God, Time, and Eternity', *Religious Studies* 14 (1979), pp. 497–503.

33   See my *God, Time and Eternity*, Pt. II, Sect. 2.

34   Especially influential among Christian philosophers has been Alvin Plantinga, *The Nature of Necessity*, Clarendon Library of Logic and Philosophy (Oxford: Clarendon Press, 1974).

35   See my 'Graham Oppy on the *Kalam* Cosmological Argument', *Sophia*, 32 (1993), pp. 1–11.

36   William A. Dembski, *The Design Inference: Eliminating Chance through Small Probabilities*, Cambridge Studies in Probability, Induction, and Decision Theory (Cambridge: Cambridge University Press, 1998), pp. 184–85. For an alternative approach see Robin Collins, 'A Scientific Argument for the Existence of God: The Fine-Tuning Design Argument', in Michael J. Murray (ed.), *Reason for the Hope Within* (Grand Rapids, MI: William B. Eerdmans, 1999), pp. 47–75.

37   John Barrow, *The World Within the World* (Oxford: Clarendon Press, 1988).

38   Parsons's blanket rejection of the principle of indifference is unwarranted. What Earman and Salmon point out is that, in cases in which the same situation can be

described in two different ways involving quantities which are non-linearly related to each other, our calculation of the probability of some outcome can lead to incompatible answers if we assume that all outcomes are equally possible. Parsons needs to show that the case of fine-tuning falls in this category and that the uncertainty that this would introduce into the outcome would be sufficient to affect seriously the claim that a life-permitting universe is extraordinarily unlikely. For a defence of the principle of indifference see George Schlesinger, *The Intelligibility of Nature* (Aberdeen: Aberdeen University Press, 1985), ch. 5; for its application to fine-tuning arguments see Collins, 'Scientific Argument for the Existence of God', pp. 67–72.

39   John Leslie, *Universes* (London: Routledge, 1989), p. 17.
40   John C. Polkinghorne, *Serious Talk: Science and Religion in Dialogue* (London: SCM Press, 1996), p. 6.
41   T. Rothman and G.F.R. Ellis, 'Smolin's Natural Selection Hypothesis', *Quarterly Journal of the Royal Astronomical Society*, 34 (1993), pp. 201–12.
42   I owe this point to Robin Collins.
43   Ludwig Boltzmann, *Lectures on Gas Theory*, trans. Stephen G. Brush (Berkeley: University of California Press, 1964), pp. 446–48.
44   John D. Barrow and Frank J. Tipler, *The Anthropic Cosmological Principle* (Oxford: Clarendon Press, 1986), pp. 561–5.
45   On the customary semantics such so-called 'counterpossibles' all turn out to be trivially true because there is no broadly logically possible world in which the antecedent is true and, hence, no antecedent-permitting world in which the consequent fails to be true. But I take it as evident that the proposition 'If God did not exist, the universe would not exist' is non-trivially true and the proposition 'If God did not exist, the universe would (nonetheless) exist' is non-trivially false. For important attempts to deal more adequately with such counterpossibles than the Lewis–Stalnaker semantics allow, see Linda Zagzebski, 'What if the Impossible Had Been Actual?', in Michael D. Beaty (ed.), *Christian Theism and the Problems of Philosophy* (Notre Dame, IL: Notre Dame University Press, 1990), pp. 165–83; Brian Leftow, 'God and Abstract Entities', *Faith and Philosophy*, 7 (1990), pp. 193–217.
46   Mann points out that 'mathematical truths are all equally necessary, hence all equally entail all others, yet mathematicians rightly assume that some mathematical propositions explain why others are true'. See William E. Mann, 'Modality, Morality, and God', *Noûs*, 23 (1989), p. 86. Van Inwagen even suggests that it is far from obvious that broadly logically necessary beings cannot stand in asymmetrical causal relations with each other:

> It is not ... easily demonstrable that just any necessary being would be an independent being. Anyone who wanted to demonstrate this conclusion would have somehow to prove the impossibility of cases like the following one. Suppose that A is a necessary being and that A causes the existence of B and that it is necessary that A cause the existence of B. Then B will be a necessary being – B will exist in all possible worlds, since A exists in all possible worlds, and, in every possible world in which it exists, causes B to exist in that possible world – but B will nonetheless depend upon A for its existence. (Peter Van Inwagen, *Metaphysics* [Boulder, CO: Westview Press, 1993], p. 108)

The issue of the dependence relation between certain necessary entities and God has been at the heart of recent discussions of divine aseity and abstract objects. See, for example, Richard Brian Davis, *The Metaphysics of Theism and Modality*,

American University Studies V/189 (New York: Peter Lang, 2001) and the therein cited literature.

47 See p. 96, my emphasis.

48 Richard Taylor, *Ethics, Faith, and Reason* (Englewood Cliffs, NJ: Prentice-Hall, 1985), p. 83.

49 Ibid., pp. 83–84.

50 For discussion see Davis, *Metaphysics of Theism*.

51 For contemporary defences see, for example, Robert M. Adams, *Finite and Infinite Goods* (Oxford: Oxford University Press, 2000); Philip Quinn, *Divine Commands and Moral Requirements* (Oxford: Clarendon Press, 1978); Janine Marie Idziak, *Divine Command Morality: Historical and Contemporary Readings* (Lewiston, NY: Edwin Mellen Press, 1980).

52 When Swinburne, *Existence of God*, pp. 176–77, says that such principles are analytic, he is clearly using the term idiosyncratically as a synonym for 'necessarily true'. His claim is merely that such principles are true in every possible world and therefore inexplicable. They are clearly not analytic in the sense that their predicates are deducible from their subject terms.

53 Frank Jackson, *From Metaphysics to Ethics* (Oxford: Clarendon Press, 1998), pp. 4–5. Naturalists face what Jackson calls a 'location problem' in finding a place in the generally accepted naturalistic account for entities like moral values. For Jackson's own attempt at serious metaphysics concerning moral values, see pp. 119–29. Jackson's 'entry by entailment thesis' does not seem to work for moral principles, since, if they are necessarily true, they are entailed by *any* account. Jackson takes no notice of divine command morality, which would subvert his claim that moral properties and descriptive properties cannot be necessarily co-extensive and yet distinct.

54 See my remarks in *Five Views on Apologetics*, ed. Steven B. Cowan, Counterpoints (Grand Rapids, MI: Zondervan, 2000), pp. 126–28, 316–17.

55 John A.T. Robinson, *The Human Face of God* (Philadelphia: Westminster, 1973), p. 131.

56 See my *Assessing the New Testament Evidence for the Historicity of the Resurrection of Jesus*, 2nd edn, Studies in the Bible and Early Christianity 16 (Lewiston, NY: Edwin Mellen, 2002), chs. 5, 9.

57 Raymond E. Brown, *The Death of the Messiah*, 2 vols (Garden City, NY: Doubleday, 1994), vol. 2, pp. 1240–1.

58 See also Byron R. McCane, '"Where No One Had Yet Been Laid": The Shame of Jesus' Burial', in Bruce Chilton and Craig Evans (eds), *Authenticating the Activities of Jesus*, New Testament Tools and Studies 28/2 (Leiden: Brill, 1999), pp. 431–52, who argues for the historicity of Jesus' entombment, which McCane maintains was a dishonourable burial by delegates of the Sanhedrin.

59 See my *Assessing the New Testament Evidence*; also Stephen T. Davis, *Risen Indeed* (Grand Rapids, MI: William B. Eerdmans, 1993).

60 I know of no New Testament scholar who would accept Parsons' claim in his note 38 that I Corinthians 15:6b–c was part of the tradition, since it breaks the rhythm of the formula and reflects a chronologically later perspective. It should be noted that group hallucinations are very rare, so this incident adds just one more straw to the cumulative weight of the evidence.

61 See my detailed exegesis in *Assessing the New Testament Evidence*, ch. 4, in response to Parsons' note 40.

62 For an account see S.L. Zabell, 'The Probabilistic Analysis of Testimony', *Journal of Statistical Planning and Inference*, 20 (1988), pp. 327–54.

63 For example, if on the morning news we hear reported that the pick in last night's lottery was 7492871, this is a report of an extraordinarily improbable event, perhaps one out of several million, and even if the morning news' accuracy is known to be 99.99 per cent, the improbability of the event reported will swamp the probability of the witness's reliability, so that we should never believe such reports.

64 J.S. Mill, *A System of Logic*, 2 vols (London, 1843), Bk. 3, ch. 25, § 6, cited in Zabell, 'The Probabilistic Analysis of Testimony', p. 331. Thus, to return to our example in the previous note, the probability that the morning news would announce the pick as 7492871 if some other number had been chosen is sufficiently remote that it is rational to believe such testimony to the wildly improbable event in question.

65 Even this needs some finessing, however. As Wainwright has argued elsewhere, we need not show that the probability of the Resurrection on the evidence and background information is greater than the probability of no Resurrection on the same evidence and information. Rather, what we must show is that the probability of the Resurrection is greater than any of its alternatives. For the collective probability of all these alternatives taken together is meaningless, since the disjunction of all these alternatives is not itself an alternative.

66 John Earman, 'Bayes, Hume, and Miracles', *Faith and Philosophy*, 10 (1993), p. 303. For example, scientists are investing long hours and millions of dollars hoping for an observation of an event of proton decay, though such an event has never been observed.

67 Ibid., p. 301.

68 See p. 68.

69 William Lane Craig and Gerd Lüdemann, *Jesus' Resurrection: Fact or Figment?*, ed. Paul Copan and Ronald K. Tacelli (Downer's Grove, Ill: InterVarsity Press, 2000).

70 See p. 122.

71 Alvin Plantinga, *Warrant and Proper Function* (Oxford: Oxford University Press, 1993); idem, *Warrant: the Current Debate* (Oxford: Oxford University Press, 1993); idem, *Warranted Christian Belief* (Oxford: Oxford University Press, 2000).

72 See my brief discussion in Moreland and Craig, *Philosophical Foundations* ch. 7.

73 Psalm 34:8.

74 Matthew 7:8.

75 See p. 152.

76 See Alvin Plantinga, 'Pluralism: A Defense of Religious Exclusivism', in Philip L. Quinn and Kevin Meeker (eds), *The Philosophical Challenge of Religious Diversity* (New York: Oxford University Press, 2000), p. 189. Plantinga even concedes that such a lapse in confidence could result in the loss of warrant for one's Christian beliefs, but he insists that it need not do so.

77 See p. 152.

78 See Keith Yandell, *The Epistemology of Religious Experience* (Cambridge: Cambridge University Press, 1993), pp. 15–32, where he distinguishes five types of religious experience. Yandell claims that Jain and Buddhist experiences are not even experiences of the divine but rather of the self; hence, these diverse experiences could all be veridical because they are not of the same thing (ibid., pp. 281–313).

79 Romans 8:15–17.

80 Craig, *Five Views*, pp. 29–30.

81 Alvin Plantinga, 'The Foundations of Theism: A Reply', *Faith and Philosophy*, 3 (1986), pp. 310–11.

Chapter 12

A Reply to my Critics

Antony Flew

Introduction

The debate in Madison, Wisconsin which stimulated the production of the present book took place on 18 February 1998. The summons to produce this final chapter was received less than a month before the third anniversary of that event, while the opportunity to make some final alterations and additions was granted to me almost exactly one year after that. During those four years I came across materials which, at first sight, appeared to call for some fairly radical rethinking about relevant issues. Later and closer examination of these materials revealed that the rethinking actually required of me was not, after all, very radical. But, since the present chapter is likely to be my last substantial publication in the philosophy of religion, and since my first and by far most widely circulated publication in this area first appeared over 50 years ago[1] I am in academic honour bound to begin this chapter by indicating what those materials were, or are, and what consequent new thinking seemed to be required.

Challenge To Think Anew

The first of these new materials consisted in newspaper and broadcast reports of researches which were said to have shown that some medical patients had enjoyed some form of consciousness at times when they were clinically brain-dead. But, just as soon as I was able to study the reports of the researchers themselves, it became clear to me that these researches did not establish what so many journalists, but not the researchers themselves, had claimed that they had established.

The second thing to which it seemed that I must attend was the publication of Michael J. Behe's *Darwin's Black Box: The Biochemical Challenge to Evolution*.[2] This book was presented by its author and his publishers as having developed a new and more powerful form of Argument to Design. I was saved by the friendly intervention of Richard Dawkins from publishing a favourable review of this book, and thus making a public fool of myself. For Dawkins told me that before publishing such a review I must first read Kenneth Miller *Finding Darwin's God*.[3] Miller, like Behe, is a devout Christian. But that does not stop him from destroying Behe's argument point by point and making scathing comments on Behe's failure to attend to relevant research findings in what was, after all, Behe's own field. (It was, of course, that fact which had led me to believe that I ought to take notice of his book.)

Mention of Kenneth Miller's book provides an occasion to point out that it is entirely reasonable for a cradle Catholic, such as Miller himself, to see as evidencing reasons for maintaining beliefs which he already holds considerations which would not constitute good evidencing reasons for adopting those beliefs in the first place. For instance, the acceptance of the Big Bang cosmology may not provide a good, or even any sort of, evidencing reason for believing that 'in the beginning' the universe was created by God. But for those who do already have some sort of sufficient reason for holding the essential Roman[4] Catholic doctrine that the universe had a beginning and will have an end, its acceptance surely does provide empirical confirmation for the first part of that belief.

It was his commitment to this essential of his Roman Catholic faith which led Aquinas to write and to publish his pamphlet *De aeternitate mundi contra murmurantes*. For what had originally provoked those murmurings of 'heresy, heresy' was the fact that his 'Five Ways' – ways, hopefully, of proving the existence of God – did not at the same time even attempt to prove that the universe was 'in the beginning' created by God. To these rumours Aquinas responded in that pamphlet by insisting that while being, regrettably, unable to provide a rational demonstration of the truth of this proposition, he himself, of course, believed it. For it was then, as it still remains, an essential of the Roman Catholic faith.

Another example is provided by the fine-tuning argument. As will become apparent later, I do not myself believe that this constitutes a substantial evidencing reason for believing that the creator, if such there was and is, creates and sustains the universe partly or mainly or solely in order that it should contain human beings. But for anyone who, like Kenneth Miller, does already believe that this was, and is, a or the main purpose which the creator had and still has in mind, it is entirely reasonable to welcome the fine-tuning argument as providing confirmation for that antecedent belief.

The third of these stimuli to new thinking was David Conway's *The Rediscovery of Wisdom: From Here to Antiquity in Quest of Sophia*.[5] In this book Conway attempts to defend what he describes as 'the classical conception of philosophy'. That conception is:

> [T]he view that the explanation of the world and its broad form is that it is the creation of a supreme omnipotent and omniscient intelligence, more commonly referred to as God who created it in order to bring into existence and sustain rational beings such as ourselves who, by exercising their intellects, can become aware of the existence of God and thereby join their Creator in the activity of contemplating God, in which God is perpetually and blissfully engaged.[6]

Conway further contends that this Aristotelian God, of whose existence and nature he believes it is possible to learn by the exercise of unaided human reason – as a finding, that is, of natural, as opposed to revealed, theology – this being nevertheless possesses 'most of the usual defining characteristics of omnipotence, omniscience, immateriality, and so on'. But to assert this is, he insists, a very different thing from maintaining that the teachings of any one of the three great monotheistic systems of religion – Judaism, Christianity and Islam – includes any items of self-revelation by that God.

What Conway does not point out is the fact that and the reasons why the teachings that are peculiar to any or all of those three great monotheistic systems of religion are not included among, and cannot be derived from, the defining characteristics of that Aristotelian God. The reason is that, absent revelation to the contrary, an omnipotent and omniscient creator God could not reasonably have been expected to create and sustain any universe which was not to that creator God's own complete satisfaction.

Surely to anyone who was, for the first time and without prejudice, entertaining the hypothesis that our universe is the creation of an omnipotent and omniscient God it would appear obvious that everything which occurs or does not occur within it must, by the hypothesis, be precisely and only what its creator wants, indeed causes, to occur or not to occur. What scope is there for creatures in such a universe to defy the will of their creator? What room is there even for a concept of such defiance? For a creator to punish creatures for what, by the hypothesis, that creator necessarily and as such (ultimately) causes them to do would be the most monstrous, perverse, unjust and sadistic of performances. Absent revelation to the contrary, the expectations of natural reason must surely be that such a creator God would be as detached and uninvolved as the gods of Epicurus. Indeed, some Indian religious thinkers not prejudiced by any present or previous Mosaic commitments are said to describe their monotheistic God as being, essentially and in the nature of the case, 'beyond good and evil'. For as Einstein was to put it:

> Nobody, certainly, will deny that the idea of the existence of an omnipotent, just, and omnibeneficient personal God is able to accord man solace, help, and guidance .... But, on the other hand, there are decisive weaknesses attached to this idea in itself, which have been painfully felt since the beginning ... if this being is omnipotent then every occurrence, including every human action, every human thought, and every human feeling and aspiration, is also his work. How is it possible to think of holding men responsible for their deeds and thoughts before such an almighty Being? In giving out punishment and rewards he would be ... passing judgment on himself.[7]

The concept of God presented by Conway is thus deistic rather than theistic and not so much that of Aristotle as, at most, Aristotelian. Deists believed that the existence of their God could commend itself to the human mind by its own inherent reasonableness, without either being supported by appeals to alleged divine self-revelations or imposed by religious institutions. Deism is usually taken to include an insistence that God, once the work of creation is completed, leaves the universe generally subject to no divine laws other than the laws of nature, although perhaps sometimes providing rather distant and detached endorsement of the fundamental principles of justice.[8] The best known manifestations of deism occurred in the thought of the eighteenth-century Enlightenment, and especially that of Voltaire.

The writings of Aristotle himself contain no concept of a single omnipotent and omniscient personal being, making demands on his human beings for our obedience, much less threatening us with an eternity of extreme torture for what he perceives as unforgivable disobedience. The closest which Aristotle's God comes to prescribing or proscribing any kind of human conduct – and it is almost as far as it could possibly be from actually doing so – is when, in the *Nicomachean Ethics*, not Aristotle's God but Aristotle tells us that 'the divine life, which surpasses all other in blessedness, consists in contemplation'.[9] So when we find Aquinas concluding, after presenting an Aristotelian argument for a First Cause or a Prime Mover, that 'This we call God'[10] we may well agree, but only with the caveat 'But in a very different understanding of the meaning of the word "God"'.

Swinburne's definition, which has become the agreed starting point for most philosophical discussion of God's existence, not only in the United Kingdom but also more generally throughout the English-speaking world, reads:

> ... a person without a body (that is a spirit), present everywhere, the creator and sustainer of the universe, able to do everything (that is omnipotent), knowing all things, perfectly good, a source of moral obligation, immutable, eternal, a necessary being, holy and worthy of worship.[11]

This definition embraces several different defining characteristics, not all of which are mutually entailed and only one of which – that of being a necessary being – is explicitly and unequivocally a characteristic of Aristotle's God. There is therefore room for importantly different, even if closely related, senses of the word 'God'.

The main effect on me of reading Conway's book was of being forced to realize more fully the enormous difference between the nature of the God who might be discovered by a successful natural theology and of those Gods perceived as revealing themselves in the *New Testament* and in the Qur'an. For in both those two very different media of revelation[12] God is revealed as predestining His human creatures to choose to behave: not only when they will in fact choose to act in ways which He intends to reward with an eternity of bliss; but also when they will in fact choose to act in ways which He intends to punish with an eternity of torture.

Nowadays it appears to be widely assumed that this appalling doctrine is peculiar to a handful of self-confessed Calvinists and has been, and could, *consistently* be abandoned by other truly believing Christians. Certainly Calvin himself was uninhibited in insisting that God must be the ultimate author of human sin, as of everything else, and he was understandably impatient with those who failed to see this as a logically necessary consequence of Christian fundamentals: 'The ears of some are offended when one says that God willed it. But I ask you, what else is the permission of him who is entitled to forbid, or rather who has the thing in his own hands, but an act of will?'[13]

This doctrine of divine predestination which, as Calvin said, offends some ears, certainly offended the ears of all members of my own family and of all the other believing Christians whom I ever met before I went to university. When I first learned of the existence of belief in this doctrine, I was assured that, in the twentieth century, it was maintained only by Calvinists, whom we never met. When in 1950 I became a lecturer in the University of Aberdeen I was disappointed to discover that there were, by then, no Calvinists to be found even in the once solidly Calvinist Kirk of Scotland.

But the doctrine of predestination is quite certainly biblical. For St Paul, who clearly had a first-class philosophical mind, saw at once and without hesitation the logically necessary implications of maintaining that the universe and everything and everyone in it was created and is sustained by an omnipotent and omniscient personal being who nevertheless punishes creatures inordinately for delinquencies of which he himself is necessarily the necessitating cause:

> For the scripture saith unto Pharaoh, Even for this same purpose have I raised thee up, that I might shew my power in thee, and that my name might be declared throughout all the earth. Therefore hath he mercy upon whom he will have mercy, and whom he will he hardeneth.
>
> Thou wilt say then unto me, Why doth he yet find fault? For who hath resisted his will? Nay but, O man, who art thou that repliest against God? Shall the thing formed say to him that formed it, Why hast thou made me thus? Hath not the potter power over the clay, of the same lump to make one vessel unto honour and another unto dishonour? What if God, willing to shew his wrath, and to make his power known, endured with much longsuffering the vessels of wrath fitted to destruction: and that he might make known the riches of his glory on the vessels of mercy, which he had afore prepared unto glory, even us, whom he hath called, not of the Jews only but also of the Gentiles?[14]

Luther, to his credit, made clear during his controversy with Erasmus that he was appalled by these predestinarian implications. He nevertheless realized that they are inescapable:

> Common sense and natural reason are highly offended that God by his mere will deserts, hardens, and damns, as if delighted in sins and such eternal torments, he who is said to be of such mercy and goodness. Such a concept of God appears wicked, cruel, and intolerable, and by it many men have been revolted in all ages. I myself was once offended to the very depth of the abyss of desperation, so that I wished I had never been created. There is no use in trying to get away from this by ingenious distinctions. Natural reason, however much it is offended, must admit the consequences of the omniscience and omnipotence of God.[15]

Later, Luther addresses himself to the question: 'Why then does He not alter those evil wills which He moves?' Understandably, if unsatisfactorily, Erasmus receives no answer:

> It is not for us to inquire into these mysteries, but to adore them. If flesh and blood take offence here and grumble, well, let them grumble; they will achieve nothing; grumbling will not change God! And however many of the ungodly stumble and depart, the elect will remain.[16]

The (not very near) nearest which Luther comes to any solution to what he sees as these mysteries is to appeal to faith:

> The highest degree of faith is to believe He is just, though of His own will he makes us ... proper subjects for damnation, and seems (in the words of Erasmus) 'to delight in the torments of poor wretches and to be a fitter object for hate than for love.' If I could by any means understand how this same God ... can yet be merciful and just, there would be no need for faith.[17]

Today, many thoroughly instructed Roman Catholics may be surprised to learn that the same appalling doctrine of divine predestination has been, and presumably still is, an essential element in their faith.[18] Thus the *Summa Theologica* contains a Question of 'Predestination' in which the Angelic Doctor lays it down that:

> As men are ordained to eternal life through the providence of God, it likewise is part of that providence to permit some to fall away from that end; this is called reprobation ... Reprobation implies not only foreknowledge but also is something more ....[19]

What, and how much that something more is, the *Summa contra Gentiles* makes clear:

> ... just as God not only gave being to things when they first began, but is also – as the conserving cause of being – the cause of their being as long as they last ... so He also not only gave things their operative powers when they were first created, but is also always the cause of these in things. Hence if this divine influence stopped every operation would stop. Every operation, therefore, of anything is traced back to Him as its cause.[20]

This is spelt out more fully in two later chapters:

> God alone can move the will, as an agent, without doing violence to it .... Some people ... not understanding how God can cause a movement of our will, have tried to explain ... authoritative texts wrongly; that is, they would say that God 'works in us, to wish and to accomplish' means that He causes in us the power of willing, but not in such a way that He makes us will this or that ... these people are, of course, opposed quite plainly by authoritative texts of Holy Writ. For it says in Isaiah (36:2)[21] 'Lord, you have worked all your work in us'. Hence we receive from God not only the power of willing but its employment also.[22]

The Angelic Doctor, however, is always the devotedly complacent *apparatchik*. He sees no problem with the justice of either the inflicting of infinite and everlasting penalties for finite and temporal offences or of their being inflicted upon creatures for offences which their creator makes them (choose to) commit. For:

> In order that the happiness of the saints may be more delightful to them and that they may render more copious thanks to God ... they are allowed to see perfectly the sufferings of the damned ... the Divine justice and their own deliverance will be the direct cause of the joy of the blessed, while the pains of the damned will cause it indirectly ... the blessed in glory will have no pity for the damned.[23]

There is a second reason why it is mistaken to insist that the creator endowed human beings – 'made in his own image' – with free will, thus ensuring that God is not responsible for our making the sinful choices which we so perversely and persistently do make. This reason is that predestinationists do not, in fact, deny that we are members of a kind of creatures who can, and therefore cannot but, make choices – some made by the agents of their own free will and some made under various forms and degrees of coercion and constraint. If, and in as far as, any predestinationists do deny free will, it is only in some factitious misunderstanding of the colloquial meaning of the term 'free will', a misunderstanding introduced in a vain attempt to refute the charge that the God of Judeo-Christian and Islamic theism must be recognized as necessarily being one causally necessitating His creatures to choose – though free of any of this worldly coercion or constraint – to do deeds for which He proposes to punish them with an eternity of torture. Luther had his own characteristically vehement way of dismissing this 'free will defense'[24] of divine justice:

> Now by 'necessarily' I do not mean compulsorily but by the necessity of immutability (as they say) and not of compulsion. That is to say, when a man is without the Spirit of God he does not do evil against his will, as if he were taken by the scruff of his neck and forced to do it, like a thief or a robber carried off against his will to punishment, but he does it of his own accord and with a ready will.[25]

Those who know of the Church of England only in its present (in more than one sense) secular decline will perhaps be surprised to learn that, once upon a time, its Commission on Doctrine unhesitatingly affirmed 'that the whole course of events is under the control of God' and appreciated that 'logically this involves the affirmation of that there is no event, and no aspect of any event, even those due to sin and so contrary to the Divine will, which falls outside the scope of His purposive activity'.[26] The same doctrine was spelt out in the only recently abandoned *Book of Common Prayer*. There, in Article 17 'Of Predestination and Election', every worshipper was invited to ask himself or herself whether he or she was one of the Elect, of those who, as such, 'can feel in themselves the working of the Spirit of Christ, mortifying the works of the flesh, and their earthly members, and drawing up their mind to high and heavenly things' or whether he or she is a 'curious and carnal person' predestined to damnation.

God Conceived as an Arbitrary Cosmic Despot

At this point it needs to be said, loud and clear, that, even if it were possible to show that the predestinarian conclusions which St Paul, Aquinas, Luther, Calvin and others drew from their theistic premises do not follow – which obviously, I believe that it is not – it is still urgently necessary to insist against them all that the imposition of any eternal punishment for the sins of even the most monstrously and extensively wicked of us mortal human beings would be so inordinately disproportionate to the necessarily finite offences of 'those people'[27] as to make it necessary to refuse to accept such impositions as exercises of divine *justice*.[28]

Once the condemnation of the majority[29] of the human race to eternal torture is recognized as being an unjust exercise of arbitrary power, it begins to be possible to see the God of traditional Christianity as being, like the God of Islam, an infinitely terrifying oriental despot ever concerned to manifest and exercise His power by insisting on total obedience and constant worship from His creatures.

But how, it may be objected, does this idea of God as an oriental despot square with the accepted Swinburnian definition of the word 'God'?[30] Two of the characteristics listed by Swinburne immediately raise questions for me – that of being perfectly good and that of being a source of moral obligation. When in my fifteenth year – during the later 1930s – I myself first ceased to be a believer it was because it seemed to me then, as it still does, that the claim that this universe was created and is sustained by a being who is omniscient and omnipotent and yet at the same time, in any everyday understanding of the word, perfectly good is utterly incompatible with manifest and undenied facts about the universe.

This objection was, at the time when I first went up to Oxford, known to Christians, as no doubt it had been long before and would be long after, as the 'Problem of Evil'. I remember the main argument which was offered in attempts to solve it at the meetings, weekly in term-time, of the Socratic Club – an organization founded by C.S. Lewis and, in my time, always chaired by Lewis himself. The key idea of this apologetic was that what might be seen as a logically lower-order evil, for instance injury, is the logically necessary precondition of what might be seen as a logically higher-order good, in this case that of forgiveness.[31] It was only after attending, and being involved in, many discussions in the Socratic Club that I went on to publish my suggestion that what Hume rather than Laplace was the first to call 'the religious hypothesis' is in principle neither verifiable nor falsifiable.[32]

What I now still see as the contradiction between the fact of the enormous evils in this universe and the claim that this universe is created and sustained by an omnipotent, omniscient and perfectly good God is, by some philosophical theologians, resolved by metaphysically identifying goodness with reality. This manoeuvre ultimately derives from Plato's identification in *The Republic* of the Form or Idea of the Good with the Form or Idea of the Real. It was this and only this peculiar and, to me, wholly unacceptable semantic equation which enabled Leibniz, in his *Theodicy*, to demonstrate to his own satisfaction that a universe in which the majority of the human race are destined to unending extremes of torture is the Best of All Possible Worlds. Similar metaphysical manoeuvres are presumably required in order to introduce interpretations of the terms 'love' and 'just' which will permit the truth of Craig's[33] contention that it is just for God to punish with eternal torture those of His creatures who persistently reject His love and His forgiveness.[34]

So much for defining God as perfectly good. To define God as the source of moral obligation raises, as of course Swinburne himself is well aware, what has come to be called the Euthyphro question:[35] 'Is what is morally good morally good because God makes it so or does God love it because it is morally good?' It is called the Euthyphro question because in Plato's dialogue, *Euthyphro*, the participant Euthyphro is scripted to ask the parallel question: 'Is piety good because God loves it or does God love it because it is good?' In the present context the question can best be approached, and to my mind for the theist definitively answered, by quoting what Thomas Hobbes said in Chapter XI of his *Leviathan*:

> The right of nature whereby God reigneth over men, and punisheth those that break His laws, is to be derived not from his creating them, as if he required obedience as of gratitude for his benefits, but from his irresistible power .... To those therefore whose power is irresistible the dominion of all men adhereth naturally by their excellence of power; and, consequently, it is from that power that the kingdom over men and the right of afflicting them at his pleasure belongeth naturally to God almighty, not as creator and gracious, but as omnipotent. and though punishment be due to sin only, because by that word is understood affliction for sin, yet the right of afflicting is not always derived from men's sin but from God's power.
>
> This question, 'Why evil men often prosper and good men suffer adversity?' has been much disputed ... and is the same with this of ours, 'By what right God dispenses the prosperities and adversities of this life?' and is of that difficulty as it hath shaken the faith not only of the vulgar but of philosophers, and, which is more, of the saints, concerning the divine providence. ... This question in the case of Job is decided by God himself not by arguments derived from Job's sin but his own power. For whereas the friends of Job drew their arguments from his affliction to his sin, and he defended himself by the conscience of his innocence, God himself taketh up the matter; and, having justified the affliction by arguments drawn from his power, such as this, 'Where wast thou when I laid down the foundations of the earth?', and the like, both approved Job's innocence and reproved the erroneous doctrine of his friends.[36]

A Personal Confession of Perhaps Wider Interest

Here it may be of more than a narrowly personal interest if I reveal that I was, when I first announced my inability to reconcile manifest facts about the universe around us with the existence of an omnipotent, omniscient and perfectly good God, attending a boarding school founded by John Wesley for the education of the sons of his preachers and run under the auspices of the Methodist Church. Moreover, my father was a Methodist minister who was, for most of his career, a teacher of theology.

Yet no one at that time, or for many years thereafter, ever warned me that my defection from the Christian faith put me in danger of suffering an eternity of extreme torture. My father was also a first-class preacher, with a very strong sense of a mission to preach 'the Gospel of our Lord Jesus Christ'. I suspect now that the reason why that first-rate preaching won few, if any, converts was that he could not bring himself to follow the example of John Wesley by starting his sermons with the threat of extreme and unending torture, and proceeding to offer to convert salvation from that unimaginably appalling and cruel fate.

It was only a long time after my school days that I came to realize that all these committed Christians – for whom I had, and still retain, both respect and affection – must have been finding themselves in a distressing situation of a kind in which adherents of many ideological systems, both religious and secular, have found themselves in the twentieth century. They could bring themselves neither actually to reject doctrines some of the consequences of which they had begun to find altogether unacceptable nor to try to justify these consequences.

Throughout the twentieth century teachings about hell have, in at least the mainstream Protestant Churches, been progressively de-emphasized. Indeed the Church of England Commission on Doctrine, reporting in 1995, asserted that 'It is incompatible with the essential Christian affirmation that God is love to say that God brings millions into the world to damn them'.[37] The title of this work, *The Mystery of Salvation*, is peculiarly apt. For, without the threat of eternal torture, what is the promise of salvation a promise of salvation from? Regrettably, for most of us sinners, the offer of salvation from our sins as such, as opposed the offer of escape from any penalties for committing them, has little appeal.

Irreverent unbelievers may be inclined to wonder why it took Protestant Churches so long to recognize openly the incompatibility between an omnipotent love and endless torture, while readers of the present volume will note that Craig persists in a refusal to recognize it.[38] Thomas Hobbes, who must have devoted a very great deal of his time between the publication of the King James Bible in 1611 and that of his own *Leviathan* in 1651 to careful critical reading and rereading of the former work, had a contribution to make here both as a philosopher of religion[39] and as a biblical critic. For, as we have just seen, after arguing in Chapter XXXI of *Leviathan*, that omnipotent power is its own justification, Hobbes went on to argue that a more careful reading of the New Testament suggests that the Christian hell is not forever:

> And it is said besides in many places [that the wicked] shall go into *everlasting fire; and that the worm of conscience never dieth*; and all this is comprehended in the word *everlasting death*, which is ordinarily interpreted *everlasting life in torments*. And yet I can find no where that any man shall live in torments everlastingly. Also, it seemeth hard, to say, that God who is the father of mercies; that doth in heaven and earth all that he will; that hath the hearts of all men in his disposing; that worketh in men both

to do, and to will; and without whose free gift a man hath neither inclination to good, nor repentance of evil, should punish men's transgressions without any end of time, and with all the extremity of torture, that men can imagine, and more.[40]

Islam Reveals the Divine Arbitrariness More Clearly

Earlier I suggested that, once the condemnation of the majority of the human race to eternal torture was recognized as being an unjust exercise of arbitrary power, it would begin to be possible to see the God of traditional Christianity as being, like the God of Islam, an infinitely terrifying oriental despot ever concerned to manifest and exercise His power by insisting on total obedience and constant worship from His creatures.

There are two reasons why this is clearer in the case of Islam than it is in the case of Christianity. The first is that, whereas only a tiny proportion of all the sentences in the Bible express utterances directly attributed to God – even if, by the acceptance of the divinity of Jesus, those attributed to Jesus are included in the list – every single sentence in the Qur'an is supposed to have been uttered by God ('Allah' is the Arabic equivalent of the English 'God') through the mouth of the Archangel Gabriel to the Prophet Muhammad. The second reason is that the Islamic world has never enjoyed either a Reformation or an Enlightenment and, as a result, there is far less of a gulf between the actual beliefs of most Muslims today and the beliefs of Muslims in the early centuries of Islam than there is between the beliefs of the saints and the fathers in the first centuries of Christianity and the actual beliefs of most of those who see themselves as orthodox believing Christians today.

At the very beginning of the Qur'an we find a passage paralleling the passage from Romans quoted earlier:

> As for the unbelievers, alike it is to them,
> whether thou has warned them or hast not warned them,
> they do not believe.
> God has set a seal on their hearts and on their hearing
> and on the eyes is a covering,
> and there waits them a mighty chastisement.[41]

Again:

> If God had willed, He would have made you
> one nation; but he leads astray
> whom He will, and guides whom He will.[42]

And among those whom He will most certainly be leading astray are all Christians:

They are unbelievers,
who say, God is the Third of Three
No god is there but
One God
If they refrain not from what they say, there
shalt afflict those of them that disbelieve
a painful chastisement ....
... and in the chastisement they
shall dwell forever.[43]

The Consequences of Approaching Natural Theology without Theistic Prejudice

Before beginning to offer reflections on the actual materials of the debate and
the later commentaries thereon I want first to say something about my own
gross deficiencies as a debater. I was, if anything, a little surprised that only one
of the commentators complained that my 'remarks throughout the debate'
were 'more meandering and disjointed than Craig's'.[44] Another charitably
refused to particularize my many deficiencies, noting only that I was up against
'a professional debater known far and wide for his skills in oral disputation.[45]
He might have added, had he known it, that, that Madison occasion was only
the second time in my life that I had ever served as one of the two protagonists
in a formal debate. But what I most scandalously failed to make clear in my
first speech was that I should be unable to offer any substantial evidencing
reasons for believing that Swinburne's God does not exist, and able only to
argue that sufficient evidencing reasons for believing that He does exist have
not, and cannot, be produced.[46]

What I want to say now, and what I ought to have said in my first speech in
the debate, is that if we want to approach the question of the existence of the
God of what Islam knows as 'the peoples of the Book' without prejudice, as we
should approach all such disputed questions, then we need to try to approach it
as if we, as fully grown adults, were meeting the concept of that God, also fully
developed, for the first time, and as if we were now, also for the first time,
wondering whether that concept does in fact have actual application. For it is,
surely, significant that almost everyone who has ever given sustained attention
to this question has treated it as being about the concept of the logically
presupposed source of a putative self-revelation, and that accounts of those
putative self-revelations have been handed down and made familiar to those
questioners through generations of parents and pedagogues, of priests and
rabbis, of imams and ayatollahs.

I myself only acquired this insight as a result of conversations with the very
able Chinese graduate student who acted as my 'minder' in Beijing in 1990.[47]
He was, of course, familiar with that conception of God, but he had
encountered it as today anyone anywhere might happen to come upon the
notions of Aphrodite or Poseidon.[48] He had never had occasion to confront it
as what William James called a 'live option' any more than, for any of our
contemporaries anywhere, belief in the real existence of the Olympians
constitutes such an option. So, confronted by the question 'What if anything

caused the Big Bang?' his response would have been – and, indeed, it was – that if physicists cannot find the true physical answer, if there is one, then the Big Bang will have to be accepted as for us the ultimate brute fact, which explains but cannot itself be explained. And, having learned from Hume that the sentence 'Every event has a cause' is not an expression of a logically necessary truth, he had no inclination to seek a metaphysical cause.

Because of my failure to make clear my fundamental position on the unverifiability and unfalsifiability of 'the religious hypothesis', Craig very reasonably saw my insistence on the manifest incompatibility of the characteristic of perfect goodness with the characteristic of torturing eternally as an attempt to refute the teaching that a 'torturer ... runs the universe'. That it certainly was not. But I am not sure now what it was that I did then have in mind. Probably it was the thought that I might later in the debate make something of the metaphysical manoeuvre whereby Leibniz contrived to reach the conclusion that the best of all possible worlds is one in which the majority of human beings are destined to an eternity of torture.

Rowe in a lively Chapter 4 wrote:

> It is unfortunate that Flew gives up so much ground to Craig at the outset by choosing only to argue that the reasons for thinking that there is a God are inadequate. Surely the enormous amount of apparently pointless suffering in the world provides an important argument for the non-existence of God.[49]

I hope that Rowe will be satisfied when he learns from the present chapter how and why I first came to unbelief and how I remain unpersuaded by attempts to solve the 'Problem of Evil'.

The other thing which I want to say here about my first response in the debate is that I was trying to approach the old question of whether the universe was created and is sustained by God without prejudice – as my Chinese 'minder' would have approached it, and indeed did.

If once we try to approach the question of the possible causal or lack of causal explanation of the occurrence of the Big Bang disembarrassed of theistic prejudices it surely becomes obvious, in the light of all, or perhaps only almost all, our previous experience of the natural world that we should look first for a physical explanation – a physical cause – while also recognizing that it may actually not be possible for physicists living after the Big Bang to discover that physical explanation, that physical cause, if such there was. What we surely cannot do is take it as obvious, indeed perhaps a logically necessary truth, that 'from the very nature of the case, as the cause of space and time, this cause must be uncaused, timeless, changeless, and immaterial being of unimaginable power that created the universe'.[50]

If physicists are unable to find any physical explanation of the origins of the Big Bang then, absent Craig's metaphysical revelation of what supposedly has to have been its cause, we have to accept the Big Bang itself as the fundamental brute fact. For it is surely a necessary truth that all systems of scientific explanation have to end in something which explains but which is not itself explained.

Every successive stage of explanation involves showing how what is to be explained is a case of, or can be derived from, a wider regularity or set of regularities. Suppose that we notice, and are puzzled by, the fact the new white paint above our gas cooker quickly turns a dirty brown. The first stage is to discover that this is what always happens, with that sort of stove and that kind of paint. Pressing our questions to a second stage we learn that this phenomenon is to be explained by reference to certain deeper and wider regularities of chemical combination; the sulphur in the gas fumes forms a compound with something in the paint. Driving on still further we are led to see the squalor in our kitchen as, in the circumstances, one of the innumerable consequences of the truth of an all-embracing atomic–molecular theory of the structure of matter. And so on. At every stage, the explanation is in terms of something else which, at that stage, has to be accepted as a brute fact. In some further stage that fact itself may be explained but still in terms of something else which, at least temporarily, has simply to be accepted. It would therefore seem to be a consequence of the essential nature of explanation that, however much may ultimately be explained in successive stages of inquiry, there must always be some facts which have simply to be accepted with what Samuel Alexander used to call 'natural piety'!

It is often thought, by naturalists as well as by theists, that it is an unavoidable defect in every naturalistic system, and one which – if only it happened to be true – theism could remedy, that in any such naturalistic system the most fundamental laws of matter and energy cannot be susceptible of any further explanation. Yet this is not, if the system is true, a defect; nor is it one which, granted that theism is true, theism can remedy. For it is not a defect in one particular sort of system, but a logical truth about all explanations of facts. For precisely the same reason, the ultimate facts about God would have to be equally inexplicable. In each and every case we must necessarily find at the end of every explanatory road some ultimates which have simply to be accepted as the fundamental truths about the way things are. And this itself is a contention not about the lamentable contingent facts of the human condition, but about what follows necessarily from the nature of explanation.

Are There Such Entities as Substantial Spirits?

I have already raised difficulties about two of the defining characteristics of Swinburne's God: that of being perfectly good and that of being a source of moral obligation. I now want at least to hint at difficulties about that most fundamental characteristic of being 'a person without a body (i.e. a spirit)'.

This conception of God was first developed in a period – centuries, even millennia ago – when everyone believed, as many still do, that the earth, indeed the entire universe, is full of active but invisible, intangible and immaterial spirits. Everyone believed that these spirits, of whose existence and activities everyone believed that they were only too well aware, were, just because they were such agents – what philosophers would call substances.

In the present context, the meaning of the word 'substance' and of its equivalent expression 'subsistent being' can perhaps most effectively be explained with the help of two references to the works of Lewis Carroll. In *Alice's Adventures in Wonderland* we can read of Alice's dealings with the cat who kept appearing and disappearing so suddenly that it made her quite giddy. In response to her consequent protest, 'it vanished quite slowly, beginning with the end of its tail, and ending with the grin, which remained sometime after the rest of it had gone'.[51] The absurdity here arises from the fact that 'grin' is not a word for a substance. It makes no sense to talk of grins occurring without the faces of which grins constitute one possible kind of configuration.

In *Through the Looking Glass* the Red Queen orders Alice to '"try another subtraction sum. Take a bone from a dog, what remains?" Alice considered: "The bone wouldn't remain, of course, if I took it – and the dog wouldn't: it would come to bite me – and I'm sure I shouldn't remain".' So Alice reasonably thinks that nothing would remain. But the Red Queen characteristically insists that Alice '"is wrong as usual ... the dog would lose its temper, wouldn't it? .... Then if the dog went away its temper would remain!"'[52] Here again the absurdity arises from mistaking a word – in this case the word 'temper' – to be a word for a substance, which it is not.

From this consideration of Carroll's instructive nonsense it should by now have become clear that the words 'mind', 'soul' and 'personality' are, in their everyday employments, not to be construed as words for subsistent beings. This is no trifling 'merely verbal' matter since it cannot but lead to questionings about the possibility of human beings surviving their own deaths. This extremely important issue I have myself examined at some length elsewhere.[53]

The relevance or irrelevance of the insubstantiality of spirits to the religious hypothesis is not something to which I have myself ever given as much attention as I should have done. Perhaps this insubstantiality is at least part of what theologians have in mind when they tell us that it is impossible to say *what* God is only *that* He is. I only know of one article on this subject by an unbelieving philosopher. It is 'The Doings of a Bodiless God' by my friend John Gaskin. But, unfortunately, it was a contribution to a *Festschrift* and – as is the way with *Festschriften* – its publication has been, and is likely to continue to be, indefinitely deferred.

Clearing Up Confusions about Compatibilism

Keith Yandell in Chapter 1 tells us that David Yandell in Chapter 9 maintains that my 'critique of Christianity's view of hell assumes compatibilism – a controversial and powerfully criticized position'.[54] I wish he had gone on to cite some of the work of these powerful critics and to indicate what it is which he believes that I mistakenly assumed to be incompatible with what. For, had he done so, I might now be able to understand why he mistook my presentation of the traditional Christian doctrine of predestination to be something which required me to defend my own 'powerfully criticized position'. As it is, all I can do here and now is to say that all the passages from St Paul, St Thomas

Aquinas, Calvin and Luther which I either quoted in the original debate and/or have quoted in this present response to my critics were also quoted in Antony Flew's and Godfrey Vesey's *Agency and Necessity*.[55] In my 'Anti-Social Determinism', published in *Philosophy*, 1994, I was mainly concerned with the unfortunate social effects of deterministic belief. But I did there include a final theological section.

What David Yandell wrote in Chapter 9 was: 'One might also take issue with the apparent compatibilism in Flew's idea that God could "make people such that they would freely choose to do what He desired"'.[56] Reference back to the context from which David Yandell's quotation was drawn will show how very far I was from arbitrarily introducing unargued assumptions of my own. I had quoted from an article by William Lane Craig in which he had said: 'It is logically impossible to *make* someone do something *freely*.' I went on immediately to reply: 'Yes, of course it is, but I didn't say that God should *coerce* people – force them to do it. I said that the omnipotent God would be able to make people such that they would freely choose to do what He desired'.[57]

My subsequent quotations from Aquinas, Luther and St Paul should have been sufficient to show that I was not wantonly introducing an unargued assumption of my own but pointing out that this compatibilism was shared by Aquinas, Luther and St Paul. But, since it clearly was not sufficient, I will here repeat the first of my three quotations from Luther:

> Now by necessarily I do not mean compulsorily ... a man without the Spirit of God does not do evil against his will under pressure as though he were taken by the scruff of his neck and dragged into it, like a thief or a foot pad being dragged off against his will to punishment; but he does it spontaneously and voluntarily.[58]

To which Craig's immediate response was:

> Let's review those three reasons that Dr Flew offers for thinking that God does not exist. The first argument is that, if God is omnipotent, then He should be able to make creatures such that they would always choose the way that He would like them to choose. And as Dr Flew's last speech made very clear, he's presupposing here a Thomistic/Calvinistic doctrine of divine conservation and concurrence.[59]

Well, of course, I was not there, or anywhere else in that debate, trying to prove that the God of traditional Christianity does not exist. How I wish that it was possible decisively to disprove the claim that the universe was created and is sustained by the God of Calvin and Luther, of St Thomas Aquinas and St Paul. What I was trying to reveal in the debate was not that that God does not exist but, rather, how infinitely terrible are the implications if He does. Nor was I aware there or elsewhere of presupposing 'a Thomistic/Calvinistic doctrine of divine conservation and concurrence', for the simple but sufficient reason that I had never before heard of that doctrine and am not even now confident that I have appreciated what difference there is supposed to be between divine conservation and divine concurrence. What I was doing, what Aquinas was doing, and what I should have expected Craig to have been doing had he had any such authority, was appealing to a scriptural statement about the issue. And to what better authority could I myself have appealed – as I actually did – than that of St Paul, whose first-class mind enabled him to see clearly and immediately the necessary consequences of omnipotence and omniscience. I will not quote yet again the devastating passage from Romans quoted earlier.

Since I have failed to master the distinction between divine conservation and divine concurrence I am in no position directly to critique the Molinist doctrine 'that God's general concurrence is an action of God's *directly on the effect* and not on the secondary agents themselves ...'.[60] But I can perhaps usefully suggest that it would appear to be an ancestor of the concept of libertarian free will, which is defined as something the operations of which are neither immediately nor ultimately necessitatingly caused, and hence are in principle unpredictable. Since the reason for introducing this concept is to refute the doctrine of predestination there is no point in introducing it into our vocabulary unless it is at the same time possible to show that we humans are indeed all endowed with free will in this new, factitious sense of the term 'free will'.

We are, most emphatically, not entitled to assume that all human beings are endowed with free will in this understanding of the meaning of the term 'free will' just because we do know that we human beings are, naturally and inescapably, agents. We human beings are, that is to say, members of a kind of creature who, as such, can and therefore cannot but make choices between those different alternative possibilities of action or abstention from action which are, from time to time, open to each one of us as an individual. Some of these choices are made of the agents' own free will whereas others are made under various kinds and degrees of coercion and constraint. It is indeed logically impossible to *coerce* some agent into performing some particular action of his or her own free will. But to say that is not the same thing as saying, nor does it entail, that there were not necessitating, possibly divine, causes for that agent being the agent who performed that action of his or her own free will.

This crucial point about the essential nature of libertarian free will is obscured by Craig. For the argument in his first rebuttal was: 'God's omnipotence does not mean that he can do things that are logically impossible. It is logically impossible to *make* someone *freely* do something. Libertarian freedom *entails* freedom from causal restraints'.[61] I can and do unreservedly accept the first of these three propositions. For what it expresses unequivocally is a logically necessary truth. The second sentence is less unequivocal, for it expresses a logically necessary truth only if the word 'freely' is not construed in its ordinary, everyday, non-technical sense as being as near as makes little matter equivalent to 'voluntarily'. But the third sentence is a philosophical can of worms. For libertarian freedom does not, of course, entail freedom from (earthly) coercion and constraint but does entail the absence of any immediate or ultimate necessitating causation of that libertarian freedom itself. The necessary sorting out of this confusion is perhaps best begun by introducing a crucial distinction first made by Hume in his essay 'Of National Characters':

> By *moral* causes, I mean all circumstances which are fitted to work on the mind as motives or reasons .... By *physical* causes I mean those qualities of the air and climate, which are supposed to work intensibly on the temper, by altering the tone and habit of the body ....[62]

The first thing we need to become clear about is what is wrong with Craig's third sentence: 'Libertarian freedom *entails* freedom from causal restraints.' In the first place, the expression 'freedom from causal restraints' is ambiguous as between the two crucially different senses of the word 'causal', distinguished by Hume. Second, and even more important, it fails actually to stipulate what an endowment with libertarian free will is supposed to preclude – namely, necessitating, and possibly divine, causes not only of being the agent who chooses to perform some actions of his or her own free will but also of being the agent who, in different and less happy circumstances, chooses to perform other actions under some kind of coercion or constraint.

The second thing we need to become clear about is the significance of Luther's statement before the Diet of Worms: 'Here I stand. I can no other. So help me God.' These most famous words of the archetypal Protestant hero are not to be interpreted (as the French would say if only they spoke English) at the foot of the letter. For Luther was not claiming to have fallen victim to a sudden paralysis – God help him. To say, in the everyday sense of 'could not have done otherwise', that I could not have done otherwise is not merely not inconsistent with, but actually presupposes, the truth of the assumption that, in a more fundamental sense, I could. What, as really we all know, Luther meant – and indeed said – was not that he was afflicted with a general paralysis, and hence unable to withdraw, but that none of the alternative courses of action open to him was, to him, acceptable.

Again, consider people who, unlike Luther before the Diet of Worms, act not of their own free will, but under some kind and degree of external compulsion or constraint. Take, to re-employ a favourite fictional example, the case of the man who receives from the Godfather 'an offer which he cannot refuse'. Unlike the errant *mafioso* who is, without warning, gunned down from behind and in that moment ceases to act and to choose, the victimized businessman does have a choice. Is it to be his signature or his brains on the deed to transfer his property to 'The Organization'? Yet, because the alternative rejected was even more intolerable than that accepted, we say that those victims who did put their signatures where the Godfather insisted that they should be put had no choice – that they could not have done otherwise than they did.

My third suggestion in the present context is that anyone proposing to speak either of God endowing human beings with free will or of influences on the will (conceived as a philosophical substance) would be well advised to take note of a very relevant paragraph in the great chapter 'Of Power' in Locke's *Essay Concerning Human Understanding*. In it Locke speaks of putting an end to that:

... unreasonable, because unintelligible, Question, viz. *Whether Man's Will be free, or no.* For if I mistake it not, it follows from what I have said, that the Question itself is altogether improper; and it is as insignificant to ask, whether Man's Will be free, as to ask, whether his Sleep be Swift, or his Vertue square ... and when anyone well considers it, I think he will as plainly perceive, that *Liberty*, which is but a power, belongs only to Agents, and cannot be an attribute or modification of the Will, which is also *but A Power.*[63]

It is, finally in the present context, high time, and perhaps overtime, to raise the question of when and how and by whom the concept of libertarian free will was first introduced. This is a question which really ought to have occurred to the Yandells after they had read my quotations from Aquinas, Luther and – above all – St Paul, and before they began to accuse me of maintaining, without offering supporting argument, 'a controversial and powerfully criticized position'. Who was it by introducing the concept of libertarian free will became the first incompatibilist, and when did they do this? Presumably it was someone worried, and very understandably worried, by the appalling theological implications of compatibilism. St Paul, on the other hand, who had never heard of libertarian free will or of incompatibilism therefore has a claim to have been the first compatibilist.

What Is So Special about Human Beings?

In his first speech Craig asked:

> ... if there is no God, then what's so special about human beings? They're just accidental by-products of nature which have evolved relatively recently on an infinitesimal speck of dust lost somewhere in a hostile and mindless universe and which are doomed to perish individually and collectively in a relatively short time.[64]

Well, for a start, and it is by no means a frivolous start, I have to say that I am not myself so committed to the practice of the new sin of specie-ism as to be worried sick about the ultimate extinction of our species. But that is not to say that I am not concerned, and much more concerned that most people seem to be, about threats to its survival through the next century or three.

Next, if it really was sensible in a matter of this kind to assess importance by reference to relative size, then the fact that the Planet Earth is, as Craig insists, relatively small would be a reason for doubting, rather than believing, that an all-wise and all-powerful being has chosen it as the stage for what He himself is supposed to reckon to be the most important goings-on in the universe.

Then again, it is surely negligent, and methodologically perverse, so immediately to conclude that there is nothing special about our species; and this without even asking whether it actually does have any relevant peculiarities. Once this important question is posed, it becomes obvious that it does have more than one such peculiarity. For as Sophocles famously sang, 'Many are the wonders of the world but none more wonderful than man'.

One of the things which is 'so special about human beings' precisely is that we are members of the uniquely peculiar species whose members can and therefore cannot but make choices between the alternative possible courses of action or abstention from action with which they are from time to time confronted. Another equally remarkable peculiarity is that we are, as human beings, capable of some measure of conscious rationality, both theoretical and practical.

I have here to mention parenthetically, that on this point Draper argued: 'First, not all human beings are equally rational. So if rationality is what makes us special, then not all humans are equally special. Second, some human beings, because of brain damage or for other reasons, are less rational than some animals.'[65] This fallacious argument depends mainly upon confusing 'special' as an adjective meaning belonging to a species and 'special' as meaning in some way extraordinary. But it also assumes, mistakenly, both that a defective creature cannot properly be accounted a member of the species from which it to some extent defects, and that when Aristotle defined Man as the rational animal he meant – as Bertrand Russell so often mischievously suggested – always actually rational as opposed to merely capable of rationality.

Nor should anyone be allowed to get away with arguing, – as Paul Johnson argued, that 'The notion that God permits atrocity is more bearable than the grim alternative'.[66] For, as Jean-Paul Sartre once famously insisted, 'In religion there are also the damned'. I greatly admire Paul Johnson's historical works, and also find myself in strong agreement with him about almost all moral and political issues. So I find it very difficult to persuade myself that he really is so callous as to prefer a universe governed by a God intending to torture some sentient beings eternally to a Godless universe – not, of course, that any human preferences either way constitute evidencing reasons for or against the existence of such a God.

In concluding this section of my response to my critics it has to be said that the fact, if it is a fact, that we are accidental as opposed to designed by-products which have evolved relatively recently can have a very different importance for us from that which Craig suggests. For importance surely is essentially relative, and, on present assumptions, we are the only creatures relative to whom anything can be important or unimportant. Furthermore, we are the only creatures capable of knowing that Planet Earth is indeed where human life 'evolved relatively recently' and that, again relatively, it is 'an infinitesimal speck of dust ... in a hostile and mindless universe'. But what follows from this for us, the only creatures for whom, on present assumptions, anything can be important? It is, surely, that Planet Earth, though relatively tiny, is supremely important. All human life is here! It is, after all, in both the literal and the metaphorical senses, where the action is!

I suggest that the unbeliever can, and should, draw a very different moral from these facts about the relative smallness of human beings. It was the moral drawn by a most distinguished scientist in the concluding paragraph of one of the great sets of Gifford Lectures:

> If you will, man's situation is left bleaker .... Compared with a situation where the human mind ... had higher mind and higher personality ... to lean on and to take counsel from, this other situation where it has no appeal and no resort for help beyond itself, has ... an element of tragedy and pathos. To set against that, it is a situation which transforms the human ... task ... to one of loftier responsibility .... We have, because human, an inalienable prerogative of responsibility which we cannot devolve, no, not as once was thought, even upon the stars. We can share it only with each other.[67]

What Is Really, and not Merely Relatively, Morally Wrong?

I cannot but agree with Geivett's complaint that what I said in the debate left my position on the issues of moral philosophy 'unclear'.[68] But I, in my turn, am somewhat puzzled about his difficulty in reconciling my acceptance of the proposition that 'Objective values do exist' with my speaking, 'Ruse-like, of the need to explain "the evolution of norms"'.[69] For, although my speaking of the evolution of norms was no doubt Ruse-like, it was certainly not intended to carry the same implications. For what Ruse was quoted as saying in Craig's first speech[70] was certainly intended to imply that any such assertion as 'Objective values do exist' must be false whereas to me, as here opposed to Ruse, it appears obvious that it is possible to study the evolution of ideas without prejudice to the question of the validity or invalidity of those ideas. I should perhaps repeat here that what and *all* I mean when I say that I agree with the proposition 'Objectives values do exist' is that I am firm in maintaining that 'some things are really wrong'.[71] What I hold to be 'really wrong' and not just wrong for one person or wrong relative to one society are violations of the principles of what in note 8 I 'called old-fashioned, without prefix or suffix justice'.[72]

This brings us back again to the 'Euthyphro dilemma' which, according to Martin, 'can be stated as follows: does God condemn something because it is wrong or is it wrong because God condemns it?'. He continues later: 'The first horn of the dilemma entails that objective morality is possible without God. The second horn entails that objective morality is impossible with theism'.[73] Martin proceeds to work with Craig's chosen example of rape, pointing out that rape traumatizes and violates the rights of its victims and disrupts the social order. However, if such wrong-making properties provide objective grounds for God's recognizing that rape is wrong then they must, at the same time, provide human beings with equally objective grounds for recognizing this objective moral fact. He then goes on mischievously to examine biblical teachings about rape.[74]

But there is what might be seen as a third way which ought to be mentioned and which has surely often been taken by people who have faced and come to terms with the compulsive clarity of the Euthyphro dilemma. It is to think of God as somehow endorsing – lending His moral authority to – moral behaviour.

This vague notion of endorsing is and, if it is to have its desired practical effect, has to be obscure and unexamined. We can find something like it in the completely secular context of 'celebrity' endorsements of particular brands of products competing for the affections of members of the general public. It was, I suggest, an endorsement of this essentially obscure kind which the many deists among the Founding Fathers of the American Republic had in mind when they made public appeals to their non-Christian God. And perhaps some such idea of divine endorsement remains in the minds of, and has some slight influence upon, many of those who have been subjected to a moral education grounded on religious beliefs which they themselves have either never really had or have later, for almost all practical purposes, abandoned.

In the United Kingdom what moral education was provided in the state-maintained schools from 1944 until the passage of a new Education Reform Act in 1988 was supposed to be provided by a combination of short spells of worship combined with some teaching periods in Religious Knowledge. Any negative effects of this grounding of moral education upon religious beliefs in a period of progressive secularization were presumably, to some no doubt very limited extent, mitigated by the retention in some minds of this somewhat nebulous idea of divine endorsement. Early warnings from unbelievers of the imprudence of such a policy for moral education in such a period were, of course, ignored, presumably at least in part through confusion about the correct resolution of the Euthyphro dilemma.

Evidence for the Physically Impossible

In my second rebuttal I said 'When I was an active member of the Society for Psychical Research we would have had grave doubts about taking as an absolutely faithful record documents that were written, say, a year or so later than the actual event'.[75] My failure on that occasion to indicate why that statement was not merely a personal anecdote but was instead crucially relevant to the whole discussion of 'The historical facts concerning the life, death and Resurrection of Jesus'[76] was surely a most scandalous example of my incompetence as a debater.

The reason why I referred to that particular society was because it was, and is, committed to the investigation of phenomena the occurrence of which are believed to be (not, of course, logically) but practically or physically impossible. But in considering 'the historical facts concerning the life, death and Resurrection of Jesus' we are surely seeking to discover what are truly the historical facts about a putative occurrence which constitutes a – indeed, for Christians, *the* – paradigm case of the physically impossible – not just a (physically impossible) miracle, but *the* physically impossible miracle of miracles. There is surely no dispute about this. Indeed, Craig in his first speech argued that 'If Jesus did rise from the dead, then it would seem that we have a divine miracle on our hands and, thus, evidence for the existence of God'.[77]

The plain consequence is that we need to have far and away stronger evidence for the actual occurrence of a truly miraculous event than we need to have for an ordinary non-miraculous event.[78] Take the matter of the allegedly empty tomb of Jesus. This is something of which so many apologists have made so much. Craig, in his first speech, made this 'Fact 1' in his case for the Resurrection:

> *On the Sunday following his crucifixion Jesus' tomb was found empty by a group of his women followers.* According to Jacob Kremer, an Austrian scholar who has specialized in the study of the Resurrection, 'By far most scholars hold firmly to the reliability of the biblical statements about the empty tomb.'[79]

But those scholars were considering the reliability of those biblical statements as if they were statements about the occurrence of perfectly ordinary events which no one had ever suggested might have miraculous implications. In that case there would be no compelling reason to demand an explanation for their occurrence. But, even in that case, there are very good reasons to doubt the story of the empty tomb. Keith Parsons provides a very plausible account of how this story might have arisen without postulating any miracle as its cause.[80]

Draper[81] makes the important further points that the best available explanation may well not be the correct explanation and that what Craig likes to call his 'three great facts' are 'in, one respect, not so great because they are not probabilistically or explanatorily independent of each other'.[82] Suppose the tomb was empty, Draper argues: 'This could easily cause sightings of Jesus, whether or not he rose from the dead (I wonder how many more Elvis sightings there would be if his body was missing.)'[83]

What has always seemed to me the strongest argument for the Resurrection of Jesus is one to which Dr Craig appeals both in his first speech and in one of his contributions to the subsequent question and answer session.[84] His challenge was to explain how else it was that 'the original disciples suddenly came to believe in the Resurrection of Jesus so strongly that they were willing to die for the truth of that belief'.[85]

The answer came to me in a book by Jack Kent, a retired Unitarian minister of religion, which I had not seen before the debate. In his *The Psychological Origins of the Resurrection Myth*,[86] Kent contends that the alleged appearances of the risen Jesus were grief-related hallucinations. Kent's originality lies not only in his systematic application of this idea to all the relevant New Testament materials but also and mainly in his deployment of abundant recent psychological evidence showing that such extremely vivid grief-related hallucinatory experiences of the recently deceased still are, and presumably always were, quite common.

The Crucial Difference Between Two Senses of 'Experience'

The fifth argument in Craig's first speech in the debate was from 'the immediate experience of God'. 'This isn't really an *argument* for God's existence. Rather, it's the claim that you can know that God exists wholly apart from arguments simply by immediately experiencing Him. This the way in which people in the Bible knew God'.[87] In his second rebuttal he said:

> As for the immediate experience of God (V), I admit that the question is: Is my experience of God veridical? But what I want to know is, in the absence of good arguments for atheism, why deny experience? God is real to me, just as the external world is real. In the absence of good reasons to deny that experience, why am I not rational to go on believing in God?[88]

It is obvious to me now that I totally failed – it may be yet another instance of my manifest deficiencies as a debater – to make clear to Craig, and presumably also to our audience, that I was not, in what would have been a grossly abusive fashion, denying that he has experiences which seem to him to be experiences of God. What I wanted, and still want, to know are the grounds for his belief that those experiences are indeed veridical. For, unless he can produce grounds which are logically independent of his own Christian beliefs, his experiences, however vivid and persuasive they are to him, cannot constitute evidencing reasons for believing that those experiences are indeed veridical. And surely 'people in the Bible' at least believed that they had better evidencing reasons for believing in the existence and activity of the God of Abraham, Isaac and Israel than their own individual and logically private experiences. Or have I just imagined reading in the Old Testament a splendid story about the confounding of the priests of Baal?

The difficulty which Craig found in appreciating what I see as the crucial point is so widely felt that it is worth treating it here at somewhat greater length. The expression 'religious experience' is enormously comprehensive. The word 'experience' can embrace almost everything which is, in a wide sense, psychological: visions of all kinds, dreaming and waking; all the analogues of visions connected with the other senses; emotions, affections, sensations, dispositions; even convictions and beliefs. It also has a fundamental and crucial ambiguity. This ambiguity, which the generic term 'experience' shares with many of its species labels, is that between, first, the sense in which it refers only to what the subject is undergoing and, second, a sense in which it implies that there must be an actual independently existing object as well. It is therefore, as easy as it is both common and wrong to pass without warrant from what is supposed to be simply a description of subjective experience to the conclusion that this must have, and have been occasioned by, some appropriate object in the world outside.

Classic illustration both of the comprehensiveness of the expression and of the diversity of the ostensible objects of this sort of 'revelation' can be found in William James' *The Varieties of Religious Experience*. James was saved by his Yankee common sense, and by the very variety of his studies, from being misled by the ambiguity. The crucial point is put, in his usual succinct and devastating way, by Hobbes:

> For if any man pretend to me that God hath spoken to him ... immediately, and I make doubt of it, I cannot easily perceive what argument he can produce to oblige

me to believe it .... To say he hath spoken to him in a dream, is no more than to say that he dreamed that God spoke to him .... So that though God Almighty can speak to a man by dreams, visions, voice and inspiration; yet he obliges no man to believe he hath done so to him that pretends it.[89]

Could There Be Bodiless People?

In his first rebuttal Craig said that I had maintained 'that the notion of a bodiless person is impossible'. He continued: 'I have two responses to this. In the first place, notice that he gave no proof of this. He gave no argument; he just asserted that it's impossible.'[90] But the reason why I gave no proof and offered no argument for that contention is that it was not the one that I had made. What I had actually said was only that it is 'a notion I find very difficult [albeit not impossible] to understand anyway, as all the people I know are creatures of flesh and blood'.[91] The difficulty is that of applying concepts which derive their original meanings from their applications to creatures of flesh and blood to an object defined as immaterial. I believe that I was right in the debate to do no more than merely mention the difficulties of constructing a concept of a bodiless person. But to anyone interested in examining these difficulties I commend the book, particulars of which are given in note 53.

What, if Anything, Does the Fine-Tuning Argument Prove?

In the very first speech of the entire debate Robert Jastrow, the Head of NASA and the Goddard Institute for Space Studies, was quoted as claiming that the fine-tuning argument constitutes 'the most powerful evidence for the existence of God "ever to come out of science"'.[92] My only contribution to the discussion of the fine-tuning argument was to suggest that, surely, neither the propensity nor the frequency theory of probability can properly be applied outside the universe.[93] I have been reproached, no doubt deservedly, for my failure to do more.[94] But Keith Yandell has saved me from suffering any remorse on this account by doing a much better job of dealing with the probability problems than I myself could ever have achieved.[95]

Something more does however need to be said about Jastrow's claim that the fine-tuning argument constitutes 'the most powerful evidence for the existence of God ever to come out of science'. For this argument is evidence, powerful or otherwise, for the existence of God only if it can be assumed that God, if He exists, will be concerned to create a universe with people in it.

About this assumption I can say here only three things. The first is that, although it certainly provides support for any system of revealed religion, it is by the same token quite unsuited to serve as a foundation for a natural theological argument for the existence of God. The second is that a God concerned to create a universe with people in it would surely have established, for that universe, laws and constants guaranteeing that there were people in it rather than merely ensuring that it was possible that there would be. The third is that the presently available evidence suggests that the emergence of human or a closely analogous form of life was by no means a certainty but rather – as the victor said of the outcome of the Battle of Waterloo – 'a damned nice, close-run thing'. An omnipotent and omniscient being must surely be expected to have acted always in ways which guaranteed the fulfilment of His intentions rather than in ways which made it merely possible or even very likely.

Wainwright's Failure to Distinguish Two Senses of 'Experience'

Chapter 5 by William Wainwright consists largely of a critical consideration of my article 'The Presumption of Atheism', reprinted in 1997,[96] but first published 25 years earlier. The best way for me to respond in the present chapter to Wainwright's objections is, I think, to refer to a controversy about the presumption of atheism, conducted in the two 1997 and the first of the two 1998 issues of *The Journal for the Critical Study of Religion, Ethics and Society*, adding as my comment the first sentence of my final rejoinder to an earlier contribution to that 1997–8 discussion: 'Professor Geivett may be surprised to learn that I find very little in his paper ... with which to disagree.' I believe that this whole discussion, originally published in a since defunct journal, is about to be republished along with some further material, but I cannot say where or when.

Wainwright does, however, take direct exception to one thing which he maintains that I said in the debate: 'at one point Craig appeals to his own conversion experience. Flew dismisses this, arguing that Craig's experiential evidence has no force unless he can make a propositional case for his experience's veridicality.'[97] What and all that I managed to say in the actual debate – and I have, without the slightest sense of embarrassment or shame, to confess that all my arguments on that occasion were, as usual, expressed in propositions – was 'I have no doubt at all that Craig's experience appears to *him* to be of God, but this is a matter in which the subject's honest testimony is not authoritative'.[98] Earlier in the present chapter I tried to make clear that what I wanted, and still want, to know are the grounds for his conviction that what he perceives as experiences of God are indeed veridical, whereas other people's experiences of other gods are not.

Conclusion

Finally, I want, first, to confess that I now accept the reasonableness of the advice to agnostics given in the paragraph quoted by Geivett at the end of his Chapter 3,[99] and then simply to recognize the realized possibility of a dynamic and dedicated Christian faith clearly and categorically rejecting traditional teaching about hell and promising salvation not from an eternity of torture but from an eternity of death.

The particular form of Christian faith which I have in mind is that of the Jehovah's Witnesses who, throughout the twentieth century, must have been the most widely persecuted of all human sects.[100] They have been persecuted by communist and by National Socialist (Nazi) regimes as well as by other regimes of no particular ideological character. I, myself, first heard of such persecution in Malawi in 1967, from a Swedish missionary friend of the friends with whom I was staying. She reported that converts were being punished for resolutely refusing, for religious reasons, to join the party of President Kamuzu Hastings Banda. (It is believed that he wrongly identified them with a very different Watchtower movement which rose in the 1930s in West Africa.)

Perhaps the most impressive example of the courage and commitment of Jehovah's Witnesses was provided by their reaction to the 'particularly ruthless persecution which began within weeks of the Nazis assumption of power'.[101] For 'No other sect displayed anything like the same determination in the face of the full force of Gestapo terrorism'.[102] Visitors to the Sachsenhausen concentration camp, on the outskirts of Berlin, can see the memorial to the more than 850 Witnesses who were martyred there. The next largest group of martyrs was that of the Polish professors, who had been rounded up for future extermination immediately after the German armies entered Warsaw in 1939.

The abandonment of traditional Christian teaching about hell by the Jehovah's Witnesses was not – as with other denominations – a belated, tacit and usually unacknowledged afterthought. Instead it was precisely what set Charles Russell on to the founding of his sect. For 'from adolescence on' he

> ... was never to stop asking how an all-loving God could punish sinners with the infinite torments of hellfire .... To him God was his father in a pre-eminent sense, and because he had always had such a warm loving relationship with his human father ... he could never conceive of the Lord Jehovah as anything but a merciful deity.[103]

I do not know how chosen spokespersons would handle the relevant Gospel passages but the rank-and-file Jehovah's Witnesses coming to my door are certainly delighted to hear such trophies of Hobbesian biblical criticism as the one that I have already quoted in this chapter:

> And it is said besides in many places [that the wicked] shall go into *everlasting fire; and that the worm of conscience never dieth*; and all this is comprehended in the word *everlasting death*, which is ordinarily interpreted *everlasting life in torments*. And yet I can find no where that any man shall live in torments everlastingly. Also, it seemeth hard, to say, that God who is the father of mercies; that doth in heaven and earth all that he will; that hath the hearts of all men in his disposing; that worketh in men both to do, and to will; and without whose free gift a man hath neither inclination to good, nor repentance of evil, should punish men's transgressions without any end of time, and with all the extremity of torture, that men can imagine, and more.[104]

But Hobbes never mentions what perhaps he did not know – that 'Gehenna', the Hebrew word employed by Jesus and usually translated into English as 'Hell', apparently 'means literally "Valley of Hinnom", and refers to a garbage dump outside Jerusalem where rubbish was shot and burnt and where unclean animals fed on garbage'.[105]

Notes

1   This was 'Theology and Falsification', a short article first printed in the first issue of *University*, an ephemeral student journal, in 1950, and first reprinted in Antony Flew and Alasdair MacIntyre (eds), *New Essays in Philosophical Theology* (London: Student Christian Movement, 1955), pp. 96–99. It has since been reprinted at least a further 41 times, including translations into seven languages other than English. The forty-first reprinting was part of 'A Golden Jubilee Celebration' in the October/November 2000 issue of *Philosophy Now*.
2   Michael J. Behe, *Darwin's Black Box: The Biochemical Challenge to Evolution* (New York: Simon and Schuster, 1996).
3   Kenneth Miller, *Finding Darwin's God* (New York: Harper Collins, 1999).
4   For me the insertion of this qualification is not a matter of finicky scholarship but of filial piety, for my Protestant theologian father edited a collection of essays, by some of his former students, published under the title *The Catholicity of Protestantism*.
5   David Conway, *The Rediscovery of Wisdom: From Here to Antiquity in Quest of Sophia* (London: Macmillan, 2000).
6   Ibid., pp. 2–3.
7   Albert Einstein *Out of My Later Years* (London: Thames and Hudson, 1950), pp. 26–27. Einstein once attempted to escape theological wrath by insisting that he believed in Spinoza's God. He hoped that his hearers were not aware that for Spinoza the terms 'God' and 'Nature' were equivalent.
8   But not, of course, of 'social justice'. For that is not at all the same thing. See my 'Socialism and "Social" Justice' in the *Journal of Libertarian Studies*, 11: 2 (1995), pp. 76–93 and my 'Private Property and "Social" Justice', in Colin Kolbert (ed.), *The Idea of Property in History and Modern Times* (London: Churchill, 1997), pp. 113–30. It was that old-fashioned, without prefix or suffix justice which in ch. 1 of Section II of Part II of his other masterpiece *The Theory of the Moral Sentiments* Adam Smith had in mind when he began his discussion of justice by distinguishing it as virtue 'of which the observance is not left to the freedom of our own wills' but 'which may be extorted by force ....' My recognition of the rightness of doing justice and the wrongness of doing injustice is the basis of my agreement that some 'things are really wrong' (p. 65).
9   *Nicomachean Ethics*, X viii, 7.
10 *Summa Theologica*, I, (i), 13.
11 Richard Swinburne, *The Coherence of Theism* (Oxford: Clarenden Press, 1977), p. 2.
12 Mischievously I suggest that to think of these two books in this way would give those departments of media studies, which have recently proliferated in British universities, something less ephemeral and more challenging to study than any contemporary media.
13 Quoted by G.W. Leibniz in his *Theodicy* at p. 222 of the edition edited and translated by A.M. Farrer and E.M. Haggard (London: Routledge and Kegan Paul, 1951). I refer here to a secondary authority because that authority is itself a classic; and a rich compendium of both clear statements of, and frantic attempts to avoid, this Calvinist consequence.

14 Romans 9:17–24, in, of course, the King James rendering.
15 *Luther and Erasmus: Freewill and Salvation*, ed. and trans. E.G. Rupp, N. Marlow, P.S. Waterson and B. Drewery (Philadelphia, PA: Westminster, 1969), p. 130.
16 Ibid., p. 130.
17 Ibid., p. 139.
18 In the early 1950s a Roman Catholic student who had been studying for the priesthood and was still wearing elements of clerical garb – he had lost his vocation but not his faith – assured me that it was not. I drew his attention to the passages from Aquinas quoted below.
19 Aquinas, *Summa Theologica*, I, xxiii, 3.
20 Aquinas, *Summa contra Gentiles*, Book III, Supp. XLIV, 1–30.
21 Aquinas chose to quote this passage from the Old Testament rather than that from Romans quoted above because the *Summa contra Gentiles* was directed to Jews and Muslims.
22 Ibid., Book III, chs. 88–89.
23 Aquinas, *Summa Theologica*, III Supp. XCIV, 1–3. As used to be said in my day in the unhallowed other ranks of the Royal Air Force: 'F—you, Jack; I'm fireproof!'
24 I believe that this expression was first introduced into the discussion of predestination in the chapter 'Divine Omnipotence and Human Freedom', in Flew and MacIntyre *New Essays in Philosophical Theory*, pp. 144–69. This chapter begins with disgraceful misattribution to St Augustine of an argument originally presented by Epicurus.
25 *Luther and Erasmus*, ed. and trans. Rupp *et al.*, p. 139. For particulars of this book see note 15 above.
26 *Doctrine in the Church of England* (London: Church House Publishing, 1922), p. 27.
27 I note without further comment that this was the expression employed by General Lee to refer to members of the opposing Union forces.
28 When I am told by Roman Catholic friends, following Aquinas, that sins, as offences against an infinite Being are infinitely evil, and therefore deserve infinite punishment, I tend to hold my peace. For I myself would be eager to say anything however false or absurd which I was required to say under threat of even a brief period of torture.
29 See the references for Leibniz *Theodicy*, note 13 above for the justification for employing the word 'majority' here.
30 Swinburne, *The Coherence of Theism*, p. 2 quoted at p. 25 above.
31 For a sample of such an argument see the chapter cited in note 20 above.
32 Flew and MacIntyre, *New Essays in Philosophical Theory*.
33 Since all the contributors to the present volume appear to possess doctorates and to be, or to have been, tenured professors, I too shall give them only surnames, save where a given name has to be added to avoid ambiguity.
34 See p. 28.
35 For philosophical discussion of this question see Antony Flew, *An Introduction to Western Philosophy: Ideas and Argument from Plato to Popper* (London: Thames and Hudson, 1989) pp. 22–33. First published 1971.
36 Thomas Hobbes, *Leviathan*, ed. C.B. Macpherson (Harmondsworth and Baltimore; Penguin, 1968), Chapter XI.
37 See *The Mystery of Salvation* (London: Church House Publishing, 1995), p. 180.
38 See p. 28.

39   He should be recognized as having produced, for good reason, cautiously a merely suggestive empiricist version of Spinoza's equation of God and Nature. See my article 'Thomas Hobbes: 1588–1679' in D.J. O'Connor (ed), *A Critical History of Western Philosophy* (New York and London: The Free Press and Collier-Macmillan, 1964), pp. 153–69.

40   Hobbes, *Leviathan*, Chapter XLIV.

41   *The Koran*, trans. A.J. Arberry (Oxford: Oxford University Press, 1985). I give the number of the sura in Roman and of the page in Arabic numerals, II, p. 2.

42   Ibid., XVI, p. 269.

43   Ibid., V, pp. 112 and 113. Since my final revision of the present paper was made after 11 September 2001 it has become appropriate for me to refer here to my 'The Terrors of Islam' in Paul Kurtz (ed.), *Challenges to the Enlightenment* (Buffalo, NY: Prometheus, 1994) and my 'Skepticism About Religion' in Paul Kurtz (ed.), *Skeptical Odysseys* (Amherst, NY: Prometheus, 2001).

It was because I had, in the later of these two articles, which was written towards the end of 1999, 'made predictions about the likelihood of religious terrorism which have proved horribly correct' that I was invited to write 'Islam's War Against the West', in *Free Inquiry*, Spring 2002 (vol. 22, no. 2), pp. 40–44.

44   See p. 49.

45   See p. 85.

46   See the text of Leibniz' *Theodicy*, cited in note 13 above.

47   I was a guest of the Director of the Institute of Foreign Philosophy in the University of Peking, Beijing. It has preserved the old transliteration 'Peking' because the university is among the oldest in China, and its students have played an important part in twentieth-century Chinese history.

48   I will not here resist the temptation to refer to my own first trip on a Greek tourist bus. Our excellent and strongly patriotic guide wanted us to know all about the major events in her country's long history. She thus both pointed to the site of the Battle of Salamis and indicated the places where one person had had a vision of one of the Olympians and another had had a distinctively Christian vision; and she said all this – as Gilbert Ryle used to say – in the same logical tone of voice.

49   See p. 70.

50   See p. 20.

51   In *The Complete Works of Lewis Carroll* (London: Nonesuch, 1939) it is ch. 6, p. 67. This supposedly complete edition does not include Carroll's remarkable essay on 'Eternal Punishment'. I commend it to any believer troubled by the traditional teachings. It is included in the Roger Lancelyn Green edition of *The Works of Lewis Carroll* published by Spring Books in 1965.

52   Ibid., ch. 2, pp. 232–33.

53   In *The Logic of Mortality* (Oxford: Blackwell, 1987). This book, with a new Introduction, was reissued under the title *Merely Mortal? Can You Survive Your Own Death?* by Prometheus in 2000. I objected to the '*Merely Mortal?*' part of the title but Prometheus insisted that, for sound commercial reasons, it had to go in.

54   See p. 8.

55   Antony Flew and Godfrey Vesey, *Agency and Necessity* (Oxford: Blackwell, 1987).

56   See p. 134.

57   See p. 32.

58   Martin Luther, *De serve anbibio*, in *Luther and Erasmus*, ed. and trans. E.G. Rupp *et al.*, p. 19.

59   See p. 33.

60 See p. 34 (emphasis in original). I confess, not *very* shamefacedly, that the only argument of Molina which I have ever met is that to the conclusion that there can be *scientia media* (knowledge of contingent hypotheticals), which to me sounds consistent, rather than inconsistent with predestinationism. See note at Flew and MacIntye, *New Essays in Philosophical Theology*, note at pp. 155–56.

61 See p. 27 (emphasis in original).

62 David Hume, *Essays, Moral, Political and Literary*, ed. E.F. Miller (Indianapolis, IN: Liberty Press, 1985), p. 198 (emphasis in original).

63 John Locke, *An Essay Concerning Human Understanding*, ed. Peter H. Nidditch (Oxford: University Press: [1681] 1975), Book II, chap. XVI, Paragraph 14, p. 240 (emphasis and spelling in original).

64 See p. 22.

65 See p. 147.

66 Paul Johnson, 'And Another Thing', *The Spectator* (30 June 2001).

67 Sir Charles Sherrington, O.M., F.R.S. *Man on his Nature* (Cambridge: Cambridge University Press, 1940).

68 See p. 55.

69 Ibid.

70 See p. 21.

71 See p. 37. I would not, of course, agree if that proposition were to be construed as carrying any implications of divine endorsement.

72 For supporting argument see my 'How and What Morality Could and Should be Taught Today?', forthcoming in the *Proceedings of the 27th Conference on Value Inquiry*, held in Central Missouri State University in April 1999.

73 See p. 90.

74 See pp. 90–91.

75 See p. 36.

76 See p. 22.

77 Ibid.

78 For a developed argument on this point in the present context, see my 'Neo-Humean Arguments About The Miraculous', in R. Douglas Geivett and Gary R. Habermas (eds), *In Defense of Miracles* (Downers' Grove, IL: InterVarsity Press, 1997), pp. 45–57.

79 See p. 23 (emphasis in original).

80 See pp. 120–22.

81 See p. 150.

82 Ibid.

83 Ibid.

84 See pp. 23 and 43.

85 See p. 23.

86 Jack Kent, *The Psychological Origins of the Resurrection Myth* (London: Open Gate, 1999).

87 See p. 23 (emphasis in original).

88 See p. 35.

89 Hobbes, *Leviathan*, Chapter XXXII.

90 See p. 28.

91 See p. 26.

92 See p. 21.

93 See p. 39.

94 See p. 70.

95 See pp. 96–7.

96 Antony Flew, 'The Presumption of Atheism', in Philip Quinn and Charles Talisferro (eds), *A Companion to the Philosophy of Religion* (Oxford: Blackwell, 1997).
97 See p. 79.
98 See p. 31 (emphasis in original).
99 See p. 61.
100 By Cantor's Axiom for Sets the sole essential feature of a set is that its members have at least one common characteristic, any kind of characteristic.
101 J.S. Conway, *The Nazi Persecution of the Churches 1933–1945* (London: Weidenfeld and Nicolson, 1968), p. 197.
102 Ibid., p. 199.
103 James Penton, *Apocalypse Delayed: The Story of Jehovah's Witnesses* (Toronto: Toronto University Press, 1985), p. 14. Knowing what I do of the relationship between myself and my father and between him and his father I suspect that Penton fully shared Russell's difficulty in believing that a Divine Father would destine any of His children to eternal torture.
104 Hobbes, *Leviathan*, Chapter XLIV.
105 George D. Smith (ed.), *The Teaching of the Catholic Church* (London: Burns and Oates, 1948), p. 1193.

Bibliography

Adams, Robert M. (2000), *Finite and Infinite Goods*, Oxford: Oxford University Press.

Alston, William (1982), 'Religious Experience and Religious Belief', *Nous*, **16**, reprinted in R. Douglas Geivett and Brendan Sweetman (eds), *Contemporary Perspectives on Religious Epistemology*, New York: Oxford University Press, pp. 295–303.

Alston, William (1986), 'Does God Have Beliefs?', *Religious Studies*, **22**, pp. 287–306.

Alston, William (1986), 'Epistemic Circularity', *Philosophy and Phenomenological Research*, **47**, pp. 1–30.

Alston, William (1991), *Perceiving God*, Ithaca, NY: Cornell University Press.

Aquinas, Thomas (1923), *Summa contra Gentiles*, trans. English Dominican Fathers, London: Burns, Oates & Washbourne Ltd.

Aquinas, Thomas (1947–48), *Summa Theologica*, trans. Fathers of the English Dominican Province, New York: Benziger Bros.

Aristotle (1936), *Physics*, revised text with introd. and commentary by W.D. Ross., Oxford: Clarendon Press.

Aristotle (1985), *Nicomachean Ethics*, trans. Terence Irwin, Indianapolis, IN: Hackett Pub. Co.

Armstrong, D.M. (1999), 'A Naturalist Program: Epistemology and Ontology', *Proceedings and Addresses of the American Philosophical Association*, **73**, November.

Augustine (1998), *Confessions*, trans. with introd. and notes by Henry Chadwick, Oxford: Oxford University Press.

Barrow, J.D. (1988), *The World Within the World*, Oxford: Clarendon Press.

Barrow, J.D. (1991), *Theories of Everything: The Quest for Ultimate Explanation*, Oxford: Clarendon Press.

Barrow, J.D. (1994), *The Origin of the Universe*, New York: Basic Books.

Barrow, John D. and Frank J. Tipler (1986), *The Anthropic Cosmological Principle*, Oxford: Clarendon Press.

Behe, Michael J. (1996), *Darwin's Black Box: The Biochemical Challenge to Evolution*, New York: The Free Press.

Blackmore, Susan (1998), 'Abducted by Aliens or Sleep Paralysis?', *Skeptical Inquiry*, May/June, pp. 23–28.

Boltzmann, Ludwig (1964), *Lectures on Gas Theory*, trans. Stephen G. Brush, Berkeley: University of California Press, pp. 446–48.

Borde, A. and A. Vilenkin (1994), 'Eternal Inflation and the Initial Singularity', *Physical Review Letters*, **72**, pp. 3305–7.

Bosleigh, John (1989), *Stephen Hawking's Universe*, New York: Avon Books.

Boyd, Richard (1997), 'How To Be a Moral Realist', in S. Darwall, A. Gibbard, and P. Railton (eds), *Moral Discourse and Practice*, Oxford: Oxford University Press, pp. 37–39.

Brink, David O. (1989), *Moral Realism and The Foundations of Ethics*, Cambridge: Cambridge University Press.

Brown, Raymond E. (1994), *The Death of the Messiah*, 2 vols, Garden City, NY: Doubleday.

Carroll, Lewis (1965), *The Works of Lewis Carroll*, ed. Roger Lancelyn Green, London: Hamlyn Publishing Group.

Carter, Brandon (1974), 'Large Number Coincidence and The Anthropic Principle in Cosmology', in M.S. Longair (ed.), *Confrontation of Cosmological Theories with Observational Data*, Dordrecht: D. Reidel, pp. 291–98.

Collins, Robin. (1999), 'A Scientific Argument for the Existence of God: The Fine-Tuning Design Argument,' in Michael J. Murray (ed.), *Reason for the Hope Within*, Grand Rapids, MI: William B. Eerdmans, pp. 47–75.

Conway, David (2000), *The Rediscovery of Wisdom: From Here to Antiquity in Quest of Sophia*, London: Macmillan.

Conway, J.S. (1968), *The Nazi Persecution of the Churches 1933–1945*, London: Weidenfeld and Nicolson.

Craig, William Lane (1979), 'God, Time, and Eternity', *Religious Studies*, **14**, pp. 497–503.

Craig, William Lane (1979), *The* Kalam *Cosmological Argument*, London: Macmillan & Co.

Craig, William Lane (1989), 'No Other Name: A Middle Knowledge Perspective on the Exclusivity of Salvation Through Christ', *Faith and Philosophy*, **6**, pp. 172–88.

Craig, William Lane (1990), '"What Place, Then, for a Creator?": Hawking on God and Creation', *British Journal for the Philosophy of Science*, **41**, pp. 473–91.

Craig, William Lane (1993), 'Graham Oppy on the *Kalam* Cosmological Argument', *Sophia*, **32**, pp. 1–11.

Craig, William Lane (1993), 'Time and Infinity', in William Lane Craig and Quentin Smith (eds), *Theism, Atheism, and Big Bang Cosmology*, Oxford: Clarendon Press, pp. 92–107.

Craig, William Lane (1994), 'Creation and Big Bang Cosmology', *Philosophia Naturalis*, **31**, pp. 217–24.

Craig, William Lane (1994), 'Professor Grünbaum on Creation', *Erkenntnis*, **40**, pp. 325–41.

Craig, William Lane (1994), *Reasonable Faith: Christian Truth and Apologetics*, Wheaton, IL: Crossway Books.

Craig, William Lane (1994), 'A Response to Grünbaum on Creation and Big Bang Cosmology', *Philosophia Naturalis*, **31**, pp. 237–49.

Craig, William Lane (1995), 'Politically Incorrect Salvation', in T.P. Phillips and D. Ockholm (eds), *Christian Apologetics in a Post-Christian World*, Downers Grove, IL: InterVarsity Press, pp. 75–97.

Craig, William Lane (1998), 'Divine Timelessness and Personhood', *International Journal for Philosophy of Religion*, **43**, pp. 109–24.

Craig, William Lane (1999), 'The Ultimate Question of Origins: God and the Beginning of the Universe', *Astrophysics and Space Science*, **269–270**, pp. 723–40.

Craig, William Lane (2000), *Five Views on Apologetics*, ed. Steven B. Cowan, Counterpoints, Grand Rapids, MI: Zondervan.

Craig, William Lane (2000), 'Naturalism and Cosmology', in William L. Craig and J.P. Moreland (eds), *Naturalism: A Critical Appraisal*, Routledge Studies in Twentieth-Century Philosophy, London: Routledge, pp. 215–52.

Craig, William Lane (2001), *God, Time and Eternity*, Dordrecht: Kluwer Academic Publishers.

Craig, William Lane (ed.) (2001) *Philosophy of Religion: a Reader and Guide*, Edinburgh: Edinburgh University Press.

Craig, William Lane (2002), *Assessing the New Testament Evidence for the Historicity of the Resurrection of Jesus*, 2nd edn, Studies in the Bible and Early Christianity 16, Lewiston, NY: Edwin Mellen.

Craig, William Lane and Gerd Lüdemann (2000), *Jesus' Resurrection: Fact or Figment?*, eds. Paul Copan and Ronald K. Tacelli, Downer's Grove, IL.: InterVarsity Press.

Craig, William Lane and Quentin Smith (1993), *Theism, Atheism, and Big Bang Cosmology*, Oxford: Clarendon Press.

Cushing, James T. (1994), *Quantum Mechanics: Historical Contingency and the Copenhagen Hegemony*, Science and its Conceptual Foundations, Chicago: University of Chicago Press.

Cushing, James T. (1998), *Philosophical Concepts in Physics*, Cambridge: Cambridge University Press.

Davis, Caroline Franks (1986), 'The Devotional Experiment', *Religious Studies*, **22**, March, pp. 15–28.

Davis, Caroline Franks (1989), *The Evidential Force of Religious Experience*, Oxford: Clarendon Press.

Davies, Paul C.W. (1980), *Other Worlds*, London: Dent.

Davies, Paul C.W. (1983), 'The Anthropic Principle', *Particle and Nuclear Physics*, **10**, pp. 1–38.

Davies, Paul C.W. (1992), *The Mind of God: The Scientific Basis for a Rational World*, New York: Simon & Schuster.

Davis, Richard Brian (2001) *The Metaphysics of Theism and Modality*, American University Studies V/189, New York: Peter Lang.

Davis, Stephen T. (1993), *Risen Indeed*, Grand Rapids, MI: William. B. Eerdmans.

Davis, Stephen T. (1997), *God, Reason and Theistic Proofs*, Edinburgh: Edinburgh University Press.

Davis, Stephen T. (1999), 'The Cosmological Argument and the Epistemic Status of Belief in God', *Philosophia Christi* NS, **1**, pp. 5–15.

Dawson, Christopher (1958), *Religion and the Rise of Western Culture*, New York: Image Books.

Dembski, William A. (1998), *The Design Inference: Eliminating Chance through Small Probabilities*. Cambridge Studies in Probability, Induction, and Decision Theory, Cambridge: Cambridge University Press.

Dembski, William A. (1999), *Intelligent Design: The Bridge Between Science and Theology*, Downers Grove, IL: InterVarsity Press.

Denton, Michael J. (1998), *Nature's Destiny: How the Laws of Biology Reveal Purpose in the Universe*, New York: The Free Press.

Doctrine in the Church of England (1922), London: Church House Publishing.

Drange, Theodore M. (1998), 'The Fine-Tuning Argument' at http://www.infidels.org/library/modern/theodore_drange/tuning.html.

Draper, Paul (1992), 'God and Perceptual Evidence', *International Journal for Philosophy of Religion*, **32**, pp. 149–65.

Draper, Paul (2003), 'A Critique of the Kalam Cosmological Argument', in Louis P. Pojman (ed.), *Philosophy of Religion: An Anthology*, 4th edn, Wadsworth Publishing Company, pp. 42–47.

Draper, Paul (2002), 'Seeking But Not Believing: Confessions of a Practicing Agnostic', in Daniel Howard-Snyder and Paul Moser (eds), *Divine Hiddenness: New Essays*, pp. 197–214.

Earman, John (1993), 'Bayes, Hume, and Miracles', *Faith and Philosophy*, **10**, pp. 293–310.

Edwards, Paul (1996), *Reincarnation: A Critical Examination*, Buffalo, NY: Prometheus Books.

Einstein, Albert (1950), *Out of My Later Years*, London: Thames and Hudson.

Firth, Roderick (1970), 'Ethical Absolutism and the Ideal Observer', in Wilfred Sellars and John Hospers (eds), *Readings in Ethical Theory*, 2nd edn, Englewood Cliffs, NJ: Prentice-Hall, Inc., pp. 200–221.

Flew, Antony (1955), 'Theology and Falsification,' in Antony Flew and A. MacIntyre (eds), *New Essays in Philosophical Theology*, New York: Macmillan, pp. 96–99.

Flew, Antony (1964), 'Thomas Hobbes: 1588–1679' in D.J. O'Connor (ed.), *A Critical History of Western Philosophy*, New York and London: The Free Press and Collier-Macmillan, pp. 153–69.

Flew, Antony (1989), *An Introduction to Western Philosophy: Ideas and Argument from Plato to Popper*, London: Thames and Hudson. First published 1971.

Flew, Antony (1993), *Atheistic Humanism*, Buffalo, NY: Prometheus Books.

Flew, Antony (1994), 'The Terrors of Islam' in Paul Kurtz (ed.), *Challenges to the Enlightenment*, Buffalo, NY: Prometheus, pp. 272–283.

Flew, Antony (1995), 'Socialism and "Social" Justice', *Journal of Libertarian Studies*, **11** (2), pp. 76–93.

Flew, Antony (1997), 'Neo-Humean Arguments About The Miraculous', in R. Douglas Geivett and Gary R. Habermas (eds), *In Defense of Miracles*, Downers' Grove, IL: InterVarsity Press, pp. 45–57.

Flew, Antony (1997), 'Private Property and "Social" Justice' in Colin Kolbert (ed.), *The Idea of Property in History and Modern Times*, London: Churchill, pp. 113–30.

Flew, Antony (1997), 'The Presumption of Atheism', *Canadian Journal of Philosophy*, **2** (1972); reprinted in Geivett and Sweetman (eds), *Contemporary Perspectives on Religious Epistemology* (New York: Oxford University Press, 1992), pp. 19–32; revision reprinted in Philip Quinn and Charles Taliaferro (eds), *A Companion to the Philosophy of Religion*, Oxford: Blackwell, pp. 410–416.

Flew, Antony (2000), *Merely Mortal? Can You Survive Your Own Death?*, Buffalo, NY: Prometheus.

Flew, Antony (2001), 'Skepticism About Religion' in Paul Kurtz (ed.), *Skeptical Odysseys*, Amherst, NY: Prometheus, pp. 375–387.

Flew, Antony (2002), 'Islam's War Against the West', *Free Inquiry*, **22**(2), pp. 40–44.

Flew, Antony and Godfrey Vesey (1987), *Agency and Necessity*, Oxford: Blackwell.

Freddoso, Alfred J. (1988), 'Introduction,' in Luis de Molina, *On Divine Foreknowledge*, Ithaca, NY: Cornell University Press.

Fuller, Reginald Horace (1971), *The Formation of the Resurrection Narratives*, New York: Macmillan.

Gaskin, John C. A. (1974), 'God, Hume, and Natural Belief', *Philosophy*, **49**, pp. 281–94.

Gauthier, David (1987), *Morals by Agreement*, Oxford: Oxford University Press.

Geivett, R. Douglas (1993), *Evil and the Evidence for God*, Philadelphia, PA: Temple University Press.

Geivett, R. Douglas (1997), 'The Evidential Value of Miracles,' in R. Douglas Geivett and Gary R. Habermas (eds), *In Defense of Miracles*, Downer's Grove, IL: InterVarsity Press, pp. 178–95.

Geivett, R. Douglas (1997), 'A Pascalian Rejoinder to the Presumption of Atheism', *The Journal for the Critical Study of Religion*, **2**, Fall/Winter, pp. 19–35.

Geivett, R. Douglas and Brendan Sweetman (eds) (1992), *Contemporary Perspectives on Religious Epistemology*, New York: Oxford University Press.

Guillen, Michael (1983), *Bridges to Infinity: The Human Side of Mathematics*, Los Angeles, CA: J.P. Tarcher.

Guth, Alan (1997), *The Inflationary Universe*, Reading, MA: Addison-Wesley.

Habermas, Gary and Antony Flew (1987), in Terry L. Miethe (ed.), *Did Jesus Rise From The Dead?*, San Francisco: Harper and Row.

Hall, H.V. (1994), 'Hallucinations,' in R. Corsini (ed.), *Encyclopedia of Psychology*, 2nd edn, New York: John Wiley, p. 101.

Hawking, Stephen W. (1988), *A Brief History of Time*, New York: Bantam Books.

Hawking, Stephen and Roger Penrose (1996), *The Nature of Space and Time*, The Isaac Newton Institute Series of Lectures, Princeton, NJ: Princeton University Press.

Hick, John (ed.), (1964), The *Existence of God*, Problems of Philosophy Series, New York: Macmillan Publishing Co.

Hick, John (1989), *An Interpretation of Religion*, New Haven, CA: Yale University Press.

Hilbert, David, (1983), 'On the Infinite', in Paul Benacerraf and Hilary Putnam (eds), *Philosophy of Mathematics*, 2nd edn, Cambridge: Cambridge University Press, pp. 183–201. First published 1926.

Hobbes, Thomas (1968), *Leviathan*, C.B. Macpherson (ed.), Harmondsworth and Baltimore: Penguin.

Howard-Snyder, Daniel (ed.) (1966), *The Evidential Argument from Evil*, Bloomington, IN: Indiana University Press.

Hoyle, Fred (1975), *Astronomy and Cosmology*, San Francisco: W.H. Freeman.

Hoyle, Fred (1981), 'The Universe: Past and Present Reflections', *Engineering and Science*, November, pp. 8–12.

Hume, David (1975), 'An Inquiry Concerning the Principles or Morals', in *Hume's Inquiries*, L.A. Selby-Bigge (ed), with revisions by P.H. Nidditch, Oxford: Clarendon, pp. 169–323.

Hume, David (1985), *Essays, Moral, Political and Literary*, E.F. Miller (ed.), Indianapolis: IN: Liberty Press.

Idziak, Janine Marie (1980), *Divine Command Morality: Historical and Contemporary Readings*, Lewiston, NY: Edwin Mellen Press.

Isham, Christopher (1990), 'Space, Time, and Quantum Cosmology', paper presented at the conference 'God, Time, and Modern Physics', March.

Isham, Christopher (1994), 'Quantum Cosmology and the Origin of the Universe', lecture presented at the conference 'Cosmos and Creation,' Cambridge University, 14 July.

Jackson, Frank (1998), *From Metaphysics to Ethics*, Oxford: Clarendon Press.

James, William (1902), *Varieties of Religious Experience*, New York: Modern Library.

James, William (1956), 'The Will to Believe', in *The Will to Believe and Other Essays in Popular Philosophy*, New York: Dover, pp. 1–31.

Jastrow, Robert (1984), 'The Astronomer and God', in Roy Abraham Varghese (ed.), *The Intellectuals Speak Out About God*, Chicago: Regenery Gateway, pp. 15–22.

Johnson, Luke Timothy (1996), *The Real Jesus*, San Francisco: Harper.

Johnson, Paul (2001), 'And Another Thing', *The Spectator*, 30 June.

Kant, Immanuel (1900–42), *Critique of Practical Reason*, in many translations from *Kants gesammelte Schriften*, Berlin: Prussian Academy, vol. V.

Kee, H., F. Young and K. Froehlich (1965), *Understanding the New Testament*, Englewood Cliffs, NJ: Prentice-Hall.

Kenny, Anthony (1969), *The Five Ways: St. Thomas Aquinas Proofs of God's Existence*, New York: Schocken Books.

Kenny, Anthony (1979), *The God of the Philosophers*, Oxford: Clarendon Press.

Kent, Jack (1999), *The Psychological Origins of the Resurrection Myth*, London: Open Gate.

The Koran (1985), trans. A.J. Arberry, Oxford: Oxford University Press.

Kreeft, Peter and Ronald K. Tacelli (1994), *Handbook of Christian Apologetics*, Downer's Grove, IL: InterVarsity Press.

Kremer, Jacob (1977), *Die Osterevangelien Geschichten um Geschichte*, Stuttgart: Katholisches Bibelwerk.

Larue, Gerald (1983), *Sex and the Bible*, Buffalo, NY: Prometheus Books.

Leftow, Brian (1990), 'God and Abstract Entities', *Faith and Philosophy*, **7**, pp. 193–217.

Leibniz, G.W. (1951), *Theodicy*, ed. and trans. A.M. Farrer and E.M. Haggard, London: Routledge and Kegan Paul.

Le Poidevin, R. (1996), *Arguing for Atheism: An Introduction to the Philosophy of Religion*, London: Routledge.

Leslie, John (1989), *Universes*, London: Routledge.

Lewis, Hywel D. (1959), *Our Experience of God*, London: Allen and Unwin.

Linde, Andrei, Dmitri Linde and Arthur Mezhlumian (1994), 'From the Big Bang Theory to the Theory of a Stationary Universe', *Physical Review* D **49**, pp. 1783–826.

Lipton, Peter (1991), *Inference to the Best Explanation*, London: Routledge.

Locke, John (1975), *An Essay Concerning Human Understanding*, Peter H. Nidditch, (ed.), Oxford: Oxford University Press. First published 1681.

Lüdemann, Gerd. (1995), *What Really Happened to Jesus?*, trans. John Bowden, Louisville, KY: Westminster/John Knox Press.

Luther, Martin (1969), *De servo arbitrio* in E.G. Rupp, A.N. Marlow, P.S. Watson and B. Drewery, *Luther and Erasmus: Free Will and Salvation*, Philadelphia: Westminster, pp. 1–156.

Luther and Erasmus: Freewill and Salvation (1969), ed. and trans. E.G. Rupp, N. Marlow, P.S. Waterson and B. Drewery, Philadelphia, PA: Westminster.

Mann, William E. (1989), 'Modality, Morality, and God', *Noûs*, **23**, pp. 83–99.

Martin, Michael (1990), *Atheism: A Philosophical Justification*, Philadelphia, PA: Temple University Press.

Martin, Michael (1991), *The Case Against Christianity*, Philadelphia: Temple University Press.

Martin, Michael (1997) 'Atheism, Christian Theism, and Rape' at http://www.infidels.org/library/modern/michael_martin/rape.html.

Martin, Michael (1998), 'Craig's Holy Spirit Epistemology', at http://www.infidels.org/library/modern/michael_martin/holy_spirit.html.

Martin, Michael (1998), 'Why the Resurrection is Initially Improbable', *Philo*, **1** (1), Spring/Summer, pp. 63–73.

Mavrodes, George I. (1970), *Belief in God*, New York: Random House.

Mavrodes, George I. (1992), 'On the Very Strongest Arguments,' in Eugene Thomas Long (ed.), *Prospects for Natural Theology*, Washington, DC: The Catholic University of America Press, pp. 81–91.

McCane, Byron R. (1999), '"Where No One Had Yet Been Laid": The Shame of Jesus' Burial', in Bruce Chilton and Craig Evans (eds), *Authenticating the Activities of Jesus*, New Testament Tools and Studies 28/2, Leiden: Brill, pp. 431–52.

McGrath, Patrick J. (1987), 'Atheism or Agnosticism', *Analysis*, **47**, January, pp. 54–57.

Mill, J.S. (1843), *A System of Logic*, 2 vols, New York: Harper & Brothers.

Miller, Kenneth (1999), *Finding Darwin's God*, New York: Harper Collins.

Moore, A.W. (1990), *The Infinite*, London: Routledge.

Moore, George E. (1963), *Principia Ethica*, Cambridge: Cambridge University Press.

Moore, James (1994), *The Darwin Legend*, Grand Rapids, MI: Baker Books.

Morris, Thomas V. (1985), 'Agnosticism', *Analysis*, 45 October, pp. 219–24.

Moreland, J.P. and William Lane Craig (2003), *Philosophical Foundation for a Christian World-view*, Downer's Grove, IL: InterVarsity Press.

Moreland, J.P. and Kai Nielsen (1990), *Does God Exist?*, Nashville, TN: Thomas Nelson.

Naland, J.K. (1988), 'The First Easter: Evidence for the Resurrection Evaluated', *Free Inquiry*, **3** (2), Spring, pp. 10–20.

Nielsen, Kai (1971), *Reason and Practice: A Modern Introduction to Philosophy*, New York: Harper & Row.

Nietzsche, Friedrich (1954), *The Gay Science*, in *The Portable Nietzsche*, trans. and ed. W. Kaufmann, New York: Viking.

O'Connor, Timothy (2000), *Persons and Causes: The Metaphysics of Free Will*, Oxford: Oxford University Press.

Pascal, Blaise (1941), *Pensées*, New York: Modern Library.

Pennock, Robert T. (1999), *Tower of Babel: The Evidence against the New Creationism*, Cambridge, MA: The MIT Press.

Penrose, Roger (1982), 'Some Remarks on Gravity and Quantum Mechanics', in M.J. Duff and C.J. Isham (eds), *Quantum Structure of Space and Time*, Cambridge: Cambridge University Press, pp. 3–10.

Penton, James (1985), *Apocalypse Delayed: The Story of Jehovah's Witnesses*, Toronto: Toronto University Press.

Plantinga, Alvin (1974), *God, Freedom, and Evil*, Grand Rapids, MI: Eerdmans, reprinted from New York: Harper & Row.

Plantinga, Alvin (1974), *The Nature of Necessity*, Clarendon Library of Logic and Philosophy, Oxford: Clarendon Press.

Plantinga, Alvin (1983), 'Reason and Belief in God', in Alvin Plantinga and Nicholas Wolterstorff (eds), *Faith and Rationality: Reason and Belief in God*, Notre Dame, IN: University of Notre Dame Press, pp. 16–93.

Plantinga, Alvin (1986), 'The Foundations of Theism: A Reply', *Faith and Philosophy*, **3**, pp. 310–11.

Plantinga, Alvin (1993), *Warrant and Proper Function*, Oxford: Oxford University Press.

Plantinga, Alvin (1993), *Warrant: The Current Debate*, Oxford: Oxford University Press.

Plantinga, Alvin (1998), 'Degenerate Evidence and Rowe's New Evidential Argument from Evil', *Noûs*, **32**, pp. 531–44.

Plantinga, Alvin (2000), 'Pluralism: A Defense of Religious Exclusivism', in Philip L. Quinn and Kevin Meeker (eds), *The Philosophical Challenge of Religious Diversity*, New York: Oxford University Press, pp. 172–92.

Plantinga, Alvin (2000), *Warranted Christian Belief*, Oxford: Oxford University Press.

Polkinghorne, John C. (1996), *Serious Talk: Science and Religion in Dialogue*, London: SCM Press.

Price, H.H. (1969), *Belief*, London: George Allen & Unwin.

Proudfoot, Wayne (1985), *Religious Experience*, Berkeley, CA: University of California Press.

Quinn, Philip (1978), *Divine Commands and Moral Requirements*, Oxford: Clarendon Press.

Railton, Peter (1997), 'Moral Realism', in S. Darwall, A. Gibbard and P. Railton (eds), *Moral Discourse and Practice*, Oxford: Oxford University Press, pp. 137–63.

Rees, M. (1997), *Before the Beginning: Our Universe and Others*, Reading, MA: Addison-Wesley.

Rescher, Nicholas (1997), *Objectivity: The Obligations of Impersonal Reasoning*, Notre Dame, IN: Notre Dame University Press.

Robinson, John A.T. (1973), *The Human Face of God*, Philadelphia: Westminster.

Rothman, T. and G.F.R. Ellis (1993), 'Smolin's Natural Selection Hypothesis', *Quarterly Journal of the Royal Astronomical Society*, **34**, pp. 201–12.

Rowe, William L. (1998), 'Reply to Plantinga', *Noûs*, **32**, pp. 545–52.

Ruse, Michael (1989), 'Evolutionary Theory and Christian Ethics', in *The Darwinian Paradigm*, London: Routledge, pp. 262–69.

Russell, Bertrand (1955), *Human Society in Ethics and Politics*, New York: Simon and Schuster.

Russell, Bertrand and F.C. Copleston (1964), 'A Debate On The Existence of God', reprinted in *The Existence of God*, ed. with an introduction by John Hick, Problems of Philosophy Series, New York: Macmillan Publishing Co., pp. 167–191.

Salmon, Wesley C. (1989), *Four Decades of Scientific Explanation*, Minneapolis, MN: University of Minnesota Press.

Salmon, Wesley C. and J. Earman (1992), 'The Confirmation of Scientific Hypotheses', in W. Salmon *et al.* (eds), *Introduction to the Philosophy of Science*, Englewood Cliffs, NJ: Prentice Hall, pp. 42–103.

Salmon, Wesley C. *et al.* (1999), *Introduction to the Philosophy of Science*, Indianapolis: Hackett Publishing Co., Inc.

Schlesinger, George (1983), *The Intelligibility of Nature*, Aberdeen: Aberdeen University Press.

Schlesinger, George (1983), *Metaphysics*, Oxford: Blackwell.

Shalkowski, Scott (1989), 'Atheological Apologetics', *American Philosophical Quarterly*, **26**, January, pp. 1–17.

Sherrington, Charles, O.M., F.R.S. (1940), *Man on his Nature*, Cambridge: Cambridge University Press.

Smith, Quentin (1992), 'The Anthropic Coincidences, Evil and the Disconfirmation of Theism', *Religious Studies*, **28**, pp. 347–50.

Smith, Quentin (1998), 'Why Steven Hawking's Cosmology Precludes a Creator', *Philo*, **1**, pp. 75–94.

Sorabji, Richard (1983), *Time, Creation, and the Continuum*, Ithaca: Cornell University Press.

Spong, J.S. (1995), *Resurrection: Myth or Reality?*, San Francisco: Harper Collins.

Stenger, Victor J. (nd), 'Cosmomythology: Is the Universe Fine-Tuned to Produce Us?' at http://www.phys.hawaii.edu/vjs/www/cosmyth.txt.

Sturgeon, Scott (1998), 'Physicalism and Overdetermination', *Mind*, **107**, pp. 411–32.

Suckiel, Ellen Kappy (1996), *Heaven's Champion: William James's Philosophy of Religion*, Notre Dame, IN: University of Notre Dame Press.

Swinburne, Richard (1979), *The Existence of God*, Oxford: Clarendon Press. Revised edition 1991.

Swinburne, Richard (1981), 'Duty and the Will of God', in Paul Helm (ed.), *Divine Commands and Morality*, Oxford: Oxford University Press, pp. 120–34.

Swinburne, Richard (1977), *The Coherence of Theism*, Oxford: Clarendon Press.

Taliaferro, Charles (1998), *Contemporary Philosophy of Religion*, Malden, MA: Blackwell.

Taylor, Richard (1985), *Ethics, Faith, and Reason*, Englewood Cliffs, NJ: Prentice-Hall.

Toon, Peter (1986), *Heaven and Hell: A Biblical and Theological Overview*, Nashville, TN: Thomas Nelson.

van Fraassen, Bas (1980), *The Scientific Image*, Oxford: Clarendon Press.

Van Inwagen, Peter (1975), 'The Incompatibility of Free Will and Determinism', *Philosophical Studies*, **27**, pp. 185–99.

Van Inwagen, Peter (1993), *Metaphysics*, Boulder, CO: Westview Press.

Van Inwagen, Peter (1996), 'Why Is There Anything At All?', *Proceedings of the Aristotelian Society*.

Wainwright, William (1995), *Reason and the Heart*, Ithaca, NY: Cornell University Press.

Wells, George Albert (1989), *Who Was Jesus? A Critique of the New Testament Record*, La Salle, IL: Open Court.

Wigner, Eugene Paul (1967), *Symmetries and Reflections: Scientific Essays of Eugene P. Wigner*, Bloomington, IN: Indiana University Press.

Wright, N.T. (1993), 'The New, Unimproved Jesus', *Christianity Today*, Issue 37, no. 10, September 1993, pp. 22–26.

Yandell, Keith. (1991), 'The Doctrine of Hell and Moral Philosophy', *Religious Studies*, October, pp. 1–16.

Yandell, Keith (1993), *The Epistemology of Religious Experience*, Cambridge: Cambridge University Press.

Yandell, Keith (1998), *Hume's 'Inexplicable Mystery': His Views on Religion*, Philadelphia: Temple University Press.

Yandell, Keith (1999), 'Ontological Arguments, Metaphysical Identity, and the Trinity', *Philosophia Christi*, Series 2, **1** (1), pp. 83–101.

Yandell, Keith (1999), *The Philosophy of Religion*, London: Routledge.

Yandell, Keith (1999), 'God, Freedom, and Creation in Cross-cultural Perspective: Augustine, Aquinas, Ramanuja, and Madhva', *Proceedings of the Twentieth World Congress of Philosophy*, vol. 4, 147–168.

Yandell, Keith (1999), 'God and Other Agents in Indian Philosophy', *Faith and Philosophy*, vol. 16, no. 4, 544–561.

Zabell, S.L. (1988), 'The Probabilistic Analysis of Testimony', *Journal of Statistical Planning and Inference*, **20**, pp. 327–54.

Zagzebski, Linda (1990), 'What If the Impossible Had Been Actual?', in Michael D. Beaty (ed.), *Christian Theism and the Problems of Philosophy*, Notre Dame, IN: Notre Dame University Press, pp. 165–83.

Subject Index

Cosmological Argument: 5–9, 19–20, 24–7, 29–30, 31, 34, 38, 39, 40, 41–3, 51–2, 66, 71, 86–8, 97–109, 110–12, 131–4, 136–7, 141–4, 156–63, 190–92, 201–2

Disembodied Persons, Possibility of: 26, 28, 31, 34, 37, 68–9, 137–8, 162, 189, 202–3, 213

Fine-tuning Argument: 9–11, 14, 20–21, 27, 30, 39, 53–4, 66, 96–9, 116–19, 144–5, 163–8, 190, 213–14

Hell/Problem of Evil: 8, 25–6, 27, 28, 31–3, 34, 71–2, 87–8, 110, 134–6, 191, 196–200, 214–16

    Compatibilism, Arguments for and against: 27, 28, 31–3, 33–4, 41, 44, 71–3, 109, 191, 192–6, 203–7

Moral Argument: 11, 21–2, 30, 35–7, 38, 39, 44–5, 54–6, 66, 88–91, 96, 146–9, 168–73, 197, 207–10

Presumption of Atheism/Theism: 13–14, 24, 37, 39, 49, 70–71, chapter 5 *passim*, 99, 155–6, 200–201, 214

Religious Experience, Appeal To: 23–4, 31, 35, 38–9, 59–61, 69–70, 91–3, 95, 138–9, 151–3, 179–82, 211–13

Resurrection of Jesus: 11–13, 22–3, 30, 35, 36, 38, 39, 43, 56–9, 66–7, 95–6, 120–24, 131, 149–50, 173–9, 210–11